D1499462

Harmony

Fifth edition

Books by Walter Piston

Harmony
Counterpoint
Orchestration

Principles of Harmonic Analysis

WALTER PISTON

Harmony

124 5435

Fifth Edition

Revised and Expanded by
MARK DEVOTO
Tufts University

781.25
P678

W·W·Norton & Company
New York · London

This book is composed in Bembo, with display in Weiss. Typesetting and manufacturing are by The Maple-Vail Book Group. Page layout by Ben Gamit.

Library of Congress Cataloging-in-Publication Data
Piston, Walter, 1894–1976.
    Harmony.
    Includes indexes.
    1. Harmony.   I. DeVoto, Mark.   II. Title.
MT50.P665   1987   781.3   86-23901

ISBN 0-393-95480-3

W. W. Norton & Company, Inc., 500 Fifth Avenue, New York, N.Y. 10110
W. W. Norton & Company Ltd., 10 Coptic Street, London WC1A 1PU

    6 7 8 9 0

Contents

Preface to the Fifth Edition

This fifth edition of *Harmony* marks the forty-fifth year of its successful use. Ten years after Walter Piston's death, his students and their students can still take pride in the enduring vitality of his teaching. My own acquaintance with this book goes back some thirty years, and my allegiance to it remains undiminished—although some who were loyalists before I incorporated wholesale revisions into the fourth edition perhaps might not agree. By now it is plain that the book is different from what it used to be but its essential approach and its basic substance remain as they were in 1941.

The major departure of the fourth edition was the addition of seven new chapters, including four on the complicated subject of harmony after common practice, which had not been discussed in the first three editions. The core of the book, however, remains the exhaustive treatment of common-practice harmony in Part I, which will still be the basis for most one-year or two-year courses in tonal harmony. In the present edition, the entire text of Part I has been carefully examined, with a view especially to clarifying the language whenever possible. A few topics of relatively lesser importance have been deleted, and a number of duplicative examples have been trimmed. These deletions were felt necessary in order to open up a little more space in what had been a terse and detailed text; the extra room will also be perceived in the more spacious design of this edition, with wider margins for jotting down notes. The earliest chapters have all been fortified with a number of new exercises, especially Chapter 8. Some new examples also have been added to Part II.

Several new features are also apparent in the substance of the book itself. Mostly these are intended to benefit the student in developing practical skills in musical analysis, which are surely no less important than skills in written and keyboard exercises. The entirely new chapter on musical texture was written so as to clear up many difficult points encountered by the beginning student in analysis of examples from the literature; in my own experience, a good understanding of the different kinds and details of musical texture is one of the best means of preparation for advanced techniques in tonal analysis, especially Schenkerian technique. Another innovation is the rearrangement of the various chapters dealing with harmonic rhythm and the structure of the phrase, concluding with a short summary of analytical method in Chapter 13. The complete dominant ninth chord, formerly treated in a separate chapter, now appears as part of Chapter 24. Modal mixture has been moved from Chapter 5 to Chapter 14, where it is a little more timely.

For the first time, the revision of this book has been simultaneously coordinated with its companion volume, the *Workbook for Piston/DeVoto Harmony*, by Arthur Jannery of Westfield State College. Professor Jannery and I have consulted each other carefully about the short exercises that are coordinated with the first fifteen chapters, and both of us are responsible for the choice of short pieces that make up the Anthology for Analysis in the second half of the *Workbook*.

The book has long been known as an introductory textbook, but because of its comprehensive range it also serves as a reference book, and we are proud to see well-marked copies of *Harmony* in professors' bookshelves as well as on students' desktops. The editors and I have always tried to observe closely the ways in which the book is used by the musical profession and to remain sensitive to their concerns. That is why for this edition, and for the fourth as well, we have specifically solicited opinions and criticisms that would be helpful in preparing revisions. The response to this call has been heartening. Many teachers, and not a few students, wrote to me directly or to the publisher with specific details, and most of their suggestions, for which all of us are very grateful, have been adopted in this edition. As always, I will be happy to hear from anyone who wishes to offer corrections or suggestions for further revision.

Once again it is a pleasure to express my thanks to those who have given me invaluable assistance in revising this book. Leo Kraft of Queens College of the City University of New York, himself the author of a superb theory text of a different kind, bore the brunt of this task with great vigor and unfailing wisdom and good cheer. Claire Brook of W. W. Norton & Company saved me untold hours of effort and provided an editorial expertise such as I can never hope to equal; and Hinda Keller Farber, who also worked on the fourth edition, once again took a big load off my shoulders. Several chapters were individually reviewed by theory teachers at several different institutions; I am particularly grateful to Christopher Hasty of Yale, a severe but sagacious critic, and Anne Swartz of Baruch College. John Wicks of the University of New Hampshire, my daily colleague for thirteen years, made a number of helpful suggestions, including the "Swiss sixth" sobriquet in Chapter 27. Mel Wildberger's exemplary engraving of the musical examples has once again benefited the smart visual appearance of the book.

And thanks again to Lois Grossman, for patience and good advice, and for enduring the ups and downs of my two years' miscellaneous work.

Mark DeVoto
Medford, Massachusetts
September, 1986

Introduction to the
First Edition (1941)

The first important step in the study of harmony is that of clarifying the purpose of such study. Much confusion exists today as to why we study musical theory and what we should expect to learn from it. In the present writer's teaching experience this confusion of outlook furnishes the commonest and most serious obstacle to progress in all branches of musical theory.

There are those who consider that studies in harmony, counterpoint, and fugue are the exclusive province of the intended composer. But if we reflect that theory must follow practice, rarely preceding it except by chance, we must realize that musical theory is not a set of directions for composing music. It is rather the collected and systematized deductions gathered by observing the practice of composers over a long time, and it attempts to set forth what is or has been their common practice. It tells not how music will be written in the future, but how music has been written in the past.

The results of such a definition of the true nature of musical theory are many and important. First of all, it is clear that this knowledge is indispensable to musicians in all fields of the art, whether they be composers, performers, conductors, critics, teachers, or musicologists. Indeed, a secure grounding in theory is even more a necessity to the musical scholar than to the composer, since it forms the basis for any intelligent appraisal of individual styles of the past or present.

On the other hand, the person gifted for creative musical composition is taking a serious risk in assuming that his genius is great enough to get along without a deep knowledge of the common practice of composers. Mastery of the technical or theoretical aspects of music should be carried out by him as a life's work, running parallel to his creative activity but quite separate from it. In the one he is following common practice, while in the other he is responsible solely to the dictates of his own personal tastes and urge for expression.

In the specific field of harmony we must first seek the answer to two questions: what are the harmonic materials commonly used by composers, and how have these materials been used? We cannot afford in the first stages of our study to become interested in the individual composer at the expense of concentration on establishing the norm of common practice. With such a norm firmly in mind, the way will be clear to the investigation of the individual harmonic practices of composers of all periods, and especially to the scientific examination of the divergent practices noticeable in the twentieth century.

Historically, the period in which this common practice may be detected includes roughly the eighteenth and nineteenth centuries. During that time there is surprisingly little change in the harmonic materials used and in the manner of their use. The experimental period of the early twentieth century will appear far less revolutionary when the lines of development from the practice of older composers become clearer by familiarity with the music. As yet, however, one cannot define a twentieth-century common practice.

Hence the aim of this book is to present as concisely as possible the harmonic common practice of composers of the eighteenth and nineteenth centuries. Rules are announced as observations reported, without attempt at their justification on aesthetic grounds or as laws of nature. The written exercises should be performed as exemplifications of the common practice of composers and not as efforts in creative composition. The author believes that through these principles a prompt and logical grasp of the subject will be achieved.

Walter Piston

I

Tonal Harmony in Common Practice

1

Materials of Music:
Scales and Intervals

Music is indigenous to virtually every culture and every civilization. This alone suggests that the instinct for making music is fundamental to human nature. We can identify music as a ceremonial art back through three millennia or further; but music as we know it today is the youngest of the arts, essentially less than a thousand years old. In this book we will be concerned mainly with the traditions of Western art music. Western art music is the richest of all musical traditions for several reasons: its identifiable and unified historical evolution, its enduring masterworks of every type, and the endless variety of accomplishments and personalities that characterize its development. Even twentieth-century popular music, with its huge and broadly based appeal, owes more to Western art music than to any other.

In the study of music theory we are concerned with what music is made up of—what things go into a piece of music, and how they are put together. From the very beginning we will work with raw materials and with matters of form and structure. In studying these, we are aided by the fact that most music deals in precise quantities. The tones of music, after all, are carefully defined: they have exact frequencies (pitch), and in a composition they are notated with precise specifications as to duration, loudness, and other qualities.

Intervals Measured by Scales

The basic unit of harmony is the *interval*. The term describes the distance between two tones.★ When the tones are sounded simultaneously the distance is a *harmonic interval*. If the two tones are heard consecutively, the distance is a *melodic interval*.

EXAMPLE I−I

harmonic interval   melodic interval

The tones that form the interval are drawn from *scales*. The most familiar of these are the two *diatonic* scales of seven notes each, called the *major scale* and the *minor scale*. Tonal music, which includes most music written between 1700 and 1900, is based on diatonic scales.

The difference between the major and minor scales is found in the distribution of whole steps and half steps above a given starting point. The major scale that starts on C is called the C-major scale.

EXAMPLE I−2

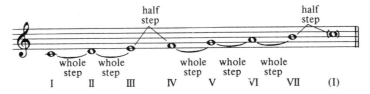

There are three different forms of the minor scale. The *natural minor scale* has three tones that are different from corresponding tones in the major scale. Some of these same tones are also found in the other forms, as shown here.

★The term *note* has historically been used interchangeably with *tone*. Many writers now prefer to reserve the word *tone* to mean an actual sound, and to use *note* to mean a symbol written on music paper as a representation of the sound. This book will not always be so fastidious about this distinction.

EXAMPLE I–3

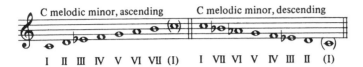

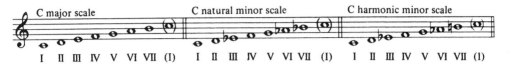

All of the possible pitches in common use, considered together, constitute the *chromatic scale*. It is made up entirely of successive half steps, the smallest interval in Western music. The example below shows segments of the chromatic scale covering the entire staff, in both ascending and descending order.

EXAMPLE I–4

From any C up to the next C, or indeed from any pitch up to the next pitch of the same letter-name, is a distance called one *octave*; counting by half steps, an octave includes twelve different pitches, white and black keys together. The chromatic scale, then, is a collection of all the available pitches in order upward or downward, one octave's worth after another.

Any particular diatonic scale is a seven-note subset of the twelve-note chromatic scale. All major scales, however, have the same distribution of whole steps and half steps, regardless of keynote. Here are all the possible major scales, each having a different pitch of the chromatic scale as its starting point. The arrangement given here, with the familiar key signatures in increasing numbers of sharps or decreasing numbers of flats, is called the *circle of fifths*, the keynote of any scale being the fifth note of the scale to the left of it.

EXAMPLE I–5

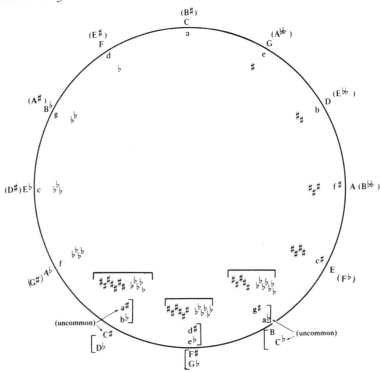

A typical melody in C major might use only notes from the C-major scale. The C-major scale, then, or for that matter any other major scale, can be considered a resource like an alphabet, in that any of its notes may be used, any number of times and in any order, to form a melody.

Scale Degrees

The seven pitches of the diatonic scale are called the *degrees* of the scale. They are customarily numbered by roman numerals I through VII, and designated by the following names:

I. *Tonic* (the keynote).
II. *Supertonic* (the next step above the tonic).
III. *Mediant* (halfway up from tonic to dominant).
IV. *Subdominant* (as far below the tonic as the dominant is above it).
V. *Dominant* (actually a dominant element in the key).
VI. *Submediant* (halfway down from tonic to subdominant).
VII. *Leading tone* (having a melodic tendency to lead to the tonic). This name is used when the distance from the seventh degree up to the tonic is a half step, as in the major and ascending melodic minor scales. When the distance is a whole step, as in the descending melodic minor scale, the seventh degree is no longer considered a leading tone and is simply called the *minor seventh degree*, although the term *subtonic* is also used.

Classification of Intervals

There are two parts to an interval's name, the general and the specific. They are combined when we speak of a "major third" or a "minor seventh." The general name of an interval is found by counting the lines and spaces included by the two notes as they appear on the staff.

EXAMPLE 1–6

| unison | second | third | fourth | fifth | sixth | seventh | octave | ninth |

The specific name of an interval (what kind of third, seventh, etc.) may be found by referring to a major scale starting on the lower of the two notes. If the upper note then coincides with a note of the scale, the interval is *major*, except in case of octaves, fifths, fourths, and unisons, for which the term *perfect* is used.

EXAMPLE 1–7

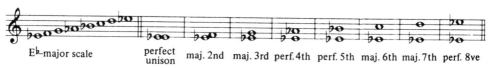

Eb-major scale   perfect unison   maj. 2nd   maj. 3rd   perf. 4th   perf. 5th   maj. 6th   maj. 7th   perf. 8ve

If the upper note does not coincide with a note of the scale, the following guidelines apply:

a. The difference between a major interval and a minor one with the same general name is one half step. The larger interval is the major, the smaller, the minor.

EXAMPLE 1–8

major   minor
third   third

b. A major or perfect interval made a half step larger is an *augmented* interval.

EXAMPLE 1–9

major   augmented   perfect   augmented
sixth   sixth   fifth   fifth

c. A minor or perfect interval made a half step smaller is a *diminished* interval.

EXAMPLE 1–10

minor   diminished   perfect   diminished
third   third   fifth   fifth

In (b) above, the C above the E♭ falls within the E♭-major scale, and therefore is a major sixth. Raising the C to C♯ makes the major sixth a half step larger, changing it to an augmented sixth.

When the lower note is preceded by a sharp or flat, the interval may be analyzed first without the sharp or flat, and the result compared with the original interval by reference to the rules above. For example, consider the interval from D♯ up to C:

EXAMPLE I—11

The scale of D♯ major, with nine sharps, is awkward to use as a measuring device. Setting aside the sharp on the D, we take the scale of D major, and find that C is one half step short of the seventh degree. The interval D to C is therefore a minor seventh. Restoring the sharp to the D, we find that the minor seventh has been made smaller by one half step, and thus according to (c) above, the result is a diminished seventh.

The major second and the minor second are identical with the whole step and half step respectively. The half step is also called the *semitone*.

Compound Intervals

An interval greater than an octave is called a *compound interval*. It may be reckoned by subtracting the octave (or octaves) and measuring the interval that remains. (The interval number is obtained by subtracting 7, e.g., 7 subtracted from a twelfth leaves a fifth.) A few compound intervals, however, such as the ninth, are characteristic features of harmonic practice and are usually called by the larger number.

EXAMPLE I—12

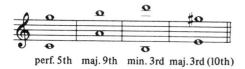

perf. 5th   maj. 9th   min. 3rd   maj. 3rd (10th)

Inversion of Intervals

The term *inversion* is applied to a variety of musical procedures. The inversion of intervals, also called *harmonic inversion*, is quite specific. In inversion of intervals equal to or smaller than a perfect octave, the lower pitch is moved up an octave, or the upper pitch is moved down an octave, with the same result:

EXAMPLE I–13

maj. 6th   inversion
            (min. 3rd)

The following results are obtained from inversion:

unisons become octaves, and vice versa;
seconds become sevenths, and vice versa;
thirds become sixths, and vice versa;
fourths become fifths, and vice versa;

and:

major intervals become minor, and vice versa;
augmented intervals become diminished, and vice versa;
perfect intervals remain perfect.

EXAMPLE I–14

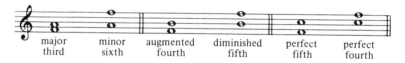

major   minor   augmented   diminished   perfect   perfect
third   sixth   fourth   fifth   fifth   fourth

The term *complementation*, borrowed from geometry, has also been applied to the procedure. A major sixth and a minor third are thus said to be complementary intervals, or simply complements.

Enharmonic Intervals

In our scale system it often happens that two intervals that look different on paper sound the same when played on the piano. This is particularly true when the intervals are sounded in isolation, away from any musical context in which the difference in their meanings would be apparent. A good example is the augmented second, which cannot be distinguished from the minor third without further evidence than the sound of the two tones. One interval is called the *enharmonic equivalent* of the other.

EXAMPLE I–15

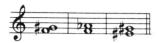

When such intervals are heard in a harmonic context, however, their differences are readily perceptible.

EXAMPLE I–16

Individual notes may also be enharmonic equivalents, for instance F♯ and G♭. Whether it is proper to use one or the other is of grammatical significance; obviously, for instance, the seventh degree of the G-major scale is F♯ and not G♭. Enharmonic key signatures are also frequently encountered, as for instance D♭ major and C♯ major (Example I–5).

EXERCISES

The exercises offered in this book can serve as suggestions for further exercises to be invented by the teacher or by the student. Of themselves, they do not provide adequate practice or training. It goes without saying that the material in each chapter must be thoroughly assimilated before you proceed to the next. Do as many exercises as necessary until you feel completely in control of the material.

   1. Name the following intervals:

2. With F♯ as the lower tone, construct these intervals: min. 3rd; aug. 6th; dim. 5th; perf. 4th; aug. 2nd; maj. 7th; min. 9th; aug. 5th.

3. With D♭ as the upper tone, construct these intervals: dim. 5th; maj. 9th; dim. 7th; min. 2nd; aug. 4th; perf. 5th; min. 6th; dim. 3rd.

4. Write out and name enharmonic equivalents of the intervals in Exercise 3 above.

5. From what major or minor scales could the following fragments have been taken?

6. For each of the following intervals, name at least two scales that contain both tones.

7. Construct a major scale in which C♯ is the sixth degree.

8. Construct a descending melodic minor scale with D as the tonic.

9. Name the interval from supertonic up to submediant in the harmonic minor scale.

10. *Analysis.* By searching through actual music in published scores, find two examples of unusual key signatures; find two examples each of double sharps and double flats; find three examples of scales.

11. *Analysis.* Choose a melody from one of the examples in this book and identify all of its melodic intervals.

2

Triads

Chord Factors

The combination of two or more harmonic intervals makes a *chord*. The basic chord of common-practice harmony is the *triad*, a group of three tones called *chord tones* or *factors*, obtained by placing one third on top of another.

The names *root*, *third*, and *fifth* are given to the three factors of the triad regardless of their arrangement.

EXAMPLE 2–1

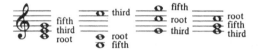

Triads on the Scale Degrees

Each degree of the scale may serve as the root of a triad. To put it another way, a triad may be constructed using any degree of the scale as its root. The triads that are so constructed are designated by the same names, and the same roman numerals, as their respective roots.

Using only the notes of the C-major scale, superposition of thirds yields the following triads:

EXAMPLE 2–2

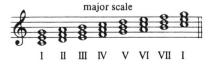

13

Triads of the minor scales will be considered in Chapter 4.

Kinds of Triads

The triads built on the various degrees of a given scale differ not only in pitch, but also in the quality of their sound. The reason is that while triads are built in thirds, some of those thirds are major and others are minor. In combination, the thirds produce four kinds of triads.

Constructing triads above a given root, we find that:

A major third plus a minor third make a *major triad*.
A minor third plus a major third make a *minor triad*.
A major third plus another major third make an *augmented triad*.
A minor third plus another minor third make a *diminished triad*.

Between the root and fifth of a major triad or of a minor triad, the interval is a perfect fifth.
Between the root and fifth of an augmented triad, the interval is an augmented fifth; of a diminished triad, a diminished fifth.

You should practice playing and listening to the four types of triads until you can easily and immediately distinguish them by ear.

EXAMPLE 2–3

maj.   min.   aug.   dim.

Inversions

A triad with its root as its lowest tone is said to be in *root position*.
A triad with its third as its lowest tone is in *first inversion*.
A triad with its fifth as its lowest tone is in *second inversion*.
All triads having the same root are identified by the same roman numeral, regardless of whether the chord is in root position or inversion.

EXAMPLE 2–4

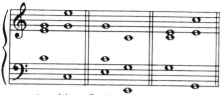

root position first inversion second inversion

Consonant and Dissonant Intervals

A *consonant interval* sounds stable and complete. A *dissonant interval* sounds unstable, calling for resolution into a consonant interval. Certainly these qualities are subjective, but it is clear that in common practice the following classification holds true:

> *consonant:* perfect intervals and major and minor thirds and sixths;
> *dissonant:* augmented and diminished intervals and major and minor seconds, sevenths, and ninths;
> *exception:* the perfect fourth is dissonant when it stands alone. It is consonant when there is a third or perfect fifth below it.

EXAMPLE 2–5

dissonant 4th consonant 4th

Major and minor thirds and sixths are frequently set apart from perfect intervals and called *imperfect consonances*. This distinction, which is important in the counterpoint of the sixteenth century, has little significance for the harmonic style of the eighteenth and nineteenth centuries.

Music without dissonant intervals is often lifeless and uninteresting, since it is the dissonant element that furnishes much of the sense of forward motion and rhythmic energy. The history of musical style has been largely occupied with the important subject of dissonance and its treatment by individual composers. It cannot be too strongly emphasized that the essential quality of dissonance is its sense of movement and not, as is sometimes erroneously assumed, its degree of unpleasantness to the ear.

Major and minor triads are consonant chords because they contain only consonant intervals. Since there are dissonant intervals in the augmented and diminished triads, those chords are dissonant.

Triads of the Major Mode

In the major mode, three triads are major—I, IV, and V; three are minor—II, III, and VI; and one is diminished—VII. It is customary in harmonic analysis to indicate all triads by their appropriate roman numerals. Although we will not use it in this book, many writers prefer the convention of writing the roman numerals of major and augmented triads in capital letters, and those of minor and diminished triads in lower case.

Four-Part Writing

Most music of the eighteenth and nineteenth centuries is conceived in terms of four-part harmony. This means four tones in each chord, and four different melodic parts. The three-part writing often observed in keyboard and chamber music frequently suggests four parts, whereas in an orchestral score, the larger number of apparent parts is most often the result of duplication in a basically four-part harmony.

Much of the study of harmony is concerned with the principles of four-part writing, and accordingly most of the exercises in this book are to be worked out in four parts or voices. The term *voices* does not necessarily mean that the parts are to be sung. It does suggest that each part should have a singable quality characteristic of all good melodic music, whether written for human voices or for instruments.

To define the four parts, we follow the convention of naming them for the four singing voices—soprano, alto, tenor, and bass—somewhat arbitrarily restricting their ranges to an approximation of the ranges of human voices.

EXAMPLE 2–6

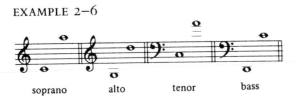

soprano   alto   tenor   bass

There is no harm in exceeding these limits occasionally, but extreme notes must be used sparingly.

Doubling

Since the triad contains but three tones (or factors), it is evident that another is needed for four-part harmony. With triads in root position, the fourth tone is normally a duplication of the root an octave or two higher, or even at the unison. This procedure is called *doubling*. Doubling of the root is most usual, but the third or the fifth may on occasion be doubled instead.

EXAMPLE 2–7

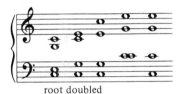

root doubled

The Leading-Tone Triad

Though of common occurrence in the first or second inversion, the triad on the leading tone is rarely found in root position and will be omitted from the earliest chapters of this book. It contains a dissonant interval, the diminished fifth, the lower tone of which is the leading tone itself, with its strong tendency toward the tonic. In later chapters, we will learn how the leading-tone triad substitutes for the dominant triad or the dominant seventh chord.

Whatever the position of the leading-tone triad, doubling of its root is avoided. Doubling of the leading tone as the third of V is also avoided; one sometimes finds the doubled leading tone as the fifth of III.

Spacing

Our harmonic sense demands an arrangement of chords which will give clarity and balance. Each chord factor must make its effect, and yet each is subordinated to the overall sonority. The distribution of the factors within the chord contributes to the presence of such qualities as sonorousness, brilliance, or intensity.

The commonest arrangement of a chord places the wide intervals at the bottom, with the smaller intervals at the top. Good four-part writing usually avoids a spacing of intervals wider than the octave, except between tenor and bass, where even two octaves' distance may sound quite satisfactory.

EXAMPLE 2–8

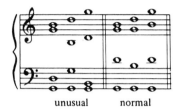

        unusual   normal

Close and Open Position

When the three upper voices are as close together as possible, the spacing is described as *close position*. Otherwise the chord is in *open position*. In close position the three upper voices are all within the range of a single octave. In open position there is a distance of more than an octave separating the soprano and tenor. Starting with a given soprano note, a root-position triad is built by giving the alto the first available chord note below the soprano. If open position is desired, the alto will not take this first available note, but will take the next below. The tenor will fall into place with the only note left. The bass will of course take the root, in whatever octave is convenient.

EXAMPLE 2–9

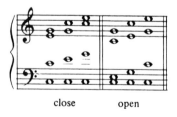

       close   open

Both close and open position have appropriate uses in all kinds of harmony. The choice between them is influenced most of all by the melodic flow of the voices. The question of ranges is also important. If the soprano is written high, close position might bring the alto and tenor too high, so that open position is more suitable. Ideally, a well-balanced chord would have all the voices in their corresponding registers, all high, all low, or all medium. This is seldom possible because the different voices will normally progress into different registers, and a compromise in the balance of voices will usually be necessary.

Notation

Most harmony exercises are written in four parts. The best way to write them is on two staves, using the four-part choral layout found in hymn books and Bach's 371 chorale harmonizations. The soprano and alto parts are always on the upper staff; the tenor and bass, on the lower. The soprano and tenor stems always point up; the alto and bass stems, down.

EXAMPLE 2–10

EXERCISES

1. The teacher will play a major scale, followed by a triad derived from that scale. The student will name the kind of triad and the scale degree that is its root.

2. Identify the following triads as major, minor, or diminished, and indicate the possible keys and scale degrees of their origins. (For example, the first triad given is major, IV of B major, I of E major, V of A major.)

3. Write three different spacings in a standard four-voice arrangement of each of the following triads. Use root position only, doubling the root.

4. Write in four parts, in both close and open position, the following triads, using root position with the root doubled:

    a. IV in B♭ major
    b. V in C♯ major
    c. VI in E major
    d. III in D major
    e. II in F major
    f. IV in A major
    g. I in E♭ major
    h. VI in G♭ major
    i. VII in G major
    j. II in A♭ major

5. By the use of accidentals only (sharps, flats, or naturals), write each of the following triads in three additional ways, altering them so as to illustrate in each case the four types—major, minor, augmented, and diminished.

6. Keeping the soprano constant in each case, rearrange the inner voices of the following chords, so that a close position triad becomes open, and vice versa. Make sure that only the root is doubled.

7. With G♯ as the soprano note, write in four parts the following chord forms:

    a. a major triad in first inversion, with its fifth in the soprano
    b. a dissonant triad with its third in the soprano
    c. a triad in second inversion, in the key of E
    d. a triad whose root is the mediant of a major scale
    e. a triad in open position, with its root in the soprano
    f. a minor triad in close position
    g. an augmented triad with its third doubled
    h. a consonant triad in the key of B major
    i. a diminished triad in major mode
    j. a triad in first inversion, with the subdominant in the bass

8. *Analysis.* Examine the excerpt from a traditional hymn given below. Put an "X" over all chords that are not triads. For all that are triads, label those in root position with "R" and those that are inverted with "inv." Finally, identify each triad with an appropriate roman numeral. How many triads are in root position? How many in first inversion? In second inversion? What factors are doubled in each triad? What kinds of triads are more abundant than others?

Old Hundredth, attributed to Louis Bourgeois, c. 1551★

Him   serve with mirth, his praise forth tell; Come ye be-fore Him and   re - joice.

★Version from *The Book of Hymns* of the United Methodist Church, 1964 (No. 21, second half)

3

Harmonic Progression in the Major Mode: Principles of Voice Leading

Harmonic progression is one of the principal resources of coherence in tonal music. The term implies not just that one chord is followed by another, but that the succession is controlled and orderly. In common practice, some harmonic successions are used more often than others, and the ways in which chords are connected follow certain procedures.

In any progression, it is generally true that the choice of tones in the individual chords is of less importance than the relationship of the two roots to each other and to the scale from which they are drawn. The chord's relationship to the scale is also the chord's location in the tonality, identified by the scale degree serving as root; in other words, the scale degree identifies the *function* of the chord. Hence, harmonic progression can be expressed as root succession, which is represented by the roman numerals indicating the scale degrees upon which the chords are built.

Table of Usual Root Progressions

The following generalizations are based on observations of usage by composers in common practice. They are not proposed as a set of strict rules to be rigidly adhered to.

I is followed by IV or V, sometimes VI, less often II or III.
II is followed by V, sometimes IV or VI, less often I or III.
III is followed by VI, sometimes IV, less often I, II, or V.
IV is followed by V, sometimes I or II, less often III or VI.
V is followed by I, sometimes IV or VI, less often II or III.
VI is followed by II or V, sometimes III or IV, less often I.
VII is followed by I or III, sometimes VI, less often II, IV, or V.

It is important to appreciate the different qualities of these progressions, qualities which do not readily lend themselves to verbal
description. As a first step in comparing root progressions, one can
place them into three categories:

a. root motion by a fourth or fifth;
b. root motion by a third (or sixth);
c. root motion by a step (or seventh).

Triads with roots a fourth or fifth apart will have one note in common. By far the most important such relationship is the the progression
V–I, generally considered the strongest harmonic relationship in tonal
music. One can easily sense the strength of this progression by playing
the bass alone.

EXAMPLE 3–1

V   I   V   I

Other progressions with root moving down a fifth (or up a fourth)
seem to have a comparable but lesser effect.

EXAMPLE 3–2

VI   II   II   V   III   VI   I   IV

Root movement down a fourth (or up a fifth) gives the reverse of the progressions above. Comparison shows their effects to be distinctly different. The IV–I progression is the most important of these; it acts rather like a counterbalance to the V–I relationship.

EXAMPLE 3–3

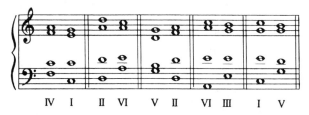

IV   I   II VI   V   II   VI III   I   V

Triads with roots a third apart will have two notes in common; in other words, they will differ by only a single note. Because they involve so little change, such progressions are considered weak. In the major mode, a root progression of a third will mean a change from a major triad to a minor, or vice versa. When the root moves up a third, the root of the second chord has just been heard as the third of the first chord (weaker); when the root descends a third, the root of the second chord comes as a new note (stronger).

EXAMPLE 3–4

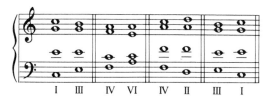

I   III   IV VI   IV II   III   I

When the root proceeds by step, the second chord will consist of a completely new set of notes, and hence will have the effect of introducing a new harmonic color. Stepwise root progressions are considered strong, although not all to the same extent; the strong IV–V and VI–V, for example, are frequently encountered, whereas II–I, relatively weaker in root position, is seldom used. (See Example 3–5.)

Root motion by seventh can ordinarily be considered as root motion by the complementary interval, the step, in the opposite direction; likewise, root motion by a sixth is comparable to root motion by a third.

EXAMPLE 3–5

In exercises in root position, root motions of intervals wider than a fifth are not often used, except the octave, which is sometimes used to help obtain a new spacing.

The comparative description of root motions should not be considered as either prescriptive or exhaustive. Nor should "weak" progressions be equated with "undesirable," because they form an important resource of contrast. While strong progressions are used more often than weak progressions, their uses are different and must be understood in context.

To get a good sense of how all these progressions sound, and of how they are similar or different, you will find it very useful to play them repeatedly on the piano, in open and close position, in every spacing you can think of, and in every key. As you acquire a thorough appreciation of the sound of the different progressions, you will find it much easier to incorporate them effectively into your written exercises.

Connection of Chords: Two Rules of Thumb

The smooth connection of chords is primarily a melodic process, in which the structure of chords as simultaneously-sounding horizontal parts must continually be taken into account. Composers in the common-practice period were always attentive to such linear considerations, even in music that is primarily chordal.

Our study of the connection of chords will necessarily begin by using root-position triads in four parts, with all four voices moving together at the same time, or note against note (Latin, *punctus contra punctum*, from which the word "counterpoint" derives). The following Rules of Thumb describe the simplest means of connecting two triads in root position, with a maximum smoothness of linear movement from chord to chord, and the individual parts moving as short a distance as possible.

Rule of Thumb 1. If two triads have one or more tones in common, these *common tones* are usually repeated in the same voice, the remaining voice or voices moving to the nearest tones of the second chord.

EXAMPLE 3–6

C: I   V

In the example, G is the common tone, so it is repeated in the same voice, the alto. The other two voices move to the nearest position available—C down to B, E to D.

Exception: In the progression II–V, when the fourth degree is in the soprano of II, it is customary not to repeat the common tone, but to move the upper three voices down to the next available position. (This motion may, but need not, be used when the fourth degree is in the alto or tenor.)

EXAMPLE 3–7

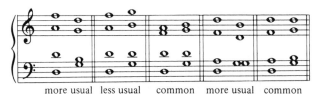

more usual   less usual   common   more usual   common

Rule of Thumb 2. If the two triads have no tones in common, the upper three voices move in opposite direction to the motion of the bass, but always to the nearest available position.

EXAMPLE 3–8

IV V   II III   III IV

Exception: in the progression V–VI, the leading tone moves up to the tonic, while the other two voices descend to the nearest position in the chord. The third, rather than the root, is doubled in the triad on VI. This exception always holds true when the leading tone is in the soprano of V; when it is in an inner voice, either the Rule or the exception may apply.

EXAMPLE 3–9

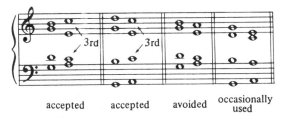

accepted   accepted   avoided   occasionally used

If the Rules of Thumb are followed strictly, the connection between the chords will be correct according to the practice of voice leading in harmonic progression. The two chords are connected as smoothly as possible, so that one seems to flow into the next.

EXAMPLE 3–10

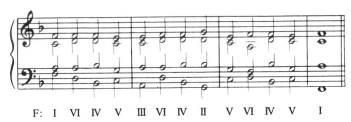

F: I   VI   IV   V   III   VI   IV   II   V   VI   IV   V   I

The example above is in close position. The following shows the application of the Rules of Thumb to the same root succession, but beginning in open position. You will note that the voice leading is identical in both versions; the soprano and alto of Example 3–11 are merely a harmonic inversion of the same voices in Example 3–10.

EXAMPLE 3–11

F: I   VI   IV   V   III   VI   IV   II   V   VI   IV   V   I

Improving the Exercise: Beyond the Rules of Thumb

The two solutions given above, which are correct but rather dull musically, are a good demonstration of both the usefulness and the limitations of the Rules of Thumb. One should therefore try to discover what additional musical interest may be gained by departing from the Rules of Thumb from time to time. In such departures, the first place to consider is the soprano line, which is instinctively heard as a melody and so must be constructed more carefully than the inside voices.

  When the root is repeated, it is advisable to change the position of at least two or all three of the upper voices, for variety.

EXAMPLE 3–12

(all three upper parts change)

A change from open to close position, or vice versa, whether the roots are different or not, is often a good way to obtain a new soprano note.

EXAMPLE 3–13

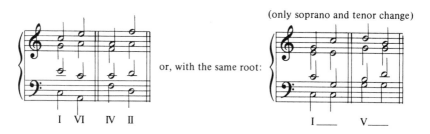

or, with the same root:

(only soprano and tenor change)

  The occasional use of a triad without fifth, usually composed of three roots and one third, may help to free the soprano line. It is not advisable to omit the third, as that leaves the empty sound of the open fifth.

EXAMPLE 3–14

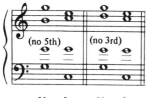

Doubling the third or fifth instead of the root is another means of making more notes available for the soprano part. A chord composed of root, fifth, and doubled third is generally preferred to one of two roots and two thirds. The leading tone should not be doubled when it is the third of V; it may be doubled when it is the fifth of III.

EXAMPLE 3–15

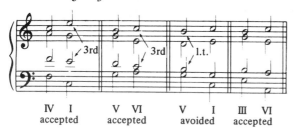

Conjunct and Disjunct Melodic Motion

As the voices are given more freedom of movement, attention must be given to the ways in which they may move, both as regards the shape of each melodic line and the ways in which the lines move relative to each other. The terms *conjunct* and *disjunct* motion are used to describe the movement of a single line by step and by skip respectively.

EXAMPLE 3–16

A good melodic line contains mostly conjunct motion, with disjunct motion used judiciously for variety. At this stage of our study, augmented and diminished intervals, and any melodic intervals wider than a sixth, are better avoided. Skips of a third, fourth, or fifth may be used freely in the soprano line, but too many skips make for angularity, rather than for the desired flowing quality. In root position, the bass is more likely to have skips than the other parts, while the alto and tenor as a rule have few, if any, melodic intervals larger than a fourth.

More will be said on the subject of melody in Chapter 7.

Rules of Motion

Unlike the Rules of Thumb, which are general guidelines, the rules discussed here are more rigorous, not to be broken except in certain special circumstances.

Relative to each other, two voices may move in three ways: in contrary motion, in oblique motion, or in similar motion.

In *contrary motion*, the voices move in opposite directions:

EXAMPLE 3–17

In *oblique motion*, one voice remains stationary while the other moves:

EXAMPLE 3–18

In *similar motion*, both voices move in the same direction:

EXAMPLE 3–19

In similar motion, if the two voices remain the same distance apart, they are said to be in *parallel motion*. (A major third followed by a minor third is still considered a succession of parallel thirds, even though the thirds are unequal in size.)

EXAMPLE 3–20

parallel sixths

Two voices in parallel motion are closely similar melodically, and may be regarded as a single voice with duplication. Parallel intervals of the unison, octave, and perfect fifth have been systematically avoided by composers of the eighteenth and nineteenth centuries, whenever it has been their intention to write a texture of independent voices.

EXAMPLE 3–21: Avoided Parallels

unisons   octaves   perfect fifths

Parallel perfect fifths and octaves are avoided between all pairs of voices, but are considered especially objectionable between soprano and bass. Consecutive motions such as fifth to twelfth, unison to octave, and vice versa, are also generally avoided.

EXAMPLE 3–22

Parallel thirds and sixths are common. Parallel fourths are used if supported by parallel thirds below.

EXAMPLE 3–23

See Ex. 6–12

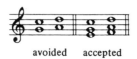

avoided   accepted

The movement of voices relative to one another aims at maintaining their independence as separate parts. The maximum of independence is furnished by contrary motion, but it is obviously not possible for four parts to move in four different directions. Oblique motion is useful to contrast a moving voice with one that is standing still. In similar motion, care must be taken that the movement is not so consistently similar that one part is merely a companion to the other, without individuality of its own.

The Direct Octave and Fifth

Composers in the common-practice period were careful about any approach by similar motion to the intervals of octave and perfect fifth. These intervals thus approached are called *direct octaves* or *direct fifths*, or in some texts, *hidden octaves*, *covered octaves*, etc. While such matters form an important part of the study of counterpoint, the prominence of these intervals as constituents of chords, especially when located between the outside voices, bass and soprano, requires special attention in elementary harmony.

An octave or perfect fifth is not usually approached by similar motion with skips in both voices.

EXAMPLE 3–24

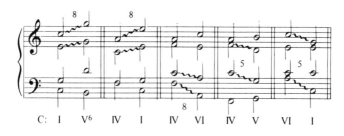

C: I   V⁶   IV   I   IV   VI   IV   V   VI   I

Exception 1: In changing the spacing of the same harmony, direct fifths approached by skip may be freely used.

EXAMPLE 3–25

always accepted

(The example above, consisting of a single harmony, does not constitute harmonic progression.)

Exception 2: In the V–I progression, particularly in a final cadence, the direct fifth may be used when the leading tone skips down to the fifth degree, but only when the leading tone is in an inner voice (alto or tenor).

EXAMPLE 3–26

accepted   accepted   avoided

The same kind of voice leading in comparable progressions, having the same intervallic relationship but on other scale degrees, such as III–VI or I–IV, is also generally satisfactory.

When the direct motion proceeds by step in one voice and skip in the other, several combinations are possible. The direct octave and fifth are permitted between soprano and bass when the soprano moves by step and the bass by skip. In upward movement, the preferred motion to a direct octave is with the soprano moving by a minor second, acting as a leading tone (c in Example 3–27), although in some cases the whole step motion is quite acceptable (*d, f*). On the other hand, the direct fifth or octave arrived at by skip in the soprano and step in the bass gives undue prominence to the perfect interval, and this kind of direct motion is generally avoided (*j, k, l*). Direct fifths or octaves with skip in one voice and step in the other are freely employed between any other two voices. Example 3–27 shows a variety of these different combinations.

EXAMPLE 3–27

(Of course, direct octaves or fifths arrived at by steps in both voices are the same thing as parallel octaves or fifths.)

Treatment of the Leading Tone

The leading tone is unlike any other degree of the diatonic scale in its audible tendency to move upward to the tonic. This property necessitates special treatment for the leading tone when it is in the soprano voice. (Though of frequent occurrence in inversion, the leading-tone triad is hardly ever used in root position, and thus the leading tone will not appear in the bass in root-position progression.) In V–I and V–VI, if the leading tone is in the soprano, it will, as a rule, lead to the tonic note in the second chord. If the leading tone is in an inner voice, it may ascend to the tonic or it may descend. (See Example 3–28.)

The interval formed by the leading tone and the fourth degree below (augmented fourth) or the fourth degree above (diminished fifth) is called the *tritone*, i.e., three whole-tone steps. It has a peculiar kind of sound and was looked on with disfavor in the era of strict counterpoint, when it was referred to as *diabolus in musica* (devil in music). The roughness of its effect was softened or avoided with consistent skill. For the present, one should avoid writing either the augmented fourth or the

EXAMPLE 3–28

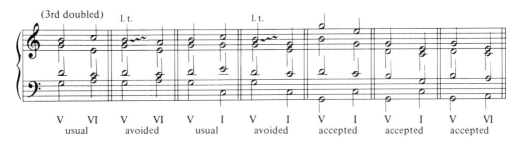

diminished fifth as a melodic interval; as harmonic intervals, both are regular components of the leading-tone triad and of the supertonic triad in the minor mode, to be discussed in the next few chapters.

Overlapping and Crossing

When two voices move upward in similar motion, the lower voice should not move to a position higher than that just vacated by the upper voice. Otherwise the ear might follow an apparent melodic progression between the two voices, which are said to be *overlapping*. The corresponding rule holds for descending movement.

EXAMPLE 3–29

It is apparent that direct motion to or from a unison is prevented by this rule. Commonly accepted, however, is the special case in which the leading tone in the tenor rises to the tonic with the dominant bass also ascending; the situation is hardly different from the comparable progression in contrary motion.

EXAMPLE 3–30

E.g., Ex. 6–35

The movement of one voice from a position below another voice to above it, or vice versa, is called *crossing*. It is a common occurrence in instrumental music, but also occurs occasionally in contrapuntal vocal music, including Bach's chorales. Because it is sometimes confusing to the ear, crossing is better avoided at this stage in our study, although an occasional crossing between the alto and tenor voices does no harm.

EXAMPLE 3–31

Similar Motion of Four Voices

As a general rule, all four parts should not move in the same direction when the triads are in root position. This rule may be relaxed in final cadences, when a particular soprano note is desired (such as in Example 3–26). In such cases, at least one part must move by step.

Quick Summary of Motion Rules

1. Avoid parallel motion of perfect fifth, perfect octave, or unison, between any pair of voices, but especially watch out for them between the outer voices, soprano and bass (Example 3–22).
2. Avoid consecutive motion between perfect fifths or octaves and their respective compounds (Example 3–22).
3. Avoid similar motion to a perfect fifth or octave when both voices skip (Example 3–24), except in certain special cases (Examples 3–25, 3–26).
4. Avoid similar motion to a perfect fifth or octave between the outer voices, when the bass steps and the soprano skips (Example 3–27).
5. Avoid overlapping and crossed voices (Examples 3–29, 3–31).

6. In root-position progressions, avoid motion of all four voices in the same direction, except in final cadences (Example 3–26).

7. In V–I or V–VI in root position, if the leading tone is in the soprano, it must progress upward by half step to the tonic note (Example 3–28).

Working on the Exercises

The written exercises in this book are designed to present specific musical problems and to introduce you to certain types of chords; but most of all they are designed to resemble, in a rudimentary way, what composers do—writing music. At first you will not think that your exercises have much in common with the music you know best; they will mostly consist of a slow manipulation of many different rules. As you get better at doing them and can find musical answers more quickly, you should try to think of how you can actually hear the exercises as short fragments of music. The rules are important, and there may seem to be too many of them at first; but what you can bring to your exercises musically should become the most important thing.

In this and the next chapter, you should write at least two versions of exercises that call for a considerable number of chords. The first version should be a "dull version," one that closely follows the Rules of Thumb given above, even though the result may be poor melodically, as in Examples 3–10 and 3–11. This will help to familiarize you with the principles of connection of triads and will then serve as a basis for a "better version" containing departures necessary to obtain a better soprano line. (See pages 28–30.)

Here again is the "dull version" that we obtained in Example 3–10, together with a "better version" (Example 3–33).

EXAMPLE 3–32

F: I VI IV V III VI IV II V VI IV V I

EXAMPLE 3–33

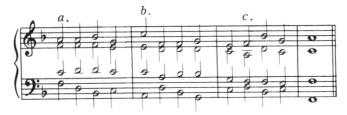

- *a.* Starting with the third in the soprano places the voices in the middle of their range and gives them a little more room in which to move.
- *b.* The doubling of the third in III avoids the repetition of the note A on the first beats of two successive measures. The three upper voices then move down, treating the III–VI progression as analogous to II–V.
- *c.* The VI has the doubled third, as is usual in the progression V–VI. This offers the choice of repeating the common tone F in either tenor or soprano, as well as the opportunity to change from close to open position.

The following is a third version of the same series of triads. Identify and analyze the departures from the basic procedure.

EXAMPLE 3–34

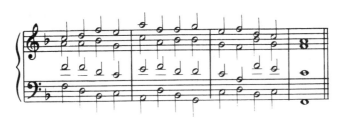

Here are two fine examples of root-position writing. Study them carefully, with attention to unity, variety, smooth connection, and melodic shape.

EXAMPLE 3–35: Chopin, *Nocturne*, Op. 37, No. 1

Eb: I IV I IV I V I V I IV I V VI V⁷ I

EXAMPLE 3–36: Brahms, *Ich schell mein Horn ins Jammertal*, Op. 43, No. 3

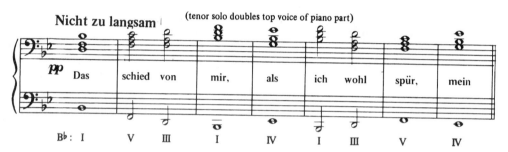

Bb: I V III I IV I III V IV

I III V III II VI II VI V of VI VI V I

You will notice that roman numerals have been included with these examples. Analytical symbols have been provided for most of the examples in this book that are taken from actual works, even though some of these symbols may not be immediately understood. All such indications will be clarified in subsequent chapters.

EXERCISES

1. Write, in four parts, three different versions of each of the following harmonic progressions, in root position:

    a. V–VI in E major
    b. IV–V in D major
    c. I–VI in F♯ major
    d. VI–V in C major
    e. V–I in A major
    f. II–V in E♭ major
    g. VI–IV in B♭ major
    h. II–V in G major
    i. III–VI in C♯ major
    j. V–VI in A♭ major

2. Add soprano, alto, and tenor parts to the following basses, using triads in root position. Make two versions of each, the first a "dull" version complying strictly with the Rules of Thumb for connecting triads, the second version containing departures from the Rules of Thumb so as to ensure a good melodic soprano part.

In this type of exercise, as in all the harmonization exercises in this book, it is essential to provide a root analysis shown by roman numerals, as in the examples.

a.

b.

c.

d.

3. Locate the broken rule (overlapping voices) that occurs in Example 3–10. How could it be avoided? This violation remained unnoticed in the earliest editions of this book. There is a lesson to be learned from

this: violations may escape even careful searching, especially when they do not sound obtrusive. This does not mean that it is pointless to avoid violations of the rules. It does mean that the rules are not so rigorous and hard-edged that the occasional inadvertent violation inevitably leads to a poor musical result.

    4. *Analysis.* In the excerpt below, identify and label all triads. Rewrite the excerpt so that the alto and soprano voices are inverted; this will mean transposing the alto up an octave. Now rewrite the excerpt again, placing the tenor an octave higher; some of it will be above the alto. Finally write a third rearrangement, so that the original tenor, written an octave higher, becomes the soprano, the original soprano the alto, and the original alto the tenor. How much crossing is there in this version? Compare the sound of all four versions.

Old Hundredth, attributed to Louis Bourgeois, c. 1551*

    All   peo-ple that on earth do   dwell, Sing   to the Lord with cheer-ful   voice.

*Version from *The Book of Hymns* of the United Methodist Church, 1964 (No. 21, first half).

4

The Minor Mode

Scale Differences

In the previous chapter we saw that the major mode is defined by a single set of triads. In the minor mode, several types of triads and scales are used, depending on different conditions and contexts. Repeated observation shows that in the period of common harmonic practice, music in the minor mode is rarely limited to one type of minor scale.

The distinguishing characteristic of music in the minor mode is that the tonic triad is invariably minor; the other triads may be defined flexibly. The dominant triad preceding the minor I, for example, is always a major triad, with the leading tone rising to the tonic; but under other conditions, as we will see, the dominant triad may be minor, without the expected upward motion of the leading tone. The third of V is thus usually the major seventh degree; but the fifth of III is regularly the minor seventh degree.

It is this kind of difference in the usage of the scale degrees that accounts for some of the quirks of ordinary musical notation. To take an obvious case, the three flats of the key signature of C minor indicate that the third, sixth, and seventh degrees of the scale are inflected with flat signs, in contrast to the same degrees in the scale of the parallel mode, C major; yet in all our ordinary experience of music in C minor, miscellaneous B♮s are to be found, and often A♮s as well.

The relationships between the scale degrees are summarized in the three traditional minor-scale forms:

EXAMPLE 4–1

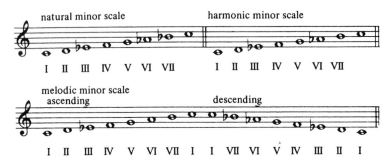

The *natural minor scale* corresponds to the key signature, as mentioned in Chapter 1, and is equivalent to the descending form of the melodic minor. It has the same notes as the relative major scale (in Example 4–1, E♭ major), but corresponding to different degrees of that scale.

The *harmonic minor scale* includes the major seventh degree, or leading tone. The distance between the sixth and seventh degrees of this scale is an augmented second; this interval is usually avoided in melodic motion, but plenty of examples can be found nevertheless.

EXAMPLE 4–2: Mozart, *Symphony No. 40*, K. 550, I

The *melodic minor scale* provides the interval pattern for much of the melodic motion of music in the minor mode. The scale includes the major sixth and seventh degrees when it ascends, and the minor sixth and seventh degrees when it descends. Stepwise melodic progression from the fifth degree upward to the tonic proceeds along the major sixth and seventh degrees; descending motion from the tonic down to the dominant most often (but not always; see Example 4–5) includes the minor seventh and sixth degrees.

Examples 4–3 and 4 show the use of a complete scale in a melody, a frequent occurrence in the eighteenth and nineteenth centuries. Throughout the common-practice period, examples may be found of the major sixth and seventh degrees used in descending order.

EXAMPLE 4–3: Beethoven, *Piano Concerto No. 3*, I

EXAMPLE 4–4: Bach, *Well-Tempered Clavier, II*, Prelude No. 6

EXAMPLE 4–5: Bach, *French Suite No. 1*, Minuet II

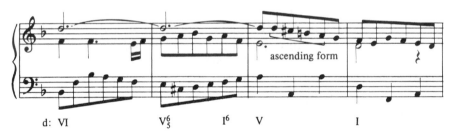

The opposite case—the minor sixth and seventh used in ascending order up to the tonic—is, however, rare until after common practice. The semitonal ascent of leading tone to tonic was such a strong convention that composers were reluctant to go against it. Most instances of such melodic progression during the common-practice period involve triads other than V and I.

The descending melodic minor corresponds to the natural minor scale; the ascending melodic minor is identical with the major scale except for the third degree. The harmonic minor scale is a sort of hybrid of the two melodic forms; it is called "harmonic" because much, though not all, of the harmony regularly used in the minor mode is made up of triads based on this scale, the remainder deriving from the melodic minor forms.

Triads in the Minor Mode

Because the sixth and seventh degrees vary according to use and context in the minor mode, it follows that there will be different kinds of triads containing one or the other of these degrees. All the possibilities are given below.

EXAMPLE 4–6

ascending forms:

descending forms:

Some elementary observations are: the tonic is the only triad in the minor mode that does not contain either the sixth or the seventh degree, and that therefore remains unchanged regardless of the type of minor scale used; four triads in the ascending melodic minor, II, IV, V, and VII, are identical with those of the parallel major mode; the whole collection includes three diminished triads, II, VI, and VII, and one augmented triad, III.

The following diagram separates the various triads into groups according to the harmonic minor scale and those triads that differ from it in the melodic minor forms.

EXAMPLE 4–7

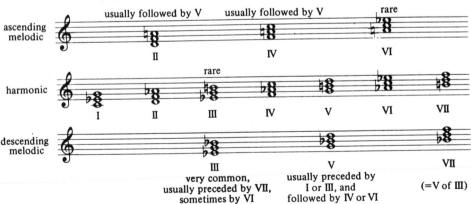

The harmonic minor scale was formerly considered to be the one scale by which all seven triads of "the minor mode" were defined. That view now seems overly simple on the one hand, and confusing on the other. The three-stave diagram above is a more accurate accounting of the triads as actually employed by composers, but it requires some explanation.

The mediant triad in the harmonic minor is traditionally the most problematic, but this augmented triad is rarely encountered in common practice. We can safely omit discussing it here; a few examples will be shown in later chapters. By far the commonest form of the mediant in the minor mode is the III major triad, whose fifth is the minor seventh degree of the scale. This triad, formed from the descending melodic minor scale, is identical with the tonic triad of the relative major scale and tends to be heard that way; its function will be discussed at the end of Chapter 5.

See Exx. 6–23, 8–27

As a general rule, the ascending melodic minor forms of II and IV (minor and major triads respectively) are used only in conjunction with the ascending melodic minor scale, when that scale appears in a clear melodic succession in one voice, from the sixth degree to the seventh degree to the tonic, usually with the fifth degree preceding as well.

EXAMPLE 4–8

c: II   V   I

EXAMPLE 4–9: Bach, Chorale No. 105, *Herzliebster Jesu*

See also Exx. 5–31, 7–7, 19–8

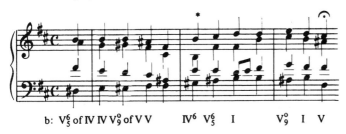

b: V$^6_5$ of IV IV V$^o_9$ of V V   IV^6 V$^6_5$ I   V$^o_9$ I   V

The ascending melodic minor form of VI, a diminished triad, is rare.

Similarly, the descending melodic minor V is generally used in conjunction with a downward scale progression beginning with the minor tonic.

EXAMPLE 4–10: Bach, Chorale No. 47, *Vater unser im Himmelreich*

d: I   V⁶ I VII⁶ I⁶   I⁶₄   V   I   V⁶ IV⁶ V (V of III)   VI IV⁶ V

See also Exx. 14–3, 26–11

See The Decline of Dominant Harmony in Chap. 30.

As mentioned before, the minor V was almost never used before the tonic triad until late in the nineteenth century; such usage is not considered common practice.

The diminished triad on the supertonic, though a dissonant triad, is used occasionally in root position, and abundantly in the other positions; its root or third may be doubled, but doubling of the fifth (the minor sixth degree) is avoided.

The diminished triad on the leading tone is of course identical with the leading-tone triad of the major mode. Its use and function in the minor mode are the same as in the major: it is seldom used in root position, and it functions like an incomplete dominant seventh chord. (See Chapters 6, 15, and 22.)

The major triad on the minor seventh degree (subtonic) is associated with major III in the great majority of cases, acting as its dominant, V of III. (See the end of Chapter 5.)

Harmonic Progression

The Table of Usual Root Progressions in the Major Mode, given on page 23, Chapter 3, applies also in the minor mode, with these differences:

I is also often followed by VII (major)
III (major) is also often followed by VII (major).
VII (major) is followed by III, sometimes VI, less often IV.
VII (diminished) is followed by I.

Voice Leading

All of the rules and procedures of motion and voice leading discussed in Chapter 3 apply with equal validity to the minor mode. The differences in scale structure in the minor mode, however, will ordinarily entail some further restrictions, for instance where motion by an augmented second is to be avoided.

A good illustration of some of these restraints may be found in the progression II–V, which can move in only two ways when the root of II is doubled; all other motions lead to an augmented second or a tritone in one of the parts, or to forbidden parallels. When the third is doubled no motion is possible without violations.

EXAMPLE 4–11

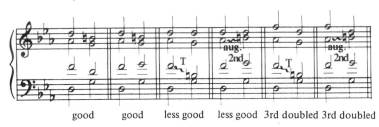

good   good   less good   less good   3rd doubled   3rd doubled

The progression VI–V is even more troublesome. If the doubled tone of VI is the root, no movement is possible except by augmented second, by tritone skip, or by forbidden parallel motion. When this progression is encountered it is best to double the third of the VI to ensure a smooth progression to V.

EXAMPLE 4–12

3rd doubled

The melodically awkward interval is sometimes unavoidable. The occasional inclusion of an augmented-second motion or a tritone motion does little harm, and if kept to an inner voice it will not disturb the progression.

Occasionally the progression I–II is encountered in root position in the minor mode, perhaps a little more frequently than in the major. When the fifth of the tonic chord is doubled it then becomes possible to move in parallel motion from a perfect fifth to a diminished fifth. This special kind of parallel-fifth motion has always been accepted between any pair of voices. It is more frequently met with in connection with the dominant seventh chord. The reverse motion—diminished to perfect fifth—is also permitted, except between the outer voices.

EXAMPLE 4–13

c: I   II   I⁶

EXERCISES

1. Write out the progressions given in Chapter 3, Examples 3–2 through 3–5, in the minor mode. Listen carefully to the results and compare with the major-mode forms.

2. Write out the progressions listed in Chapter 3, Exercise 1, according to the instructions given, but using the minor scales instead of the major.

3. Add soprano, alto, and tenor parts to the following basses. These harmonizations are to be worked out like those in Chapter 3. Write two versions of each bass, as before. Brackets indicate places where the harmony should employ the ascending or descending melodic minor scale form in one of the versions; where brackets are not given, the dominant will of course be the major form.

a.

desc.   asc.

4. *Analysis.* Find examples of ascending and descending melodic minor scales, extending through at least an octave, in works of several different composers. Find an example of a harmonic minor scale segment used melodically, with the minor sixth degree followed by the major seventh degree or vice versa.

5

Tonality and Modality

Modal Scales

Tonality is the organized relationship of pitches around a tonic. This means that there is a central tone supported in one way or another by all the other tones. Music that we say is "in the key of C major" has C as this central tone; it uses the notes of the C-major scale, but it also defines the C-major *tonality*, or key. We can also speak of tonality in a much broader sense, encompassing the whole body of major and minor scales, the various kinds of harmony based on them, and the music that uses these scales and harmonic types; thus music in the common-practice era is music that illustrates tonality generally, and is said to represent the *tonal system*.

Modality refers to the specific choice of the tones relating to a particular tonic, and thus is concerned with the different kinds of scales. The major and minor scales are the most familiar specific modalities. In addition to these, a large number of other *modal scales* can be con-

EXAMPLE 5–1

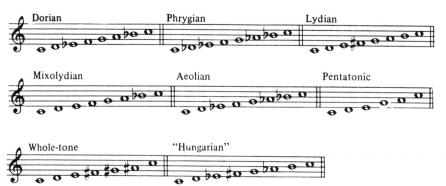

52

structed in any given tonality. Several of these scales are central to the music of the fifteenth and sixteenth centuries; we will study them in detail in Part Two of this book, in connection with their reappearance in nineteenth-century music. As illustration, a few are given on the keynote C in Example 5–1.

The *Aeolian mode* is identical with the natural minor scale; the older name, like the term *Ionian mode* for the major scale, was employed until the seventeenth century.

These modes may be transposed freely by changing the pitch of the tonic and preserving the interval relationships.

EXAMPLE 5–2

G: Dorian   E: Phrygian   B♭: Lydian   F♯: Mixolydian

Modes taken from folksongs and even oriental scales have been used by composers during the common-practice period, but only by exception.

Tonal Functions of the Scale Degrees

Tonality is not merely a matter of using only the tones of a particular scale. It is more a process of establishing the relationship of these tones to the one that is the tonal center. Each scale degree has its part in the scheme of tonality, its *tonal function.*

Once established, the tonic serves as the basis for the tonality of a work and for all the harmony that goes into it. So strong is the tonic function that it may be effectively projected by an incomplete triad, or even by the tonic root alone, as at the end of a piece when the primacy of the tonic center has already been repeatedly confirmed.

EXAMPLE 5–3: Bizet, *Carmen,* Act I

Allegro

d: I   (V of V?)   V   I

Dominant and subdominant seem to give an impression of balanced support of the tonic, like two equidistant weights on either side of a fulcrum.

EXAMPLE 5–4

I   V   I   IV   I

The above could represent the harmonic outline of many a short piece of music, the first destination being the dominant, followed by a return to the tonic, and then the subdominant to make the last tonic more satisfying and final.

Tonic, dominant, and subdominant are called the *tonal degrees* of the scale, since they are the mainstay of the tonality. In a given tonality these degrees remain the same for both modes.

EXAMPLE 5–5

C: I   IV   V   c: I   IV   V

Mediant and submediant are called the *modal degrees*. They have little effect on the tonality but define the mode, since they are different in major and minor.

EXAMPLE 5–6

C: III   VI   c: III   VI

The power of a modal degree to "color" a harmony is suggested by a tonic chord with any number of doublings of root and fifth, and only a single third degree. Such a distribution of factors is often seen in orchestral music.

EXAMPLE 5-7

The supertonic often functions as dominant of the dominant.

EXAMPLE 5-8

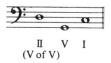

II   V   I
(V of V)

Harmonically, however, the supertonic tends to become absorbed into the subdominant chord, especially in certain positions.

EXAMPLE 5-9

II   I
(IV)

The supertonic should, therefore, be included in the list of tonal degrees, since it partakes of both dominant and subdominant characteristics, but should be distinguished from I, IV, and V as having much less tonal strength.

The seventh degree, the leading tone, for all its importance as an indicator of the tonic through its melodic tendency, does not function by itself as a generator of harmony, but rather is absorbed into the dominant chord. The progression of leading tone to tonic may be described as melodically VII-I and harmonically V-I.

In terms of harmonic roots, overemphasis on the modal degrees tends to give the effect of a mode, and a tonality, other than that intended.

The modal degrees, by their insistence, are accepted by the ear as tonal degrees of another scale.

EXAMPLE 5–10

It follows that the tonal structure of music consists mainly of harmonies with tonal degrees as roots (I, IV, V, sometimes II), and modal-degree chords (III and VI) used for variety. There are many possible variations to this generalization, but nevertheless it may be considered the norm of common practice for music remaining in one key.

Dominant Harmony

The strongest harmonic element in tonal music is the dominant function. The dominant-to-tonic succession determines the key much more decisively than the tonic chord alone. This fact is perhaps not apparent with simple triads, but should be borne in mind throughout the study of harmony. Establishment of a key or confirmation of it, reinforcing the tonic by means of dominant harmony, is an everyday occurrence. (See Examples 5–11, 12, and 13.)

The use of dominant harmony before the tonic is by no means confined to the establishment of a key. The combination may occur anywhere, but is most often found at the end of a phrase, where it is

EXAMPLE 5-11: Beethoven, *Violin Concerto*, Op. 61, I

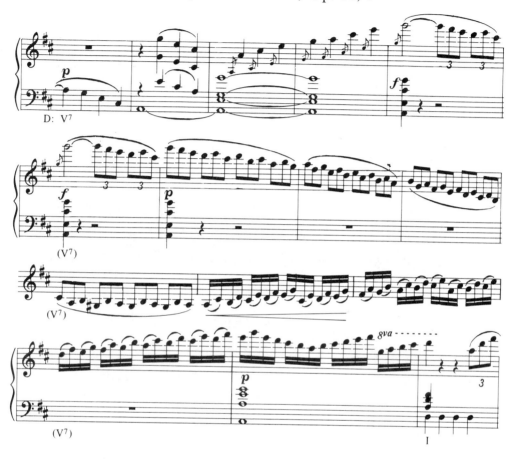

EXAMPLE 5-12: Chopin, *Prelude*, Op. 28, No. 16

EXAMPLE 5–13: Schubert, *Mass No. 5 in A♭*, Gloria

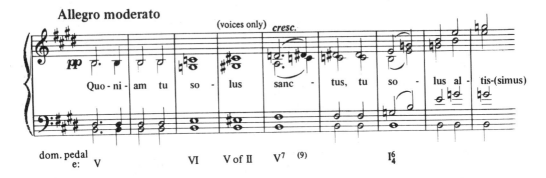

called the *authentic cadence*; virtually any work will furnish an example of this familiar progression.

EXAMPLE 5–14: Bach, Chorale No. 350, *Werde munter, mein Gemüte*

EXAMPLE 5–15: Beethoven, *Symphony No. 5*, I

The alternation of tonic and dominant for long stretches at a time, with no other harmony, occurs frequently in music throughout the Classical and Romantic periods, particularly in dance forms.

EXAMPLE 5–16: Schubert, *Ländler for the Fair Ladies of Vienna,*
        Op. 67, No. 2

D: V⁷   (9)   I   V⁷   (9)   I   V   I

EXAMPLE 5–17: Beethoven, *Symphony No. 5,* IV

C: I   V   I   V⁷   I   V⁷   I   V   I

It will be noted that the minor triad on the dominant root is almost never used in contexts such as those above. Without the leading tone, the dominant effect is drastically weakened, as the alternate analysis in Example 5–10 shows. The minor dominant commonly occurs in conjunction with the descending melodic minor scale, but in motion away from tonic harmony, not toward it.

Tonal Strength of Chords

A single chord heard by itself may be interpreted in any of several keys.

EXAMPLE 5–18

F: I	e: I
B♭: V	G: VI I
C: IV	C: III
a: VI	b: IV

This ambiguity, which will later prove advantageous to the process of modulation, is greatly lessened when two chords are heard in a harmonic progression. Each progression has certain preferred implications of tonality.

EXAMPLE 5–19

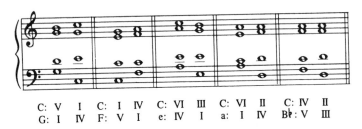

The greatest tonal strength in these harmonic progressions results from contrasting dominant harmony with subdominant harmony, with the supertonic considered as having some subdominant qualities. The presence of the tonic chord itself is not necessary to the establishment of a key. The dominant is much more important. The progressions IV–V and II–V cannot be interpreted in more than one tonality, and hence they do not need the tonic chord to show the key. The tonic following upon one of these progressions is a confirmation of what was already certain. As for the progression V–VI, it too points strongly to a single tonality, even though it is possible to hear it as the relatively uncommon progression I–II in the dominant key.

EXAMPLE 5–20

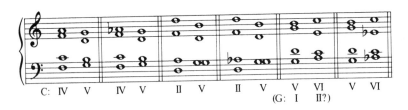

It may be necessary to hear a third chord if the harmonic progression is to define the tonality with certainty. When another chord is added to the successions in Example 5–19, they can be rendered almost unmistakably in C.

EXAMPLE 5–21

C: IV V I   I IV V   V VI III   VI II V   IV II V

On the other hand, a third chord could be selected that would confirm the alternative tonalities given in Example 5–19.

EXAMPLE 5–22

G: I IV V   F: IV V I   e: IV I V   a: I IV V   B♭: V III II

These elementary tonal units, groups of two or three chords with distinct meaning as to key, might be regarded as musical "words." As an aid in learning these *formulae* (Latin, "little forms"), you will find it helpful to write as many of them as possible in a notebook where they will be available for reference, beginning with the commonest, like II–V–I, I–IV–V, etc., and even including some that you may invent. Study them for their individual qualities, their tonal strength and direction, and look for them in actual works of music.

Variations of the formulae by differences in doubling, spacing, and choice of soprano note are resources that are already familiar.

EXAMPLE 5–23

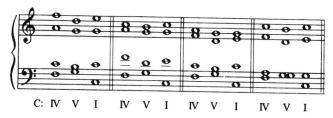

C: IV V I   IV V I   IV V I   IV V I

Change of mode from major to minor, or vice versa, does not affect the tonality of the formula, and it is one of the most important means of variation. Example 5–22 could be rewritten as follows, the only change being in the modes. The last measure shows that the results of the mode change may not always be as satisfactory as the original.

EXAMPLE 5–24

g: I IV V   f: IV V I   E: IV I V   A: I IV V   bb: V III II

Harmonic formulae exist in virtually every kind of music from the simplest textures to the most complex. Analysis of the masterworks of the eighteenth and nineteenth centuries reveals the endless possibilities for varied treatment of these harmonic structural elements. Compare the following presentations of the formula II–V–I:

EXAMPLE 5–25: Mozart, *Sonata*, K. 330, III

See also Exx.
6–14, 8–4,
8–25, 11–5,
13–13, 13–17,
15–9, 19–5 and
even 31–22

C: II⁶   V⁷   I

EXAMPLE 5–26: Chopin, *Nocturne*, Op. 62, No. 1

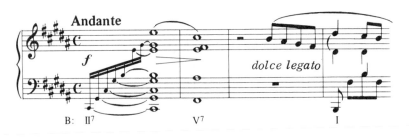

B: II⁷   V⁷   I

EXAMPLE 5–27: Beethoven, *Sonata*, Op. 13 ("Pathétique"), II

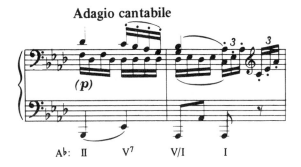

Interchangeability of Modes

The modal implications of the chord progressions are less significant than their tonal implications. Major and minor modes are not as different in usage as their two scales would seem to indicate, and it is sometimes hard to tell which the composer intends.

Fluctuation between major and minor is frequently heard in common-practice music. In the following example, the progression I–V is repeated with change of mode, a change involving but one note—the third degree. The mode change is thus brought about within the tonic chord, the dominant proceeding to the major or minor tonic with equal ease.

EXAMPLE 5–28: Beethoven, *Sonata*, Op. 53 ("Waldstein"), III

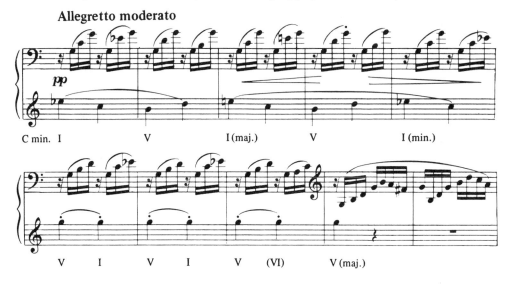

The next example is of a more unusual kind of mode change, the major subdominant proceeding to the minor tonic without the mediating force of the dominant in between.

EXAMPLE 5–29: Haydn, *Sonata No. 8*, II

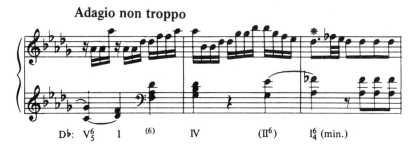

The Picardy Third

As early as the sixteenth century, it was a widely accepted convention to end a work with a major triad, even if the work had been unmistakably in minor throughout. The major third of this triad is still called the *tierce de Picardie* or *Picardy third*.

EXAMPLE 5–30: Bach, *Well-Tempered Clavier, I,* Prelude No. 4

See also Ex. 14–4

Relationship of Relative Major and Minor: The Secondary Dominant Principle

The keys of C major and A minor, to take the simplest example, are called *relative major and minor* because they have the same key signature, and for the most part use the same set of notes. In the most basic sense, the distinction between the two keys is defined by the tonic. In actual music, however, what defines the key is not just the scale used. What is important is the way the tonic triad is used—where it appears, how it associates with the dominant, and with what kind of preparation and emphasis. We have already stated that tonic and dominant are the principal harmonic elements that define tonality. Thus one might expect to be able to determine whether a given phrase, or group of phrases, or even a whole piece, is in C major or A minor by several tests: by examining initial and final chords, by comparing the relative frequency of C-major and A-minor triads, and by looking for the presence of G♯s, which would suggest the leading tone in A minor.

EXAMPLE 5–31: Bach, Chorale No. 48, *Ach wie flüchtig, ach wie nichtig*

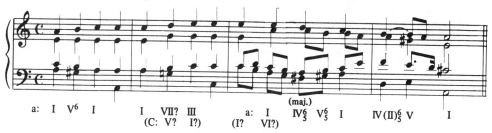

It is obvious that the example above begins and ends in A minor, the beginning and ending both being clearly marked by V–I progressions. The second measure, however, would seem to be in C major, especially if one imagines a V–I in that key comparable to the V–I of A minor in the first measure. The second measure could be interpreted as I–VII–III in A minor, but this does not account for the strong dominant feeling in C major; on the other hand, it does not seem right to say that after hearing a piece in A minor for one measure one suddenly hears it in C major for the next, and then just as abruptly hears the next two measures in A minor again.

A combination of these two interpretations allows the entire phrase to be analyzed in A minor. The second chord in the second measure is certainly the dominant of C, and C is III in A minor; therefore the dominant will be called V of III. The V of III is said to *tonicize* III, to make it momentarily heard as a tonic even while we remember that A minor is the overall tonic of the phrase as a whole. This interpretation is an application of what is called the *secondary dominant principle*.

The secondary dominant principle will be discussed thoroughly in later chapters, but it is important to introduce it early. The use of secondary dominant harmony throughout the common-practice period is one more confirmation of the importance of the dominant–tonic relationship. Since the concept of "V of . . ." can be applied to virtually any degree of the scale, it points to the possibility of a greatly magnified vocabulary of chords available in any one key.

See also Exx. 7–22, 8–27

Here is a somewhat longer illustration of the relationship shown in Example 5–31. The student should analyze it and compare the two.

EXAMPLE 5–32: Schubert, *Symphony No. 9*, II

Chromaticism and Tonality

Chromaticism is the name given to the use of tones outside the major or minor scales. Chromatic tones began to appear in music long before the common-practice period, and by the beginning of that period were an important part of its melodic and harmonic resources. Chromatic tones arise in music partly from inflection of scale degrees in the major and minor modes, partly from secondary dominant harmony, from a special vocabulary of altered chords, and from certain nonharmonic tones.

It is apparent that establishment and maintenance of a key may be a complicated procedure, especially in a long symphonic movement when the apparent tone center may change many times before returning to the original key. We have seen how tonality may be defined in short phrases, and we know from experience that, for instance, Beethoven's *Symphony No. 1 in C major* is fundamentally "in C major" even though many other tonalities may be found in it. Our study of harmony will eventually reveal much about how one key may change to another and how composers have considered tonal design in both smaller and larger contexts.

The investigation of these complexities belongs to a more advanced stage in the study of harmony, but there are two points to be aware of from the start. The first is that the parallel and relative modes, major and minor, tend to become interchangeable, even when only triads are used. The second point is that notes outside the scale do not necessarily affect the tonality. These principles may cause difficulty at first, but they should be announced early, if only to emphasize the fact that tonality is established by the progression of roots and the tonal functions of the chords, even though the details of the music may contain all the tones of the chromatic scale.

Arpeggiation of Chord Factors

All the exercises in Chapters 3 and 4 were to be written note against note, with all harmonizing voices having the same time-values as the given bass notes. From this point on, this strict limitation will no longer be required, and the upper parts may move in smaller note-values than the bass, using any of the factors of the indicated triad. Melodic motion among the factors of a single chord is called *arpeggiation*. You are urged to make use of arpeggiations in the upper parts of your exercises, to permit more flexibility of the melodic line and of the spacing of the four-part texture. Experiment with the simpler cases first, such as the motion of two notes in the soprano against one in the bass, to the nearest available triadic factor.

EXAMPLE 5–33

sometimes

To maintain proper spacing and doubling, it will usually be necessary to arpeggiate at least two voices at the same time.

The principal advantages to be gained by arpeggiation are the new possibilities for rhythm and melodic direction, both of great importance in shaping the soprano line.

EXAMPLE 5–34

It is important that arpeggiation not be thoughtlessly overused. A soprano line with too much disjunct motion, unrelieved by rhythmic contrast and without any broad contours, would soon sound as shapeless as one that hardly moved at all. In all exercises in this book, musical imagination is as important as the specified constraints. You should test your invention and judgment constantly by singing your exercises one line at a time and by trying them out on the piano.

EXERCISES

Writing exercises without key signature, using accidentals when needed, is sometimes helpful for showing the differences in mode and tonality.

1. Write the modal degrees of the following scales:

    a. A♭ minor
    b. C♯ major
    c. D♭ major
    d. G♯ minor
    e. E♭ minor

2. In which tonalities is E♭ a modal degree? a tonal degree? Answer these same questions for the notes F♯, B, G♯, and D♭.

3. Give the tonalities and modes (major and minor) of the following progressions:

4. Rewrite the following progressions, changing those that are major to minor, and those that are minor to major.

5. Write each of the following harmonic formulae in four different versions, using only triads in root position. Each version should have a different spacing.

a. C minor: VI–II–V
b. E major: II–V–VI
c. D♭ major: V–VI–IV
d. A minor: IV–V–I
e. F major: V–IV–I

6. Harmonize the following basses in four parts, root position only:

7. Construct an original chord succession, starting with a series of roman numerals, arranged with attention to the proper distribution of modal and tonal degrees, and to the quality of the harmonic progressions involved. The series should finally be worked out in four parts, with suitable meter and rhythm.

8. *Analysis*. Examine all the triads in the excerpt below, ignoring all chords that are not triads. What minor scale forms are used? What would be the result of using a different scale form? At the piano, try substituting the major sixth and seventh degrees for the minor, and vice versa. Could the excerpt be easily rewritten entirely in major?

Erhalt uns, Herr, bei deinem Wort (German, 1543)

6

The First Inversion—
The Figured Bass

Arabic-Numeral Notation

If the third of a triad is in the bass, the triad is said to be in *first inversion*, regardless of where the root may appear above it.

Adopting the method of musical shorthand developed by composers in the Baroque era, most theorists designate inversions of chords by arabic numerals showing the intervals between bass and upper voices. Thus, a triad in first inversion is represented by the figures $^6_3$, or simply ^{6}, the third being understood. With roman numerals identifying the roots, any chord in any inversion can be represented symbolically in this way.

Spacing and doubling are not prescribed by the figures. A $^6_3$ chord will of course have the third in the bass, but the root and fifth may be placed above it in any order or octave.

Though we will not discuss seventh chords until a later chapter, a

EXAMPLE 6–1

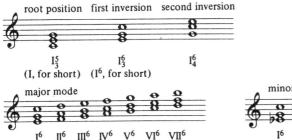

71

dominant seventh chord is shown in Example 6–2 in all of its positions to illustrate the figuring of such chords. The backward sequence (7, 6–5, 4–3, 2) of the abbreviated figuring forms a convenient memory device.

EXAMPLE 6–2

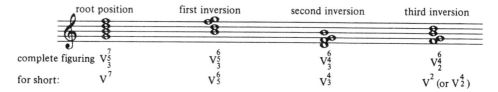

root position   first inversion   second inversion   third inversion

complete figuring $V^7_5{}_3$ $V^6_5{}_3$ $V^6_4{}_3$ $V^6_4{}_2$

for short: V^7 V^6_5 V^4_3 V^2 (or V^4_2)

Doubling

In order to obtain a fourth tone for four-part writing, the root is generally doubled when the triad is in root position. This useful rule does not necessarily apply, however, to triads in the first inversion.

The choice of which tone to double does not depend on whether the triad is major, minor, augmented, or diminished. Nor does it appear to have been, throughout this period of common practice, a question of effective sonority. Most often, the choice is based on the position of the doubled note in the tonality. In other words, tones are doubled that contribute to the solidity of the key.

The customary procedure for doubling in triads in the first inversion can be summed up as follows:

    a. If the bass (not root) of the first-inversion triad is a tonal degree (I, IV, or V; sometimes II), it is doubled.
    b. If the bass of the triad is not a tonal degree, it is not doubled, but a tonal degree in the chord is doubled instead.

EXAMPLE 6–3

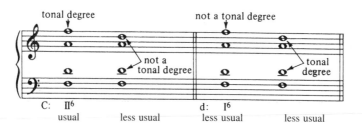

tonal degree   not a tonal degree

not a tonal degree   tonal degree

C: II^6 d: I^6

usual   less usual   less usual   less usual

Regardless of what tone is chosen for doubling, all three normal factors—root, third, and fifth—should be present in any inversion of a triad. This is because ambiguity may result if one of them is omitted. If the root is omitted in a triad in first inversion, it will most likely be heard as a root-position triad, without fifth, on the tone a third above the intended root. If the fifth is omitted, the chord might be interpreted as a second-inversion triad with missing root.

EXAMPLE 6–4

C: I⁶ or III?   I⁶ or VI₄⁶?

Voice-leading considerations may occasionally dictate the use of incomplete chords in passing; nevertheless, it remains a good rule that inverted triads in harmonically strong situations should not omit any factors.

General Effect of the First Inversion

Harmonically, considered vertically as a sonority, the triad in its first inversion is lighter, less ponderous, less blocklike, than the same triad in root position. It is therefore valuable as an element of variety when used with root-position chords. Compare the sound in the two versions of a series of triads given below.

EXAMPLE 6–5

A: I   IV   I   II   III VI   II   V   I   A: I   IV⁶   I⁶   II⁶   III⁶ VI   II⁶   V   I

Melodically, first-inversion triads permit the bass to move by step in progressions in which the roots would move by skip. It is difficult to arrange a smooth melodic line for the bass when all the chords are in root position. The bass will also possess that advantage hitherto allowed only in the upper voices, of moving from root to third, and vice versa, in the same harmony.

EXAMPLE 6–6

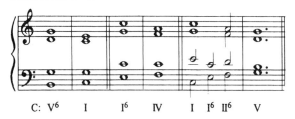

C: V⁶   I   I⁶   IV   I   I⁶ II⁶   V

EXAMPLE 6–7: Schubert, *Symphony No. 9*, II

F: I   V⁶   VI   III⁶   IV VII⁶ III VI   II⁶   V   I
                                         (I⁶?)

Rhythmically, the triad in first inversion is less weighty than one in root position. In Example 6–6 above, the progressions V⁶–I, I⁶–IV, and II⁶–V are felt as weak-to-strong rhythms, and the I–I⁶ as strong-to-weak. The student is reminded, however, that the almost inevitable presence of other factors influencing the rhythm makes it unwise to draw conclusions from a single criterion. In the following example, there can be no doubt that the rhythmic stress is on the first beat of the second measure.

EXAMPLE 6–8: Brahms, *Symphony No. 1*, II

E: I IV⁶ IV   V⁶ I

Voice Leading

There are no new principles of voice leading or of harmonic progression involved in the use of triads in the first inversion. The objective of smooth connection of the chords is ever to be kept in mind, the normal progression of the voices being always to the nearest available position. It remains a true principle of contrapuntal practice that doubling and spacing are less important than melodic movement.

EXAMPLE 6–9

G: II   I⁶   II⁶   V

    Here the stepwise contrary motion in the soprano and bass has been thought desirable enough to allow the doubling of the modal degree B in the second chord, even though that note has the added prominence of being in the outside voices.

Consecutive First-Inversion Triads

When several first-inversion triads occur in succession, there is a tendency for the parts to move in similar motion. Many examples of the following manner of voice leading may be found in the literature. (In the fifteenth and sixteenth centuries such parallel first-inversion triads were called *fauxbourdon*.)

EXAMPLE 6–10

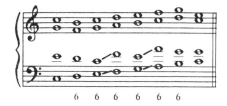

    6   6   6   6   6   6

    The direct octaves between tenor and bass can, however, be avoided, and a more balanced arrangement made:

EXAMPLE 6–11

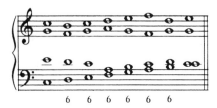

6 6 6 6 6 6

In either case, the harmonic function of the individual chords is deemphasized in favor of the parallel, linear character of the succession.

In fast tempo, a succession of parallel first-inversion triads may sound more like a triadic doubling or thickening of a single melodic line than a succession of actual harmonic progressions.

EXAMPLE 6–12: Beethoven, *Sonata*, Op. 2, No. 3, IV

C: I   IV⁶(I⁶₄)   V⁶₅ of V

Usage of the Various Triads

The first inversion of the tonic triad is one of the most useful chords, and at the same time one of the inversions most neglected by the beginner. It serves as a useful alternative where the root-position triad might sound too strong, and often provides the necessary variety when a chord is needed to follow the dominant. I⁶ is also a natural harmony to support a melody moving from tonic to dominant by skip.

Some common formulae containing I⁶:

EXAMPLE 6–13

I⁶ II⁶ V   I I⁶ IV   V I⁶ IV   IV I⁶ V

EXAMPLE 6–14: Beethoven, *Piano Concerto No. 1*, Op. 15, I

EXAMPLE 6–15: Schumann, *Carnaval*, Op. 9, *Préambule*

EXAMPLE 6–16: Mozart, *Sonata*, K. 332, I

The supertonic triad in first inversion is very common in cadences, where it precedes and introduces the dominant. It is strongly subdominant in feeling, since the fourth degree is the bass tone and usually doubled. II⁶ often follows I, whereas II in root position is generally considered an awkward progression from root-position I. In minor, the first inversion is preferred to the root-position diminished triad. This minor form is not unusual in combination with the major tonic triad.

Common formulae:

EXAMPLE 6–17

II⁶	V	I	II⁶	V	I	I	II⁶	V	VI	II⁶	I

$$\text{II}^6 \quad \text{V} \quad \text{I} \qquad \text{II}^6 \quad \text{V} \quad \text{I} \qquad \text{I} \quad \text{II}^6 \quad \text{V} \quad \text{VI} \quad \text{II}^6 \quad \text{I}$$

EXAMPLE 6–18: Schumann, *Album for the Young*, Op. 68: No. 28, *Remembrance (November 4, 1847)*

Nicht schnell und sehr gesangsvoll zu spielen

$$\text{A:} \quad \text{I} \qquad \text{II}^6 \qquad \text{V}^7 \qquad (\text{V}^2) \qquad \text{I}^6 \quad \text{V}^2 \text{ of IV} \quad \text{IV}^6 \quad \text{II}(\text{IV})^6_5 \quad \text{V}$$

EXAMPLE 6–19: Brahms, *Symphony No. 4*, IV

Allegro energico e passionato

$$\text{e:} \quad \text{IV}^6 \qquad \text{II}^6 \qquad \text{I} \qquad \text{IV}^6 \qquad \text{V}^7 \text{ of V} \qquad \text{I}^6 \qquad \text{V}^4_3 \qquad \text{I}$$

III⁶ is not usually an independent chord; it is a good example of the kind of chord made by temporary displacement of tones of some other chord, in this case nearly always the dominant. For this reason, it is considered harmonically weaker than the first-inversion triads of the tonal degrees, and must be employed carefully.

EXAMPLE 6–20

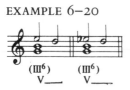

$$(\text{III}^6) \quad (\text{III}^6)$$
$$\text{V}\underline{\quad} \quad \text{V}\underline{\quad}$$

The augmented triad on III in the harmonic minor mode, mentioned in Chapter 4 as an uncommon chord in any case, is probably more often found in the first inversion than in root position. Example 6–23 shows this chord actually substituting for a dominant.

Like all other chords of the sixth, it may be found in scalewise passages of weak rhythmic value.

When it proceeds to VI, the third degree may be doubled and regarded temporarily as a dominant of the sixth degree.

Common formulae:

EXAMPLE 6–21

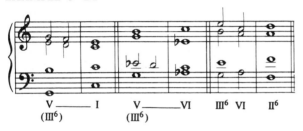

EXAMPLE 6–22: Brahms, *Violin Sonata*, Op. 108, II

EXAMPLE 6–23: Bach, *Magnificat*: No. 7, *Fecit potentiam*

EXAMPLE 6–24: Chopin, *Polonaise*, Op. 40, No. 1

A: III   II⁶   III⁶   IV⁶   V   I

The first inversion of the subdominant triad is often used after V. It furnishes a welcome change from VI when the bass moves up by step. This also avoids the false relation of the tritone between bass and soprano, likely to occur in the progression V–IV with leading tone in the upper voice.

The chord is of course valuable for relieving the weight of the subdominant in root position, retaining the strength of the root progression and at the same time imparting a melodic quality to the bass.

Common formulae:

EXAMPLE 6–25

I   V   IV⁶   IV⁶   V   I⁶   I   IV⁶   I⁶

EXAMPLE 6–26: Mendelssohn, *Symphony No. 3* ("Scottish"), I

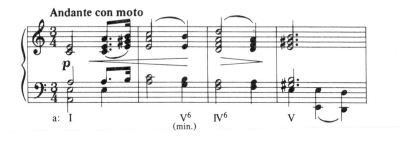

a: I   V⁶   IV⁶   V
                (min.)

EXAMPLE 6–27: Beethoven, *Symphony No. 2*, III

D: I   IV⁶   I⁶ V⁴₃ I   V

The third of the dominant is the leading tone, and placing that degree in the bass gives the bass strong melodic significance in addition to lessening the harmonic rigidity of the root-position dominant. The leading tone in the bass usually moves to the tonic, so that the next chord will probably be I, as in Examples 6–29 and 6–30.

At times the bass may proceed downward, as in a descending scale. In the minor mode, this would be the occasion for the use of the descending melodic minor scale in the bass, as in Example 6–37.

Formulae:

EXAMPLE 6–28

I V⁶ I   I   V⁶ IV⁶   I   V⁶ IV⁶

EXAMPLE 6–29: Beethoven, *Symphony No. 9*, III

B♭: I   V²   I⁶   V⁶   I   V⁶ VII⁷ V⁴₃ of V I⁶₄   V

EXAMPLE 6–30: Mozart, Overture to *Don Giovanni*, K. 527

The VI[6] chord is similar to III[6] in its inability to stand as an independent chord. It is nearly always the tonic chord, with the sixth degree as a melodic tone resolving down to the fifth. Usual exceptions to this are found in scalewise progressions of successive first-inversion triads.

Formulae:

See also Ex.
12–7

EXAMPLE 6–31

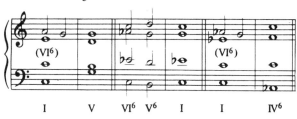

See also Ex.
22–2

EXAMPLE 6–32: Franck, *Symphony*, I

EXAMPLE 6–33: Chopin, *Waltz in E minor* (op. posth.)

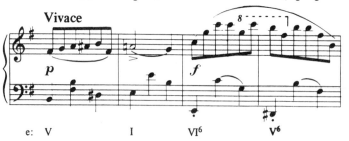

The leading-tone triad in first inversion is commonly used as a passing chord between the tonic chord in root position and its first inversion. In such a case it is rhythmically weak, hardly disturbing the effect of tonic harmony, and may be analyzed as a grouping of melodic tones above the tonic root. On the other hand, if dwelt upon or otherwise given any prominence, it may function as a true dominant, the root V being understood.

In VII⁶ the second degree is most often doubled in preference to the more strongly tonal fourth degree, but instances in which the fourth degree is doubled are numerous (Example 6–37).

Formulae:

EXAMPLE 6–34

I VII⁶ I⁶ IV   VII⁶ I⁶ II⁶ V   I⁶ VII⁶ I
(I _____ IV)

See also Exx.
4–10, 11–7,
23–14

EXAMPLE 6–35: Bach, Chorale No. 20, *Ein' feste Burg*

D: I   VI   I VII⁶ I V of V V VI VII⁶ of VI VI⁶ III IV VII⁶ I V I

EXAMPLE 6–36: Mozart, *Piano Concerto*, K. 488, III

Presto

A: I   VII⁶   I⁶   V of V⁶₄ I V

Keyboard Harmony and Figured Bass

As was suggested earlier, a certain amount of time, preferably every day, should be devoted to the practice and eventual memorization of the harmonic formulae given in each chapter. You should learn them at the piano in various spacings and in all keys. Additional constraints may be introduced, such as playing the parts with crossed hands, or not playing one of the inner parts and singing it instead. With such practice the progressions and their voice leading will become instinctive.

The advantages afforded by proficiency in keyboard harmony are considerable. The applications in improvisation are obvious, but the main value of keyboard skills is that they accustom the ear to instantaneous solutions to standard harmonic problems. Beyond the formulae, apply your technique to the realization of figured bass at the keyboard.

The figured bass had a practical use in the Baroque period, when the ever-present keyboard player required only a guide to the harmonic content of the music in order to fill in missing parts or to reinforce weak ones. The *basso continuo* was prescribed in scores up into Mozart's time, but fell out of use thereafter as the orchestra became standardized in its instrumental makeup and as the art of conducting developed. Today, specialists in Baroque performance often are trained in rapid figured-bass reading, in the interest of historical authenticity.

Although in general use in the study of harmony, the figured bass is of somewhat limited value as a written exercise. It is a good short-hand method of designating chords, but the working-out of figured basses entails no problem of choosing the appropriate harmony. The problem is solely one of distribution of given materials, correct voice leading, and construction of a smooth soprano melody. In the early stages of study, this can prove useful for written exercises, but working out figured basses at the keyboard is much more beneficial. They should be played anew each time, beginning with different soprano notes. It is extremely important that they be played rhythmically, even if very slowly.

The practice of denoting upper voices by arabic numerals also allows for the inclusion of nonharmonic tones (discussed in Chapter 8). The proper method of reading the figures consists of finding the notes by measuring intervals above the bass, and only afterwards identifying the resulting chord. With practice, the combinations of figures get to be as familiar as the chords themselves.

The full figuring for a triad in root position would be $\frac{8}{5}$, but this is used only to designate the exact doubling. The order of voices from the top down need not follow that of the numerals; the figuring is the same whether root, third, or fifth is in the soprano voice. Root-position triads are so common that this is assumed when no figure appears under the given note. Sometimes just a 5 or a 3 is given as a reminder, to make sure that a triad in root position will be used. For the first inversion, a 6 is sufficient indication, the third being thereby understood, as shown in Example 6–1.

EXAMPLE 6–37

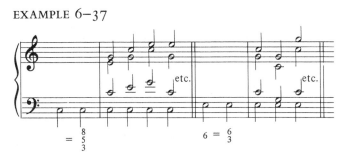

Accidentals are shown by placing the desired signs *to the right* of the numerals representing the notes to be affected. An accidental sign standing alone, or *under* a number, signifies that the third above the bass is to receive that sign. The leading-tone sharp or natural in the minor mode is indicated that way. A line drawn through the numeral has the same effect of chromatically raising the note to which the numeral refers. A straight horizontal line placed after a figure means that the note represented by the figure is maintained in the harmony to the end of the line, regardless of the change of bass; this sign will be encountered in connection with nonharmonic tones.

EXAMPLE 6–38

Not all published figured basses conform rigorously to these symbol rules. The Bach Gesellschaft Edition scores, for instance, some-

times use the sharp sign for chromatically raising a tone, or a flat sign
for lowering, when only a natural sign would be called for.

EXAMPLE 6–39

The following example shows a phrase from a Bach chorale as it
appears in the score of the *St. Matthew Passion*, together with a typical
realization in which most of the nonharmonic tones are in the bass.

EXAMPLE 6–40: Bach, Chorale No. 78, *Herzliebster Jesu*

Choral score

Continuo as given

Typical realization

with full figuring

EXERCISES

1. Write in four parts the following series of chords indicated by
symbols.

a. C minor: III⁶–I–IV

f. E♭ major: I⁶–II⁶–V

b. G major: I–I⁶–IV

g. D minor: VI⁶–V⁶–I

c. A♭ major: III⁶–VI–II⁶

h. B minor: II⁶–V–I

d. A minor: V–I⁶–IV

i. F♯ major: I–V–IV⁶

e. B♭ major: I–VII⁶–I⁶

j. D major: II⁶–V–I

2. Realize the following figured basses in four parts:

3. Realize the following figured basses in four parts, or, if you wish, just three parts. The soprano will have the rhythm indicated; the rhythm of the inner part or parts is up to you.

4. Harmonize the following basses, using root-position triads and, where appropriate, first-inversion triads:

5. Harmonize the following basses, using triads in root position and first inversion, and incorporating the soprano notes as given:

6. *Analysis.* Analyze the following excerpt by providing roman and arabic numerals. Some of the notes are not part of the harmony associated with them; indicate these with a check mark. (One of the triads, identified by the indication I_4^6, is in second inversion.)

Mozart, *Sonata*, K. 284, III

7

Function and Structure of Melody

A melody is any group of tones heard as a coherent succession. Usually, however, when one thinks of melody it is a particular melody, one with an individuality that is intended to be perceived.

That melody is so basic to the very nature of music is shown by the way we identify individual pieces. We recognize compositions by their themes or tunes, not by their harmony or form, nor by performer. When we hum or whistle to ourselves, it is melody that we hum or whistle, our recollection of the melody helping us to recreate in the mind's ear as much of the whole piece as we can.

Throughout history, melodies of every conceivable variety have been used to impart order and meaning to compositions large and small. The structure of melody and the uses of melody in music constitute an enormous and complex subject, to which this chapter will serve as a brief introduction.

Uses of Melody

The character and structure of a melody often depends on the way it is used within a piece of music. Its most important function is as a *theme*, a melody that recurs in a composition and is part of its larger organization. Often the very first music heard in a composition will also be its most important theme. (See Example 7–1.)

Not all melodies, of course, are themes; and some themes are not melodies. An interior or accompanimental part, for instance, may be

EXAMPLE 7–1: Beethoven, *Symphony No. 1*, II

very plainly melodic, even though one does not normally listen to it for its melodic individuality.

EXAMPLE 7–2: Mozart, *Symphony No. 38*, K. 504 ("Prague"), II

This is even more likely to be true of bass lines, which are so frequently written to assure a maximum of contrast with the melody in the upper voice.

EXAMPLE 7–3: Mendelssohn, *Symphony No. 4* ("Italian"), II

A principal melody may be stated entirely alone, as in Example 7–1, or it may be exposed against any type of accompaniment, whether simply chordal or busily contrapuntal or anything in between. Other things being equal, a melody in the top voice of a texture is likely to be automatically heard as the principal voice. If a middle or lower voice is to be given melodic prominence, it will normally be stressed by use of a stronger dynamic marking, by reinforcement of its instrumentation, or by lessening the activity of the surrounding accompaniment.

EXAMPLE 7–4: Beethoven, *String Quartet*, Op. 59, No. 1, I

A *countermelody* is deliberately contrasted with a principal melody both rhythmically and melodically, especially when there is little or no other melodic activity. The main countermelody in the example below is the part moving in steady sixteenth notes; the slower principal melody, sometimes above it and sometimes below, has already been heard earlier in the movement.

EXAMPLE 7–5: Berlioz, *Symphonie fantastique*, I: *Reveries—Passions*

A countermelody for a solo instrument in combination with a solo singer and additional harmonic accompaniment is called an *obbligato*; many examples appear in opera and in sacred music with orchestral accompaniment. In a vocal work, a countermelody sung above a principal melody is called a *descant*.

A *collateral part* follows along with a principal melody, often in thirds or sixths, with little or no differentiation from the contour or rhythm of the principal melody. A collateral part is used to fill out a texture or to add harmonic weight, and is commonly found in instrumental music, less often in writing for voices. In the following example, the upper melody and the collateral part just below it are scored for two flutes; elsewhere in the movement, the two flute parts are written with much more independence.

EXAMPLE 7–6: Bach, *Magnificat*: No. 8, *Esurientes*

E: I   V ⁽⁷⁾ I   V ⁽⁷⁾ I   V⁰₉ of II   II   V of II

Other melodic types and usages that may be found in various kinds of music are:

1. *Cantus firmus.* Generally associated with sacred music of the sixteenth through eighteenth centuries, this term implies a theme of regularly spaced notes without much rhythmic differentiation, usually as part of a contrapuntal composition with a faster-moving texture surrounding it. In Protestant sacred music of the Baroque era, the most familiar cantus firmi are hymns, usually called *chorales*; in Catholic sacred music of the Renaissance and earlier, cantus firmi are derived from chant, sometimes from popular tunes.

EXAMPLE 7–7: Bach, *Orgelbüchlein*: No. 37, *Vater unser im*
                 Himmelreich

d: V   I   IV⁶   V   I   IV(II)⁶₅ V ⁽⁷⁾ I

2. *Tune.* This term is useful for describing melodies containing regular groups of phrases, strong tonic and dominant cadences, and, very often, distinct rhythmic or intervallic motives. Tunes have a "closed" structure; they do not imply any continuation beyond the final phrase.

Two broad categories of tunes are songs and dances, both popular and folk. Song tunes are usually matched syllabically to a text in rhymed verse. Folksongs as a rule encompass a relatively small range (usually not more than a tenth), are easy to sing, and seldom use wide intervals, chromatic degrees, or complex rhythms. Dance tunes are melodically structured like folksongs but not necessarily as restricted; wide skips and lively rhythms frequently suggest an instrumental character.

3. A *symphonic melody* is one designed to be used as a theme in a larger work. It may be shorter than a tune and does not usually contain a strong cadence on the tonic; without such a conclusive ending, a symphonic melody lends itself to continuation when necessary. Melodies of this type are subject to changes during the course of a composition, changes which achieve thematic variety and continuity of the form, while at the same time ensuring that the original thematic identity is not lost. The process of such thematic change is called *development*, a principal resource in the so-called organic or narrative musical forms, especially the sonata and rondo forms. Symphonic melodies may be repeated in toto without essential change but in a variety of keys, as in the ritornello forms of the Baroque; or they may be used in every kind of contrapuntal combination and transposition, with or without motivic fragmentation, as in fugal technique. Or they may be fragmented and the fragments repeated with seemingly endless variety, as in Beethoven's technique (Example 7–18, later in this chapter, is an excellent illustration of this); they may be continued and extended with new phrases, as in Mozart's; they may be transformed rhythmically and metrically into new and independent guises, as in Liszt's. In the sonatas and symphonies of Viennese Classicism and nineteenth-century Romanticism, themes become the protagonists in a narrative succession of events; what they are becomes less important than what happens to them.

4. *Ostinato*. This term (Italian for "obstinate") refers to a melody that is repeated over and over again. Many ostinati are short and simple, like the alternation of tonic and dominant notes in a drumbeat pattern; an ostinato in the lowest voice that is as long as a phrase, or even longer, is called a *ground bass* or simply *ground*. Some musical forms, such as the passacaglia and chaconne, use the ground bass continuously throughout; two famous vocal examples of these types are the aria 'When I am laid in earth' in Purcell's *Dido and Aeneas* and the *Crucifixus* in Bach's B-minor Mass. A few special ground basses became the basis of a number of popular songs in the sixteenth century (romanesca, folia, passamezzo, etc.) and were adapted by many composers; twentieth-

century popular music has seen a revival of this technique (blues, boo-gie-woogie, etc.).

5. *Connective or decorative melodies.* These are plainly not themes, but serve to connect phrases, or even prominent tones within a phrase, in a smooth, flowing way.

EXAMPLE 7–8: Beethoven, *Sonata*, Op. 13 ("Pathétique"), I

EXAMPLE 7–9: Chopin, *Piano Concerto in F minor*, Op. 21, II

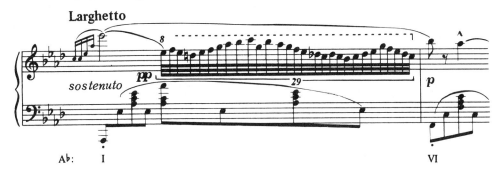

The type of melody in the Chopin example above, with its free, undivided, almost blurred succession of notes, at lightning speed, is called a *roulade.* The roulade is most characteristic of the virtuoso piano

styles of the nineteenth century, but it is often found in earlier music, including in vocal cadenzas of opera arias, where it probably originated.

6. *Figurational melody.* The successive tones in a repeated pattern are melodic just as in any other melody, but nevertheless a given figuration, especially if it contains much arpeggiation, will usually project harmony more than melody. Some figurations depend on characteristic usages of instruments; the example below could not easily be imagined played on anything but a piano.

EXAMPLE 7–10: Chopin, *Etude*, Op. 25, No. 12

Although all these melodic characteristics are important and occur frequently, one seldom finds a melody in actual music that illustrates only one of them. Some symphonies have songlike themes; others have themes that are transformed into accompanimental figures; many songs have melodies that are dancelike, and vice versa. The endless variety of these possibilities is part of the richness of the melodic art.

Shape

The distribution of tones in a melody is marked by changes of direction, by range, by high and low points, and by the variability with which all of these occur in the phrase. Together all of these aspects constitute the contour of the melody, an important determinant of its character.

A good melody will usually have a restricted range, with a high or low point that may be anywhere in the phrase. Secondary high or low points, which are common, do not usually repeat the primary high or low point. The majority of melodies seems to favor a rising–falling curve over a falling–rising curve, but there are many examples of the latter, as well as mixed curves.

EXAMPLE 7–11: Mozart, *Piano Concerto*, K. 467, II

EXAMPLE 7–12: Beethoven, *Sonata*, Op. 28, I

EXAMPLE 7–13: Bach, *St. Matthew Passion*, No. 27

Where the melody begins or ends may not be as important for defining the contour as it is for anchoring the tonality. But in general, a melody will return in the phrase to approximately the same point where it began, within a fourth or fifth at most. Melodies that start high and end low, or vice versa, are less common.

EXAMPLE 7–14: Schubert, *Nähe des Geliebten*, Op. 5, No. 2

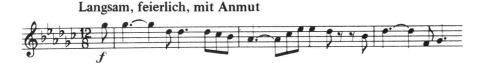

From the metric standpoint, the beginning of a melodic phrase is measured by the appearance of a downbeat, which may or may not be preceded by an upbeat. The upbeat, also called the *anacrusis*, is analogous to a weak syllable that begins a line of verse; it may include the entire beat preceding the downbeat, or just a portion of it, as in the example above.

The Motive

The name *motive* is given to a short thematic unit, melodic or rhythmic or both, which is subject to repetition and transformation. A motive is thematic because it is recurrent and recognizable; at the same time, it is not usually independent because it characteristically appears as a part of a melody.

EXAMPLE 7–15: Bach, *Clavier Concerto in D minor*, III

The motive in the example above has the pattern of two sixteenth notes followed by an eighth note, repeated regularly, and thus it is a rhythmic motive; but it is also a melodic motive, because its melodic pattern, a principal tone with lower neighbor note, is the same throughout.

In all applications of a motive one expects to find variety as well as unity, and transformations as well as literal restatements. Yet it is the amount of resemblance, not the amount of difference, that should determine whether or not we would call a particular configuration of notes motivic.

EXAMPLE 7–16: Mozart, *Symphony No. 38*, K. 504 ("Prague"), I

The long theme above shows five different versions of a motive, labeled a^1, a^2, a^3, a^4, a^5, all differing by their exact note content or duration and by their intervallic content (a major sixth between the first and second notes in a^1 and a^2, a minor seventh in a^3 and a^4, an octave in a^5). But the resemblance of contour among all of these different versions is greater than their intervallic, durational, or pitch differences, and thus we consider all of them as related versions of one motivic shape a. Another consideration is the location of these motivic statements in the measure with respect to the barline; when this is taken into account, the various a's fall into two exactly comparable two-measure patterns, which we have labeled A^1 and A^2, a classification on a higher level than that of the individual a's. The second half of the melody shows no resemblance to the a motive at all, other than the elementary relationship of four eighth notes; instead, a new motive (b^1, b^2, b^3) appears.

Motives can be even as short as a single note, though when they are longer than seven or eight notes they cannot be used as frequently or as flexibly because they occupy a larger amount of musical space. This is admittedly a matter of definition that depends on the hearer's ability to remember patterns, and on the consideration of where one thematic or formal level ends and another begins. It is most convenient to regard a motive as a unit that allows at least two statements within a phrase.

Motives are mainly an aspect of melody, and thus far they have been discussed in connection with principal melodies, but any part of a musical texture may be motivic. The term *figuration* is used to denote a repeated melodic pattern which is accompanimental or subsidiary to a principal melody (see p. 96).

EXAMPLE 7–17: Chopin, *Prelude*, Op. 28, No. 8

In the example above, an interior principal melody using a single rhythmic motive is found between two figurations, one in the right hand, the other in the left.

The contrapuntal style of the late Baroque often included a pervasive use of short motives in any or all melodic parts, as a means of achieving continuity in the individual melodic lines (Example 7–7). At the opposite extreme was one of Beethoven's favorite techniques, marked by the relentless repetition of motives as a means of extending musical time and action. The following example shows an opening melody made up of two different motives, *a* and *b*, which are then separated; in the process of development, these two motives are divided, transformed, repeated, and recombined, with all of these manipulations accounting for forty-two of the forty-six measures of the example.

EXAMPLE 7–18: Beethoven, *Leonore Overture No. 3*

All of the above is melodic, because it has note-to-note melodic continuity, and except for the four measures of sustained high G it is all thematic, because it is made up of motivic fragments of the opening theme. Yet the entire passage has melodic importance only at the points where the complete theme is stated, at the beginning and again at *sempre ff*; the rest of it is connective, a way of extending the psychological action of the theme through many measures. Even when the complete theme is not present, we sense that the music around it belongs to it because its motivic fragments mark the space. (The tonality marks the space, too, by providing a single key framework in which the theme can operate, but that is a different consideration.)

The Phrase

A musical phrase can perhaps best be defined by analogy: the phrase in music is comparable to the line in rhymed verse. The phrase shows a certain regularity in its number of measures, which is usually four or eight. Most important, the phrase is perceived as a unit of musical thought, like a sentence or clause, and it generally implies that another phrase is to follow unless it shows a certain amount of finality. The phrase is what measures the beginning and ending of a melodic unit, as well as the point of departure for the next.

The end of the phrase is called the *cadence*. The origin of this word (from the Latin *cadere*, "to fall") suggests its significance, as a kind of metric punctuation mark, not a pause but something more like a breath. Like the final syllable of a line of metric verse, the cadence is metric in function; at the same time, to continue the analogy, the cadence is always marked by a certain conventional harmonic formula, just as metric verse is ordinarily marked by rhyme.

Phrase structure is one of the most important regulators of musical time. At the most immediate level, we perceive tones as organized by rhythm and measured by meter, which is the perception of a regularly occurring pattern of strong and weak beats. From the longer viewpoint, we perceive music organized into individual movements or pieces of different forms, with a sectional structure characteristic of each type (such as the sonata-allegro form or the minuet and trio). A hierarchy of phrase structure accounts for the various levels in between these extremes. A group of measures forms a phrase; a pair of phrases forms a period; several phrases or periods form a subsection or a section. The phrases of a given piece may be very clearly separated, or they may be so overlapped and merged as to make their definition difficult; nor are all writ-ers always in agreement as to how to define the different types.

When phrases or subphrases occur together in balanced or matched pairs, that is, when the second phrase seems to complement or answer the first, the two phrases are called *antecedent* and *consequent*. The ante-cedent–consequent relationship is found everywhere in music, espe-cially in dance forms and songs. The paired relationship of phrases is so common as to suggest that it fulfills a deeply felt instinctive need, both in the metric and formal sense, like rhyme in poetry.

The following famous theme by Mozart is analyzed from the standpoint of motive and phrase:

EXAMPLE 7–19: Mozart, *Sonata*, K. 331, I

The two motives identified as *a* and *b* are distinct in rhythm and shape; other motives could be labeled in the second half of the theme. The overall form is simple: eight measures balanced by eight measures, with a two-measure extension at the end. Furthermore, one notices that measures 5–8 are very similar to 1–4, with 5–6 exactly like 1–2, and 13–16 are closer still to 5–8, again with 13–14 exactly like 1–2. Only 9–12 show significant departure from the patterns of the others, and even measure 9 shows a kinship of rhythm and shape with measure 1. The example is an elementary illustration of the skillful balance between association of similar ideas and the contrast of dissimilar ideas that is characteristic of musical form as practiced by the masters.

Harmony in Melody—Polyphonic Melody

It is not essential that all the factors of a chord be attacked simultaneously for it to be heard as harmony; and it should likewise be apparent that not all melodic successions will be purely melodic, without any sense of harmony coming from the melody itself. Most music, but particularly instrumental music, contains melodic lines that arpeggiate the factors of chords. There is no doubt that a succession of tones such as in the right-hand or left-hand part of the example below is melodic by definition, because one note follows another in time; yet it is plain that we do not hear it as a note-to-note melodic succession, for the melodic motion of these notes is subsidiary to the harmonic element when we consider the total succession of forty-eight notes.

EXAMPLE 7–20: Chopin, *Etude*, Op. 25, No. 1 ("Aeolian Harp Etude")

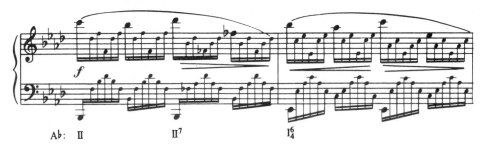

We can see what the real harmonic and melodic elements are by making an *analytical reduction*, removing repeated successions of triadic factors, and notating them as a single simultaneous chord. This leaves as the principal melodic element the succession of tones given by Chopin in large notes. The rest is all harmonic support, the progression moving smoothly with only steps and common tones except in the bass. (The apparent parallel octaves in the reduction on the next page are textural doublings, not independent parts. We will confront this topic again in Chapter 18.)

A melody may imply a polyphony of different melodic lines rather than just one line and chordal support. The melody given below suggests a *compound line*, two parts merged into one. The melodic reduction shows one way of hearing the two lines separately, allowing for the possibility that neither line, considered by itself, will necessarily

Cf. Ex. 7–13

EXAMPLE 7–21: Analytical Reduction

II   II⁷ (min.)   I⁶₄

have the integrity of the original melody, without gaps in the imagination.

EXAMPLE 7–22: Chopin, *Waltz*, Op. 64, No. 1 ("Minute Waltz")

The preceding examples of melodies in keyboard music depend at
least theoretically on the harmonic support of a left-hand part, even
though this does little more than provide a bass and perhaps some chord
factors that may already be present in the right-hand part. Music for an
unaccompanied monophonic instrument, on the other hand, can rely
on no simultaneities at all. All harmony in such music, including bass
support or at least the appearance of one, must be provided within the
melody itself.

EXAMPLE 7–23: Bach, *Sonata for Unaccompanied Flute*: I,
          Allemande

In the reduction, melodic connections between tones that are not necessarily successive, as in a compound line, are indicated by stems or beamed stems; arpeggiations are indicated by slurs. Some nonharmonic tones have been left out of the reduction; if these omissions are not understood now, they will be clearer after you have completed Chapter 8.

It often happens that a melody is stated alone, without any supporting harmony. If such a melody does not clearly imply a harmonic background, then the ear is left to imagine one, which may not always be easy to do unambiguously. Ambiguities may of course be resolved at a later point in the piece. The following example shows a four-measure melody with octave doubling, its altered restatement, and the harmonized versions of both from later in the movement, each excerpt followed by two measures of continuation to show the harmonic context. Schubert's harmonizations are perhaps not what one might have predicted from just the melodies alone, which makes them all the more satisfying for being unexpected. It is fair to say that composers are constantly faced with problems of this kind, but that they think of them not as problems but as opportunities for expression and invention.

EXAMPLE 7–24: Schubert, *Symphony No. 9*, III

To summarize, we observe that just as the faculty of musical memory enables us to assimilate all the notes of a melody as one idea, rather than as a succession of tones, so does memory enable us to hear the harmonic relationship between arpeggiated tones in a melody, even when this relationship is hidden by stepwise motion. The ear searches a melody for such a harmonic basis, instinctively fixing upon whatever triadic configuration is most prominent at a given time, and relating it to the next configuration that appears.

The following is another illustration of polyphonic melody in a keyboard texture, two parts sounding like several, with doublings and some stepwise motion, regulated by the shape of the figuration.

EXAMPLE 7–25: Bach, *Well-Tempered Clavier, I*, Prelude No. 11

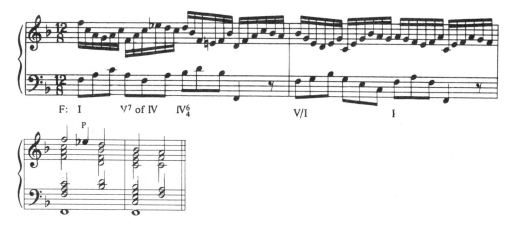

Melodic Variation

The idea of introducing changes in a melody when it is restated is certainly one of the most important principles of musical form; its most systematic manifestation, the technique of theme and variations, has existed in music for nearly four centuries. Like the other topics in this chapter, melodic variation is a vast and varied subject, which will be only introduced here.

The term *ornamentation* is used in two ways in music. In the narrow sense it refers to part of the performance practice of the late Baroque and early Classical eras, where the notes of a written melodic line would be decorated with various kinds of rapidly executed grace notes and combinations of short melodic figures. French composers of keyboard music in the mid-eighteenth century evolved the most complex usage of ornaments, both improvised and notated. A special set of symbols developed for indicating the types of figures to be played; the variety of these can be seen in the harpsichord works of Couperin and Rameau, and in some works of Bach, such as No. 5 of his *Three-Part Inventions (Sinfonias)*. Although the use of ornaments was at times so profuse as to be a stylistic mannerism, there is no doubt that they constituted a valuable resource for melodic variety. Beginning in the later part of the eighteenth century, the use of ornamental symbols declined in favor of the practice of writing out the actual notes with their appropriate time values, although some symbols such as the grace-note sign, the turn (∞), and the trill sign are still in common use, up to the present day.

In the broader sense, ornamentation of a melodic line involves adding tones to it in such a way that its original form or profile can still be discerned. A simple instance is given in Example 7–26, showing the original statement of a theme and the somewhat boisterously ornamented version that immediately follows it.

EXAMPLE 7–26: Beethoven, *Piano Trio*, Op. 97 ("Archduke"), IV

The following example shows how one melody may be ornamented in different ways in a theme with variations. The first four measures of the theme and of each of six variations are given, sometimes with some of the harmony closely attached.

EXAMPLE 7–27: Mozart, *Violin Sonata*, K. 377, II

The example shows that the variations are for the most part very similar in their overall shape to the theme itself, differing mainly in rhythm and decorative tones. In the theme, the small notes are a written-out turn; in Variation 1, the same notes become a rhythmic figure, and a few tones are added that are only a melodic step away from those of the theme. In Variation 2, the same kind of decoration occurs, but the rhythm is different. Variation 3 is like the theme with the turns removed; it appears simpler because the variational interest is all in the accompaniment, which is not shown. In Variation 4 there is a bigger difference, the octave skip in the third measure. Variation 5 achieves its principal variety by the change to major mode, Variation 6 by the change to a different meter and the use of a sprightly rhythm.

More striking, perhaps, than any differences between these variation beginnings are the similarities. These give the impression of all being united by a kind of basic shape, which we can discern by reducing the melody of the theme itself:

EXAMPLE 7–28

In the first stage of reduction, the turns and repeated notes of the first three measures have been removed, leaving only the initial notes of each measure and the arpeggiations a third above them. These upper arpeggiations are shown as stemless notes linked by slurs to their principals. In the fourth measure the lower C♯, a harmonic inner part, is included in parentheses; although not itself part of the upper melody, it seems melodically closer to the D of the third measure than does the upper A.

The second stage of reduction shows the upper arpeggiations merged harmonically with the principal tones. The reduction now consists of two separate parts, suggesting that the original melody can be analyzed as a compound line. The C♯, which was somewhat underhandedly brought into the first stage, now can be seen as having a more legitimate use, supplying an element of the compound line that was not present in the upper part alone.

The analysis is akin to the more plainly harmonic interpretation that we devised for the Chopin Etude in Example 7–20. In the Mozart example we are confronted with a melody with many tones which are decorative, and which are not part of either the essential shape of the melody or of the harmony that supports it. At the same time, these decorative tones provide much of the individuality of the different melodies in the variations. We will soon take up the function of nonharmonic tones in Chapter 8, and will consider these very important aspects of melodic structure in detail.

The Mozart variations, though well suited to the demonstration just given, are actually a less than typical example of the theme-and-variation form, because for the most part they stay very close to the theme. A more usual procedure, in Mozart's time and after, is to retain the original theme literally in only one or two variations as a secondary voice, with different countermelodies superimposed; the other variations would change the melody more substantially, and vary the supporting harmony, the meter, the mode, even the key. Viewed as a whole in the common-practice period, the best works using the theme-and-variation form are marked by extreme departures from the melodic outline of the theme. For instance, one would probably find it difficult, on first hearing, to perceive the melodic relationship between the theme and the melody of the third variation of Brahms's well-known Haydn set.

EXAMPLE 7–29: Brahms, *Variations on a Theme of Haydn*, Op. 56

The variation sets of Bach, Mozart, and later composers show that where the variations depart significantly from the melody, the element of unity among the variations is provided principally by the supporting harmony and the phrase structure, though these too may be subjected to variation. The most famous examples of this type are Bach's *Aria with 30 Variations* (the "Goldberg Variations"), which are variations on a thirty-two-measure ground bass, and Beethoven's *33 Variations on a Waltz by Diabelli*, Op. 120.

Approach to Melodic Analysis

Analysis of a melody should begin with the determination of its phrase and subphrase boundaries, including cadence and subcadence, and where the first downbeat occurs. Motivic subunits of rhythm or interval pattern may then be considered, and their possible correlation with changes of harmony. Melodic climaxes, as well as rhythmic stresses, are often related to important harmonic changes.

An attempt should be made to determine the harmonic structure of the melody, where one is apparent, from the melodic characteristics alone. The reduction through successive levels to uncover the fundamental underlying motion of the melody is also useful, though many melodies will prove to be not readily susceptible to this kind of analysis. (Better not attempt it anyway until after you have completed Chapter 8, Nonharmonic Tones.)

When a melody is considered as an element of a complete texture in a given passage, its internal structure can be seen more clearly in relation to the whole. It is important, however, to appreciate the qualities of structure that may be discerned by studying melodies in isolation. Melody is, to a greater extent than any other aspect, the wellspring of the compositional process, in which the individualities of the composer's inspiration are most apparent.

EXERCISES

1. Analyze the following melodies from the standpoint of shape, phrase, rhythm, motive structure, and internal harmony. Summarize your findings about each melody in a short paragraph, accompanied by examples or diagrams.

g. **Allegro agitato ed appassionato** (Liszt)

2. Examine a work or movement in theme-and-variation form. Choose three variations and compare them with the original theme. What are the differences? What are the similarities?

3. Compose melodic fragments so as to fill the blanks appropriately in the following melodies.

a. **Tempo di menuetto** (Schubert)

b. **Allegro** (adapted from Haydn)

c. **(Andante)** (J. S. Bach)

d. (Schumann)

4. *Road maps.* Construct melodies using the indicated rhythms and using only notes that are factors of the triads indicated.

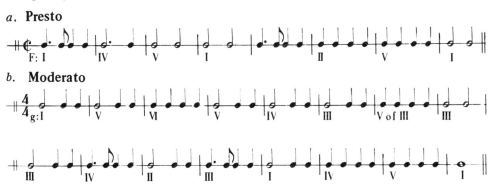

a. **Presto**

b. **Moderato**

c. **Menuetto**

d. **Mazurka**

5. *Road map.* Construct two melodies in A major, each eight measures long, one in $\frac{3}{4}$ and the other in $\frac{4}{4}$, to the following specifications:

  a. Each melody contains exactly twenty notes.
  b. The tonic degree appears seven times.
  c. The dominant degree appears six times.
  d. Two notes are dotted.
  e. The overall range of the melody is not more than a twelfth.

6. *Road map.* Construct a melody in C major, $\frac{3}{8}$ time, eight measures long, in which the following fragments appear, not necessarily in the order given.

7. *Road map.* Construct a melody in $\frac{6}{8}$ meter, eight measures long, in which each of the motives ♩.♫ and ♩ ♪ appears at least three times, plus another rhythmic motive of your own choice, which appears twice.

8. *Road map.* Construct a melody in $\frac{3}{4}$ meter, sixteen measures long, entirely out of ♩ or ♩. At least three times, use a motive having the rhythm of ♩♩♩, with the first two notes the same pitch and the third note either a third or a fourth below. (The last beat of the final measure may be ♩..)

8

Nonharmonic Tones

It is obvious that most music contains melodic tones that are not members of the chord against which they are sounded. Literally, there is no such thing as a nonharmonic tone, since all tones sounding together create harmony. But the language of music has grown like any other language. Certain harmonic forms become established through usage, and we sense the presence of these as a kind of skeleton, or harmonic framework, upon which the complex melodic structure of music rests.

Melodic Dissonance

We have observed before that polyphonic music is two-dimensional, that is, vertical and horizontal. Polyphony suggests that the ear can perceive a harmonic relationship between two tones sounded simultaneously, and a melodic relationship between two tones sounded successively. The combination of these is the contrapuntal relationship, and the ear's perception of counterpoint is simultaneously harmonic and melodic. The most plainly chordal music must have melodic relationships in its successive tones and a contrapuntal relationship between its separate voices; the most elaborate linear polyphony will have contrapuntal relationships between its melodic lines and harmonic relationships between its simultaneous tones.

In the previous chapter we saw that melodic successions can imply harmony, the simplest case being when successive melodic tones are factors of a chord. The arpeggiation of a triad necessarily means disjunct motion, because the factors of a triad are not adjacent tones in the scale. Conjunct or stepwise motion implies the dissonant relationship of adjacent tones, because the major second and minor second are dissonances. The other side of this coin is that any dissonant interval may be resolved into a consonant interval by the stepwise motion (by either a major or a minor second) of one of its factors; to put it another way, dissonant tones connect consonances. These empirical facts are the basis of the theory and practice of counterpoint.

Until now we have considered triads as fixed entities in musical texture, their factors moving only to change the spacing, or to the next harmony. Melodic motion that produces dissonant intervals has up to now been excluded from our consideration. In this chapter we will investigate dissonances arising in melodic motion. These dissonances are called *nonharmonic tones*. The discussion above shows that stepwise melodic motion, the most basic type of melodic motion, can both generate and resolve dissonances. Our purpose here will be to discover how these occur and how they fit into the structure of melody and harmony.

The study of harmony presupposes that during the period of harmonic common practice, composers were so chord-minded that they only wrote melodies with harmonic implications. This does not mean that every melodic tone is a chord factor; we can easily determine which melody notes are chord factors and which are not. Understanding melody in terms of harmony is the point of view recommended in this book, the other more linear aspects being left for the study of counterpoint and melodic analysis. This pedagogical conceit, however, is also a warning. Neither harmony nor counterpoint is complete in itself as a description of composers' practice.

The Passing Tone

A melodic skip may be filled in with tones on all intervening steps, either diatonic or chromatic; these are called *passing tones*.

EXAMPLE 8–1

The interval filled in by passing tones is not necessarily an interval between two members of the same chord.

EXAMPLE 8–2

Passing tones are rhythmically weak, and yet may occur anywhere in the measure, on any beat or fraction of the beat. The "accented passing tone" occurring on the strong beat is really a weak appoggiatura, discussed later in this chapter. In the example below, the passing tones are unaccented even though they fall on the beat.

EXAMPLE 8–3: Beethoven, *Sonata*, Op. 10, No. 3, IV

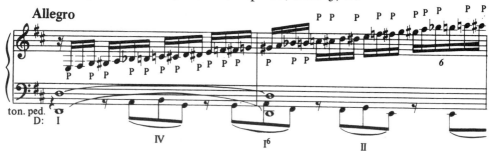

Passing tones may be employed in any voices, even in different voices at the same time, although if more than two passing tones are used simultaneously it may appear that the entire chord is moving. In applying these resources in the exercises it is recommended that they be used discreetly at first, so as to preserve the clarity of the harmonic structure. After nearly three centuries, the works of Johann Sebastian Bach remain the supreme models of balance in the use of all nonharmonic tones.

EXAMPLE 8–4: Bach, Chorale No. 369, *Jesu, der du meine Seele*

In the minor mode, the sixth and seventh degrees, when they are used as passing tones, will be derived from the melodic scale, ascending or descending.

EXAMPLE 8–5

The Neighbor Note

The *neighbor note* (the commonly used synonym *auxiliary tone*, or simply *auxiliary*, will also be employed in this book) is a tone of weak rhythmic value which serves to decorate a stationary tone. It is approached by either a half step or a whole step from the tone it decorates, to which it returns.

EXAMPLE 8–6

EXAMPLE 8–7: Bach, *Brandenburg Concerto No. 3*, I

A change of harmony may take place as the neighbor returns to the main tone.

EXAMPLE 8–8: Wagner, *The Flying Dutchman*, Act I, Spinning Song

The neighbor note is not always a diatonic note, but is frequently altered chromatically to bring it a half tone closer to the main tone. When it is below, it has the character of a temporary leading tone of the scale-degree it attends.

EXAMPLE 8–9: Mozart, *Sonata*, K. 331, I

The upper and lower neighbors combine to form a melodic turn of five notes around a central tone.

EXAMPLE 8–10: Schumann, *Carnaval*, Op. 9: No. 5, *Eusebius*

The five-note grouping shown in the example above is often found with the third note omitted. Such a configuration is called a *double neighbor note*, implying that it is a single tone decorated by two neighbor notes.

EXAMPLE 8–11: Berlioz, *Symphonie fantastique*, II: *A Ball*

Two or three neighbor notes occurring at the same time in similar motion make a chord which might be termed a *neighbor chord* or an *auxiliary chord*.

EXAMPLE 8–12: Liszt, *Les Préludes*

The *incomplete neighbor note* (labeled IN) results when either the initiating or the returning principal tone is omitted. It is a component of the escape tone and reaching tone formulae, discussed below, but it is also seen independently from them. In the following example, the incomplete neighbors are decorations to the arpeggiated factors of the tonic triad.

EXAMPLE 8–13: Beethoven, *Sonata*, Op. 31, No. 1, II

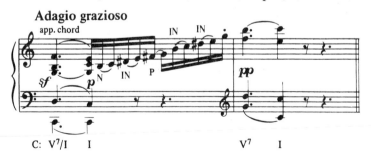

Many instances of grace notes are incomplete neighbor notes of the leading-tone type, comparable to the example above.

Like the passing tone, the neighbor note is not always a dissonant tone; it is consonant when it is a component of a fifth moving to a sixth and back again. When neighbor to the fifth of a triad in root position, it remains consonant with the third of the triad, becoming itself the root of a triad in first inversion; the harmonic progression resulting from this is very weak, if it has even taken place at all, thus confirming the nature of the consonant neighbor note as a melodic tone.

EXAMPLE 8–14

C: I (VI⁶) I

The Anticipation

As its name implies, the *anticipation* is a kind of advance sounding of a note. It is rhythmically like an upbeat to the tone anticipated, to which it is usually not tied.

EXAMPLE 8–15: Mozart, *Symphony No. 34*, K. 338, I

A very characteristic use of the anticipation is before an appoggiatura, discussed below (Example 8–23).

The anticipation is ordinarily shorter in time value than the principal tone, as in the preceding example; sometimes the two may be of equal length, as with the figurational anticipations in the example below.

EXAMPLE 8-16: Bach, *St. Matthew Passion*, No. 36

E: I   V$_3^4$ of VI VI   V$_5^6$ of VI

The anticipation in the cadence shown below, with the tonic sounding simultaneously with its own leading tone, is an example of the so-called *Corelli clash*.

EXAMPLE 8-17: Handel, *Concerto Grosso*, Op. 6, No. 5, IV

b: V^7 I   IV   V   I

The Appoggiatura

All nonharmonic tones are rhythmically weak, with the single exception of the *appoggiatura* (plural, *appoggiature*). The derivation of the term (from the Italian *appoggiare*, "to lean") gives the best clue to its character. It gives the impression of leaning on the tone into which it finally resolves, by half or whole step. The rhythm of the appoggiatura followed by its note of resolution is invariably strong-to-weak. The following example should be compared with Example 8-13 for its difference in rhythmic effect.

EXAMPLE 8-18: Beethoven, *Violin Sonata*, Op. 12, No. 2

The force of the appoggiatura depends on the way in which the ear perceives it as relating to the surrounding harmony. Ordinarily the appoggiatura will resolve to a consonant factor of the chord. An additional consideration is the question of preparation. The appoggiatura is a smoother, less emphatic component of the melodic line when it is self-prepared, the same pitch appearing before it either as a factor of the preceding harmony (*a* in the example below) or as a nonharmonic tone (*b*). The next smoothest preparation of the appoggiatura is by step from above or below (*c, d*). It is not prepared if it enters by skip (*e*).

EXAMPLE 8–19

The appoggiatura is special among the nonharmonic tones in being characterized by different types of preparation. In general, the other nonharmonic tones are intrinsically prepared, like the passing tone and the suspension, and the quality of their dissonance cannot be expected to vary except insofar as they are used in combination in different voices at the same time. The preparation or nonpreparation of dissonance is less a rule of counterpoint than an aspect of style, and may be inconsistent in different works by the same composer.

EXAMPLE 8–20: Bach, *Well-Tempered Clavier, I*, Prelude No. 24

EXAMPLE 8–21: Bach, *Well-Tempered Clavier, I*, Fugue No. 24

In arranging an appoggiatura with a four-part chord, it is customary to avoid doubling the note of resolution, especially when the appoggiatura is not in the upper voice. The note of resolution is doubled in the bass in chords in root position, the appoggiatura being far enough above to be clearly followed melodically.

EXAMPLE 8–22

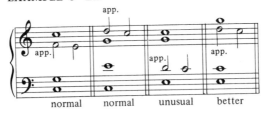

EXAMPLE 8–23: Beethoven, *Sonata*, Op. 7, IV

The harmony may change as the appoggiatura resolves, the new harmony incorporating the expected tone of resolution.

EXAMPLE 8–24: Schumann, *Album for the Young*, Op. 68: No. 41, *Northern Song*

The appoggiatura may be below the note toward which it is tending. Commonest of this type is the leading-tone appoggiatura to the tonic.

EXAMPLE 8–25: Chopin, *Prelude*, Op. 28, No. 8

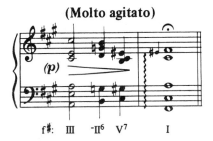

f#: III   –II⁶ V⁷   I

The preceding example is a nineteenth-century survivor of eighteenth-century notational convention, which employed a special ornamental symbol resembling the grace note but lacking the diagonal cross-stroke. To avoid confusion, most modern editions write out the appoggiatura and resolution with their proper note-values.

EXAMPLE 8–26: Beethoven, *Sonata*, Op. 2, No. 1, III

Like the neighbor note, the appoggiatura is often found as a chromatically altered scale degree. The alteration increases the tendency toward its destination, like a leading tone moving to a tonic (Example 8–18).

The rarely used augmented triad on III in the minor mode contains a built-in appoggiatura.

EXAMPLE 8–27: Schubert, *Andantino varié for Piano Four Hands*, Op. 84, No. 1

b: I V of III III⁶   V⁴₃ of III III   V   III⁵⁺   VI   II (IV)⁶₅   I⁶₄   V
                                               (V⁵⁺ of VI)

A most pungent form of appoggiatura is that of the lowered seventh degree, descending minor, standing for the sixth degree against the leading tone in dominant harmony. This creates the somewhat unusual interval of the diminished octave in what is called a *simultaneous cross-relation.*

EXAMPLE 8–28: Bizet, *l'Arlésienne,* Suite No. 1: No. 4, *Carillon*

See also Exx. 5–27, 8–8, 11–13, as well as 28–30 and 31–61

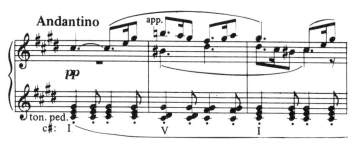

Several appoggiature sounding together make an *appoggiatura chord.* The most familiar is the dominant chord sounded over a tonic bass. This so-called V/I, read "five over one," is common in cadences (Example 8–13). In the following example, not the root but the third of the triad is the tonic component underneath the appoggiatura chord, as is shown by the resolution.

EXAMPLE 8–29: Beethoven, *Sonata,* Op. 13 ("Pathétique"), I

The Suspension

The *suspension* is a tone whose natural progression has been rhythmically delayed. (See Example 8–30.) The suspension occurs on the strong beat or on the strong portion of a weak beat, but is rhythmically weak with respect to the tone that prepares it, because of the tie. It is not attacked at the same time as the harmony with which it is dissonant,

EXAMPLE 8–30

and thus differs from the prepared appoggiatura. (It is worth noting that this difference was considered important in the strict counterpoint of the sixteenth century, which permitted the suspension but not the appoggiatura.)

EXAMPLE 8–31: Couperin, *Harpsichord Pieces, Book II*, Sixth Order: *Les Barricades mystérieuses*

In many situations, however, the distinction between suspension and prepared appoggiatura is not possible to make, nor is it of any consequence. In the following example, the repeated notes in the second violins are clearly not tied over the barline, and the preparation of each suspension is equal to half the length of the measure; the first bassoon, not shown in the example, doubles an octave below the second violins, in sustained notes tied over the barline.

EXAMPLE 8–32: Mozart, *Piano Concerto*, K. 467, II

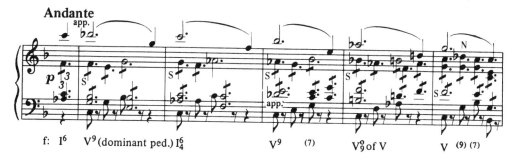

f: I⁶   V⁹ (dominant ped.) I⁶₄   V⁹   (7)   V⁰₉ of V   V (9) (7)

The resolution of the suspension is usually to the scale step below, but the upward resolution is not infrequent. If the suspended note is a leading tone, or a chromatically raised tone, it will have a natural resolution to the note above. (Compare Example 8–25.)

EXAMPLE 8–33: Beethoven, *String Trio*, Op. 3, VI

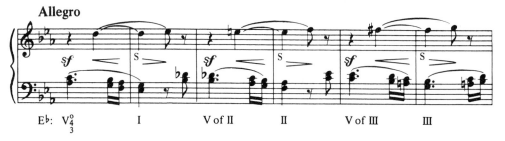

When several tones are suspended at once, they constitute a suspended chord, so that there may be two harmonies heard at the same time, a familiar effect in cadences.

EXAMPLE 8–34: Brahms, *Intermezzo*, Op. 117, No. 2

Escape Tone and Reaching Tone

The *escape tone* and *reaching tone*, in their most characteristic forms, are interpolations between suspensions and their resolutions, and in comparable resolutions of appoggiature. Their essential shape consists respectively of step followed by skip and vice versa, the second motion always in opposite direction to the first. The *escape tone* is a note that reverses direction of the melodic movement and then returns by skip. On the other hand, the reaching tone is the result of having gone too far, so that it is necessary to turn back by step to the note of destination.

EXAMPLE 8–35

melodic movement   melodic movement

EXAMPLE 8–36: Haydn, *String Quartet,* Op. 76, No. 3, III

EXAMPLE 8–37: Mozart, *Sonata,* K. 533, II

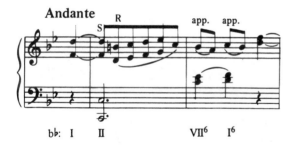

The French equivalent *échappée* is used in many books instead of *escape tone.* What we call *reaching tone* was formerly called *cambiata* (Italian for "exchanged") because of its supposed resemblance to the *nota cambiata* of sixteenth-century counterpoint, but this term is now obsolete.

The escape-tone and reaching-tone patterns may be used to bridge any melodic progression of a second, up or down. It is not necessary for the initiating tone to be a dissonance. When the escape tone proceeds from a chord tone, it will of course be dissonant with the chord; the reaching tone will be dissonant with the chord of destination.

Successive Nonharmonic Tones

Nonharmonic tones may occur in succession, their normal resolutions being overlapped with or interrupted by the next tone. A resolution may be postponed by the interpolation of a harmonic note that is not the note of resolution, as in the case of the escape tone and reaching tone. Such linear combinations are called *ornamental resolutions*. Delayed resolution of nonharmonic tones is a familiar resource of melodic vitality, particularly in music with prominent contrapuntal elements.

The suspension does not usually resolve on a fraction of a beat. In normal rhythmic movement the amount of time a note is suspended is at least the value of one whole beat or pulse. There are, however, a

EXAMPLE 8–38

EXAMPLE 8–39: Handel, *Suite No. 3*: II, Fugue

EXAMPLE 8–40: Bach, *Well-Tempered Clavier, II*, Fugue No. 5

number of ornamental resolutions of the suspension that may provide melodic activity before the actual note of resolution arrives. Besides the escape tone and reaching tone, these ornamental resolutions may occur in the form of neighbor note or anticipation, or there may be a chord tone inserted between the suspension and its resolution.

The following familiar example shows a normal melodic progression through a third via a passing tone, interrupted by the interpolation of an appoggiatura. This is the most usual kind of explanation for the "incomplete passing tone."

EXAMPLE 8–41: Verdi, *La Traviata*, Act I, "Sempre Libera"

Sometimes one will encounter a "free" tone, a tone clearly not belonging to the prevailing harmony and without any apparent direct or postponed resolution. Such a tone may have an implied connection with another voice in the texture. In the following example, the A in the bass marked with the arrow appears at first sight to be a dangling tone interposed in a C-major triad; but without much effort one can hear it as an anticipation of the third of the IV which follows it, as though by octave transfer to the alto voice.

EXAMPLE 8–42: Bach, *Well-Tempered Clavier, II,* Prelude No. 1

C: I   V⁷ of IV IV⁷   II⁶

The Pedal

The *pedal* (sometimes *pedal point* or *organ point*) is a tone, either the tonic or dominant degree, that persists in one voice throughout several changes of harmony. The pedal is the one exception among the nonharmonic tones in that it is not melodic. It tends to render the harmonic rhythm static, and this effect is offset somewhat by the use of chords dissonant with the pedal. A typical pedal will be at some moment foreign to the harmony with which it sounds, though it customarily begins and ends as a member of that harmony. It is perhaps most often used in the bass, but it may appear as the upper voice, as an inner part, or any combination of these.

The term *pedal* originated as descriptive of the natural procedure of holding down an organ pedal key while improvising on the manuals above. As subsequently developed by composers, however, the device seems far from the implications of its name. It is often broken into rhythmic patterns and decorated by other tones, even attaining thematic significance in ostinato figures.

The strength of tonality inherent in the pedal makes it a very effective device for establishing or maintaining a key, even though the accompanying harmony may go far afield. One of the commonest usages of the dominant pedal is as a preparation for the recapitulation section of a movement in sonata-allegro form, or in a slow introduction just before the exposition; similarly, the tonic pedal appears frequently in the coda section to reinforce the finality of the key.

The following example shows the climax of a coda section with a particularly piquant blend of tonic pedal and dominant harmony. The

EXAMPLE 8–43: Beethoven, Overture to *Fidelio*

dominant seventh is distributed between the upper strings, four horns, and all the woodwinds; the tonic pedal, in four octaves, is played by cellos, basses, timpani, and two trumpets.

In the next example, Verdi uses a variety of chromatic harmonies to underscore the tolling of a midnight bell.

EXAMPLE 8–44: Verdi, *Falstaff*, Act III, Scene 2

Più mosso (Andante sostenuto)

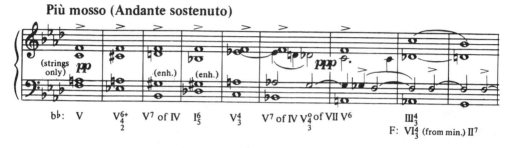

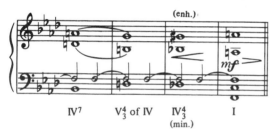

When the pedal is of short duration, with only one or two dissonant harmonies, it may be possible to regard it as the prolongation of a single chord, the intervening harmony appearing as a chord of nonharmonic tones.

EXAMPLE 8–45: Clementi, *Sonatina*, Op. 36, No. 4, I

Con spirito

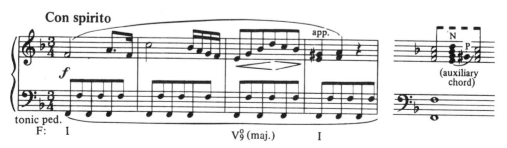

Though the pedal may be as short as a single measure, it may extend much longer, even through an entire piece. Examples of such lengthy pedals should be analyzed for their effect on the harmonic rhythm and the general tonal scheme. Pedal-point pieces can be short and relatively simple harmonically, like Schubert's song *Die liebe Farbe* (*Die Schöne Müllerin*, No. 16), or of considerable length with much contrapuntal activity, like the fugue that concludes Part III of Brahms's *German Requiem*, thirty-six measures of $\frac{4}{2}$ time in moderate tempo.

A double pedal is sometimes used, tonic and dominant usually in the form of a drone bass, making the key even more secure. The drone of the following example is maintained through the entire piece.

EXAMPLE 8–46: Tchaikovsky, *The Nutcracker: Arabian Dance*

Application

The practical application of the principles of nonharmonic tones involves two different processes, one analytical and one constructive. The first will be called into play during the process of choosing chords to fit a given bass or soprano melody, and deciding which are essential notes and which are nonharmonic tones. The experience of harmonic analysis of compositions will prove helpful in this respect.

The constructive process should be based on the hypothesis that the harmony is the origin of the melody. The steps would be as follows:

1. Choose a key and a succession of roots as the basis of a phrase. Let us take, for example: A major, I–IV–II–V–I.
2. Construct a bass melody accommodating these roots, allowing the possibility that the third of the triad may appear for greater melodic flexibility and smoothness.

EXAMPLE 8–47

A: I (6) IV II V⁶ (5) I

3. Add three upper voices in a simple harmonization of the indicated scheme.

EXAMPLE 8–48

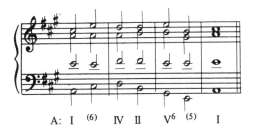

A: I (6) IV II V⁶ (5) I

4. Consider the various possibilities of nonharmonic tones that may be applied, beginning with the simplest. It may be desirable to rearrange the distribution of chord factors that was arrived at in the previous step.

EXAMPLE 8–49

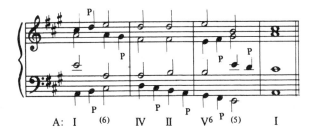

A: I (6) IV II V⁶ P (5) I

5. After the simpler amplifications of the basic texture have been decided upon, more advanced embellishments may be added to any or all parts. The number of possibilities at this stage is practically without limit, but there is no merit in striving for complexity for its own sake.

EXAMPLE 8–50

A: I (V$^4_3$) I^6 IV (V$^4_3$ of II) II   V$^6_{(5)}$ V   I

EXERCISES

From this point on, make a serious effort to incorporate nonharmonic tones into all your written exercises unless otherwise instructed. The exercises in this chapter have specific instructions and suggestions about how to do this; later chapters will take nonharmonic tones for granted, and you should always consider them as an important resource, particularly in the construction of a good melody. In conjunction with the analysis you provide in your written work, indicate your use of these nonharmonic tones by means of appropriate symbols already shown in this chapter. (After the first few exercises, you won't have to indicate every passing tone.)

    1. Apply the five-step process given above to the following root successions, using each as the basis of a four-measure phrase. Give careful consideration to the rhythm of the root changes.

    a. B♭ major: I–VI–II–V–VI–V–I
    b. C♯ minor: I–V–I–IV–II–V–VI
    c. G major: I–V–I–IV–I–V–III–VI–II–V–I

    2. Realize the following figured basses in four parts, with nonharmonic tones added to the upper parts. Most of the time, the upper parts will move at the same speed as the changes of figures. (Remember that 5— indicates a root-position triad with the upper parts sustained while the bass moves; in the same way, 6— indicates the upper parts of a first-inversion triad with the bass moving.) The first measure of *b* is already provided, to get you started.

3. Realize the figured basses given below, using the melodies provided.

4. The soprano and bass lines given below are to be rewritten by dividing the melody notes, using the given rhythm and the nonharmonic tones indicated. (The given note must be one or the other of the tones resulting from the division. When no nonharmonic tone is indicated in the division, the two notes will be arpeggiated chord tones.) Complete the exercise by providing appropriate inner parts.

5. Harmonize the following unfigured basses, employing nonharmonic tones in the added parts.

6. The following soprano melody with unfigured bass is to be completed with inner parts. A few fragments of these have been provided.

7. Construct a bass for the following melody according to the rhythm and nonharmonic tones indicated.

8. Examine ten examples from earlier chapters in this book and identify their nonharmonic tones.

9. *Analysis.* A root analysis of the following example is already given. Identify all the nonharmonic tones.

Schumann, *Andante and Variations*, Op. 46

9

Harmonization of a Melody

Harmonization of a given soprano melody is one of the most valuable exercises in the study of harmony. At the level of an elementary skill, the mental steps involved in harmonization make it one of the most effective types of ear training. As part of one's mature musicianship, the ability to harmonize a melody involves hearing and manipulating entire phrases and understanding their formal implications.

During the common-practice period, nearly all melodies were of harmonic origin. They were either evolved from chord tones, with the addition of nonharmonic melodic tones, or they were conceived as having harmonic meaning, expressed or implied. So the process of harmonization does not mean invention as much as it means discovery, in a sense, of the harmony implied by the melody.

Good harmonization, then, requires a consideration of the alternatives among available chords, the reasoned selection of one of these alternatives, and the tasteful arrangement of the texture of the added parts with due regard for consistency of style. All of these criteria involve musical choices, and it will rarely be possible to say that of possible choice there is one that is the best; more likely there will only be some choices that are clearly better than others.

At first, we shall consider the harmonization process using only triads, leaving for later in this chapter the incorporation of nonharmonic tones.

140

Analysis of the Melody

In order to find the chords available for consideration, begin by determining the harmonic possibilities suggested by the melodic tones, individually and in groups. The first question is, of course, the tonality of the melody. A few melodies of restricted range may offer the possibility of different keys and modes, even if we limit ourselves to triads in root position.

EXAMPLE 9–I

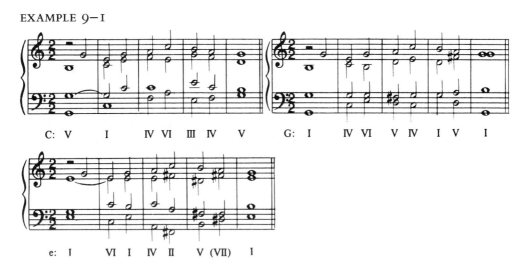

Determination of the key depends first of all upon the analysis of the ending of the phrase. At present we shall consider only two possibilities, ending on the dominant chord, and ending with V–I, the authentic cadence. In the example above, the final note was interpreted in turn as dominant of C, tonic of G, and mediant of E. Tonalities containing one flat or more were not acceptable because of the B♮ in the melody, and keys of two or more sharps were ruled out since C♮ was present. The absence of F made it possible to choose keys containing either F♯ or F♮. In the E-minor version, the leading-tone triad in root position was used for the soprano note A, and is here clearly a form of dominant harmony, although not the most satisfactory dominant chord that could be used.

Having decided on the key and having marked the roman numerals of the last two chords, one should next consider the frequency of change in the harmony. With triads in root position the rate of change will be fairly constant, but there are two ways to escape from the regularity of one chord for each soprano note: by melodic skip and by sustained tones.

Melodic Skips

When a melody moves by skip, it is often advisable to use the same harmony for both notes.

EXAMPLE 9–2

G: I_____V

Exceptions to this will usually arise from questions of harmonic rhythm. If one of the two notes involved in the skip falls on a weak beat, then a change of harmony is recommended.

EXAMPLE 9–3

G: I V VI IV   I   V

Such a rhythmic effect is generally placed so that the second chord falls on the first beat of a measure, giving rise to the often-stated rule that it is better to change root over a barline. However, the same progression might have occurred quite naturally within the measure, without the durational stress the second chord received before.

EXAMPLE 9–4

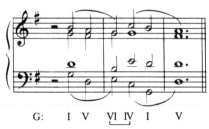

G: I V   VI IV I   V

Sustained Tones

A melodic tone may be sustained through one or more chord changes, as a common tone of each of the chords used.

EXAMPLE 9–5

G: I   VI IV   V III VI   V

It is also possible to have melodic movement in the inner voices without change of root, and sometimes this will be desirable.

EXAMPLE 9–6

G: IV   V   I   V

Available Chords

After an appropriate tonality is chosen and a preliminary decision is made as to the general frequency of chord changes, each note of the given melody should be examined as a potential chord tone. These possibilities should actually be written down, as a roman-numeral listing, in order to see all the alternatives.

EXAMPLE 9–7

root third fifth

In working with a given bass only one chord was available for each tone, since the bass notes were at the same time the roots of the triads. When an upper voice is given, each tone offers a choice of three triads, since the given tone may be the root, the third, or the fifth.

This step is shown applied to a short soprano part:

EXAMPLE 9–8

Selection of Chords

In determining the possible choices of chords, it may be helpful to review the Tables of Usual Root Progressions in Chapters 3 and 4.

Let us first consider only root-position triads. Starting with the last measure of the preceding example we can at once eliminate the VI and the IV, as we wish to end the phrase with either V or I. Since I remains, the cadence will be an authentic cadence, so we choose V to precede the I. The VII, seldom used in root position in any case, would be a particularly poor substitute for V here because it would give a doubled leading tone, and parallel octaves with the bass in the last chord. In measure 4 we can also eliminate VII in favor of the stronger IV or II. In measure 3 either I or VI could serve for the whole measure. In measure 2 the VII's can be struck out, since they would be absorbed by the V of measure 1, with too much dominant harmony resulting. Also the II will prove a troublesome choice for the second beat of measure 2, as it would make parallel octaves if followed by I, and would not give a very satisfactory bass interval if followed by VI. So we conclude that measure 2 had better contain either IV–V or II–V. These eliminations leave the following alternatives:

EXAMPLE 9–9

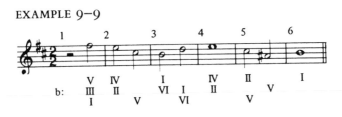

Considering what we now have from the standpoint of unity and variety, and harmonic rhythm, we see that the only chance to use VI is in measure 3, and that the progression V–VI would provide a good contrast with the cadential V–I. So we eliminate the I from measure 3, and as a result decide that we had better use I in the first measure for unity, so that the final chord will not be the only appearance of the tonic. In measure 4 both IV and II could be included under the same soprano note, adding variety of melodic and harmonic rhythm, in which case we would not use II in measure 5, but keep V for the whole measure.

The above reasoning brings us to the conclusion below, with the resultant bass part. It is obviously not the only conclusion possible, but appears to be a good one. Comparison of the two melodic curves shows a good amount of contrary motion, a quality to be sought between soprano and bass.

EXAMPLE 9–10

The inside parts may require irregular doubling and changes of position. Care should be taken to make the connections as smooth as possible and to avoid parallel octaves and fifths.

EXAMPLE 9–11

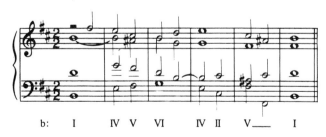

When first-inversion triads are included, there will be further possibilities for shaping the bass melody, although these will not guarantee

a better result. The II⁶ in the fourth measure of the following, for example, is rather weak without motion of the bass.

EXAMPLE 9–12

b: I   (6)   II   V⁶   VI⁶   (5)   IV   II⁶   V   I

The examples above illustrate the logical steps in the construction
of a harmonic background for a given melodic part. It is inadvisable to
omit any of these steps in favor of a harmonization that presents itself
spontaneously, even though such a harmonization might prove to be a
superior choice. The weighing of the pros and cons of each detail and
of the whole constitutes a profitable experience and practice which even
the person with a gift for improvisatory harmonization cannot afford
to miss.

Contrapuntal Approach:
Melody and Bass

In the method of harmonization just described, the final selection of
chords was based chiefly on voice leading within chord progressions.
The bass line emerged as a result of this selection process; even though
some of the details of the bass line, such as beginning and ending on
the tonic note, may have been kept in mind from the start, we were
concerned with the bass primarily as a succession of roots, and not as
an independently conceived melody with its own melodic shape.

The shape of the bass line will inevitably become more important
to the harmonization when first-inversion triads are included in the
allowable chords. Let us see what possibilities are made available when
we plan the harmonization by considering the melody and bass line
together.

First of all, since we are using only triads in root position and first
inversion, there will be only four intervals possible between soprano
and bass; octaves, perfect fifths, thirds, and sixths, including their compounds. Dissonant intervals are necessarily excluded. (The two excep-

tions, the augmented fifth and the diminished fifth, will occur relatively seldom, when III or II in the minor mode, or VII in either mode, is used in root position.) These intervals can be classified by their possible application under our restricted conditions:

a. A fifth (or twelfth, etc.) between soprano and bass means that the triad will be in root position.
b. A sixth (or thirteenth) between soprano and bass means that the chord will be a first-inversion triad.
c. An octave (or double octave) between soprano and bass will mean either a root-position or a first-inversion triad; if the latter, the third will be doubled.
d. A third between soprano and bass will mean either a root-position or a first-inversion triad, with no specifications as to doubling.

With this repertory of possible intervals in mind, let us now construct several bass lines against a given melody, focusing our attention principally on the melodic characteristics of the bass and only secondarily considering what the roots of the resulting chords will be. We choose here a four-measure phrase ending with a half cadence, or cadence on the dominant. The cadential bass note, therefore, will preferably be the dominant note F, though we may also consider the leading tone, the bass of the dominant triad in first inversion, as a somewhat weaker alternative.

EXAMPLE 9–13

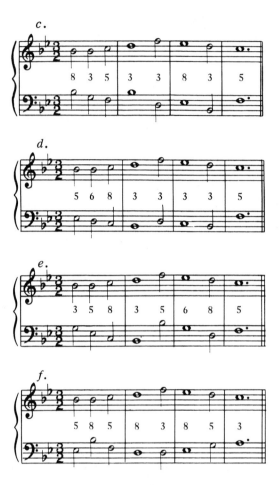

In *a* we see the possibility of harmonization entirely in root-position triads. The bass is melodically dull; it is made up entirely of skips, the tonic note appearing five times, and it sounds like nothing so much as an "elementary exercise bass" similar to those used first in Chapter 3. This is precisely what we are trying to avoid in the two-part approach.

Solution *b* is a definite improvement. The tonic appears three times, but only near the beginning of the phrase, where it may be strongly asserted to contrast with the dominant harmony at the end. Following the third tonic note, the bass moves smoothly. Three parallel sixths in a row are not too many, though four might be; it is desirable to keep soprano and bass independent in their motion most of the time. The repetition of the F at the end of the bass descent is a melodic weakness, and its harmonization, which must be III⁶–V, is also weak.

Solution *c* is better still. There is a good deal of contrary motion between the two parts, though not so much as to seem automatic. The G in the first measure helps take the bass away from the tonic, making the return of the tonic in the second measure somewhat less repetitive than in *b*. The skip down to D and the answering step to E♭ gives the bass a wider range than in *b*, the return to E♭ helping to maintain the balance of the curve. The B♭ in the third measure makes a strong approach to the cadential F, although it might be considered to contribute too much additional tonic to what has gone before, especially if the D in the second measure were to be harmonized as a first-inversion I.

Solution *d* shows an even more imaginative beginning. The tonic note does not appear until the second measure, but it is clearly the goal of the bass line and thus all the stronger when it does appear. The second and third measures duplicate the last three notes of the beginning, an undesirable repetition somewhat offset by the different rhythm. In addition, these measures show four thirds in succession. These could not be harmonized with all root-position triads without an excessive manipulation of the inner parts in order to avoid parallel fifths and octaves; on the other hand, all first-inversion triads would not be very suitable, since VI⁶, with B♭ in the bass, is weak before V at the end. The likely harmonization for these two measures would be I–I⁶–VII⁶–I, which eliminates the excess of parallel motion but also employs too much tonic harmony.

Another nontonic beginning appears in solution *e*. With a bass-line tonic goal comparable to that of *d*, two skips in a row without returning is not a fault here. But the remainder of the bass melody does not have enough conjunct motion to offset the skips, and the direct octave on D in the third measure, implying either a weak III or a I⁶ with doubled third, is not a good idea.

In *f* the oblique motion of fifth to octave is natural enough, but its implication of IV–I with the tonic note in the soprano sounds like a plagal cadence at the wrong point in the phrase. The repeated D in the second measure affords less contrast than in the second measure of *a*, *b*, or *c*, and would probably best be given the same harmony for both notes, so as to avoid the weak I–III relationship; for this purpose I⁶ with doubled third is not as strong as root-position I would be, and the only other alternative, III, is more static than I⁶ and somewhat weak after V. The ending, VI–V⁶ or VI–VII, is inevitably less satisfactory, as is the implied melodic tritone on successive downbeats of the last two measures.

Plagal cadence: see Chap. 11

By choosing and combining the best motions from these six solutions, selecting appropriate harmonies where a choice exists, and constructing suitable inner parts, we might arrive at a harmonization like the following:

EXAMPLE 9–14

Bb: IV I⁶ VII⁶ I   I⁶ IV I   V

It should be borne in mind, however, that other satisfactory or even better solutions might be devised, since the six bass lines we examined in detail obviously do not exhaust all possibilities, even within the restrictions of note-against-note triads in root position and first inversion.

Use of Formulae

It was advocated in the discussion of tonality (Chapter 5) that groups of two or three chords might be learned as commonly recurring formulae or harmonic "words." A vocabulary of such words is extremely useful in the planning of a harmonization. One recognizes an upper voice in one of the formulae as part of the melody, and the consideration of alternative chords becomes the consideration of alternative formulae.

EXAMPLE 9–15

This group of notes, instead of being regarded as four isolated chord tones, could be considered as the familiar upper voice of a number of formulae, such as these:

EXAMPLE 9–16

G: IV I V I   II III V VI   IV I V VI

Or, if chords in the first inversion are included:

EXAMPLE 9–17

G: IV III⁶ V VI   IV⁶ I VII⁶ I⁶   VII⁶ I⁶ II⁶ VI

Harmonization and Nonharmonic Tones

Analysis of a given melody will usually suggest the character of the harmonization, the kind of harmonic rhythm that would be suitable, and the possible use of nonharmonic tones. A melody of pronounced rhythmic and motivic construction, for instance, will usually be best accommodated by changes of harmony that coincide with either the length of the motive or the basic pulse of the measure; less often such a melody will prove suitable for note-against-note harmonization. On the other hand, melodies of slow or moderate tempo, moving for the most part in equal time values, are well adapted to note-against-note harmonization, the harmonic rhythm generally matching the melodic rhythm.

Before harmonizing a melody, sing it through repeatedly, in order to understand its phrase structure and to estimate the range of possible harmonic rhythms best suited to it. The ideal to be kept in mind is consistency of texture, with motion in the given part being balanced at different times by motion in the other parts. There is nothing duller than a pedestrian harmonization that is correct in all details of voice leading but that adds nothing of interest to support the given melody.

We may consider various ways of harmonizing the melody given below, beginning with two opposite approaches.

EXAMPLE 9–18

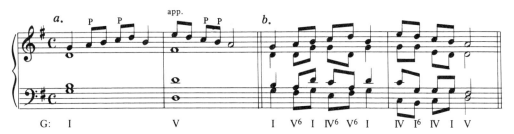

The harmonization given in *a* above involves minimal harmonic activity, only two chord changes against eleven soprano notes with rather insipid nonharmonic tones. The melody has a shape, but the texture does not convincingly support it. The harmonization in *b*, on the other hand, has a maximum of harmonic activity, and the texture is completely homophonic; the harmonic rhythm and the melodic rhythm are identical in all parts, and the same kind of texture would become rhythmically wearying if continued for very long.

EXAMPLE 9–19

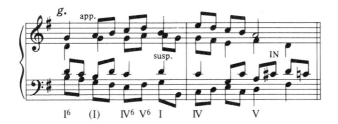

In *c* we have a harmonic rhythm of quarter notes in the first measure, half notes in the second. This is much better than *a* above, but with everything in root position, and smaller note-values only in the melody, this harmonization sounds rather wooden and plodding. With first-inversion triads included, *d* has a better bass than *c*, but the lack of eighth-note motion in the lower parts is still very noticeable.

A big improvement may be noticed in *e*, which has the same harmonic rhythm as *c* but with the addition of a bass line which is well contrasted with the given melody in both rhythm and contour. At the half cadence, where the melody holds firm, the motion of the bass is matched in an inner voice. The harmonization illustrates how much a texture may be enriched by passing tones alone; except for the escapetone D in the first measure, these are the only nonharmonic tones present. The next example, *f*, is very similar to *e*, but the eighth-note motion in the bass is uninterrupted, and there is more activity in the inner parts. Passing tones are the only nonharmonic tones, but they sometimes occur simultaneously with arpeggiations as well as with other passing tones in different voices.

Many other possibilities for the use of nonharmonic tones are easy enough to find, even restricted to the eighth note as the smallest time value. The harmonization given in *g* is perhaps too busy, with some contrapuntal values that might be questioned. Such a texture might well be satisfactory, in part depending on the tempo, but it also involves aspects of style, whether instrumental or vocal or a combination of the two.

EXERCISES

1. Harmonize the following melodies in four parts, note against note, without nonharmonic tones. Use triads in root position and first inversion. Write two versions of each harmonization, making use of the alternative choices indicated.

2. Harmonize the following melodies in four parts, using triads in root position and first inversion. Write two versions of each, the first without any nonharmonic tones, the second a substantially different harmonization making use of nonharmonic tones in the added parts.

3. Harmonize the following soprano parts, observing the nonharmonic tones indicated. Other nonharmonic tones may be introduced in the added voices.

4. Harmonize the following soprano parts, first making a careful melodic analysis to determine the nonharmonic tones present.

5. Add three upper voices to the following basses, forming triads in root position and first inversion.

6. Harmonize the following phrases drawn from chorale melodies, using triads in root position and first inversion, and arpeggiations and nonharmonic tones having note-values no smaller than the eighth note. Under the fermata, all the lower voices must have the same note-values as the soprano note.

e . Nun danket alle Gott .

f . O Gott, du frommer Gott

7. *Analysis*. Analyze the following excerpt, taking care to indicate all nonharmonic tones.

Bach, Chorale No. 5, *An Wasserflüssen Babylon*

10

The Six-Four Chord

When the notes of a triad are so arranged that the original fifth becomes the lowest tone, the triad is said to be in the second inversion, and in this position is known as the *six-four chord*, the intervals between the bass and the upper voices being sixth and fourth.

EXAMPLE 10–1

Since the fourth is a dissonant interval when its lowest tone is in the bass, the six-four is an unstable chord. In its characteristic usages it is the product of melodic motion between two stable harmonies, and thus can be considered as a grouping of nonharmonic tones.

The Cadential Six-Four Chord

By far the commonest type of six-four chord is the familiar tonic six-four preceding the dominant chord in a cadence. This is the *cadential six-four chord*. It has the cadential effect of a dominant chord in which the sixth and fourth above the bass form appoggiatura to the fifth and third respectively, while at the same time the ear's attention is attracted to the tonic degree as the moving tone. Thus the tonic six-four used in this way shares tonic and dominant properties simultaneously, and for this reason it is a harmonically strong chord even though it must be resolved.

EXAMPLE 10–2

I^6_4 V
(V_____)

In four-part writing the bass of the cadential six-four chord is doubled, since it is the inactive tone, and also since it is the real root of a dominant chord in root position.

Compare the example above with the following closely related effects for their relative dissonance values.

EXAMPLE 10–3

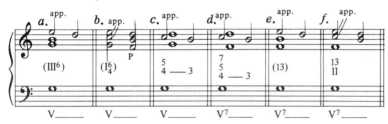

As might be expected for a chord containing two appoggiature, the cadential six-four chord, with its resolution to the dominant chord, has the rhythmic value of strong-to-weak. In its most characteristic form it marks a strong downbeat, directly following the barline. The harmony preceding the cadential six-four chord is one that would normally precede the dominant, as in IV–V, II–V, sometimes VI–V (especially in minor), or even I–V in a weak-to-strong progression. The dominant chord itself is a less satisfactory preparation for the cadential six-four.

EXAMPLE 10–4

See also Exx.
5–29, 22–7

EXAMPLE 10–5: Wagner, *Die Meistersinger*, Act I, Scene 1

Mässig

C: IV   VII⁶₅   V of VI   IV   I⁶₄   V   I
         (II⁶₅ of VI)

EXAMPLE 10–6: Mozart, *Sonata for Piano Four Hands*, K. 497, II

Andante

B♭: I   II⁶   I⁶₄   V

When the chord before the cadential six-four chord is tonic, the progression is nevertheless felt as weak-to-strong, since the root change is actually I–V.

EXAMPLE 10–7: Beethoven, *String Quartet*, Op. 18, No. 2, II

Adagio cantabile

C: I   V⁴₃   I   I⁶₄   V

Chords on V and III are less appropriate to introduce the cadential six-four chord, because of the static harmonic rhythm or the weakness of the progression itself.

EXAMPLE 10–8

The sixth or the fourth, or both, may occur as suspensions, tied over from the previous beat, instead of as appoggiature. In this case the harmonic rhythm remains weak-to-strong, while the melodic rhythm of the voices involved becomes strong-to-weak.

EXAMPLE 10–9

In the next example, the chord on the first beat of the second measure could be described as a supertonic six-four chord, but the sixth is a suspension and the fourth an appoggiatura, so that the basic harmony of the first two beats is really VI.

EXAMPLE 10–10: Mozart, *Piano Quartet*, K. 478, II

Although the sixth and fourth are by origin nonharmonic tones, they may function as principal melodic tones with further embellishment. Thus the E in the second measure of Example 10–11, the sixth of the chord, is decorated by the appoggiatura F♯ and the auxiliary D♯.

EXAMPLE 10–11: Brahms, *Intermezzo*, Op. 117, No. 3

In keeping with the contrapuntal character of the sixth and fourth, care is usually taken to observe their natural resolution to the step below. The following resolutions represent exceptions to this rule, although they are not infrequently encountered.

EXAMPLE 10–12

EXAMPLE 10–13: Mozart, *String Quartet*, K. 421, II

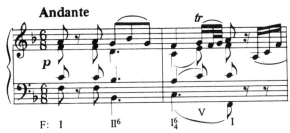

EXAMPLE 10–14: Schubert, *Symphony No. 8* ("Unfinished"), I

Other harmonies may be interpolated between the six-four chord and its resolution to the dominant. The quality of suspense inherent in the cadential six-four is retained by the ear until the dominant is reached.

EXAMPLE 10–15: Bach, Chorale No. 252, *Jesu, nun sei gepreiset*

EXAMPLE 10–16: Berlioz, *Nuits d'été*, Op. 7, No. 4, *L'Absence*

This effect of suspense is carried to the extreme in long, developed concerto cadenzas, which are inserted between the cadential six-four chord and the expected dominant. In such cadenzas, which typically last for several minutes, the six-four suspense is chiefly symbolic; it is usually entirely forgotten by the time the dominant finally arrives.

The Auxiliary Six-Four Chord

When the root of a triad remains stationary while its third and fifth rise one degree and return, an auxiliary six-four chord is formed. It differs from the appoggiatura type in that it is weak rhythmically, the sixth and fourth entering from below in the manner of neighbor notes. A simple analysis of one root for all three chords is always possible, the sixth and fourth being nonharmonic tones. The subdominant six-four is probably the commonest example of this type.

EXAMPLE 10–17

EXAMPLE 10–18: Chopin, *Etude*, Op. 10, No. 5

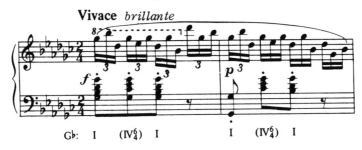

Many examples may be found which are melodically like those above but which differ rhythmically, with the six-four on the strong beat of the measure, that is, like an appoggiatura six-four. In such a metric position, with the particular melodic preparation, this appoggiatura six-four has weak harmonic value and will not be mistaken for a cadential six-four.

Cf. Ex. 19–11   EXAMPLE 10–19: Clementi, *Sonatina*, Op. 36, No. 6, II

The Passing Six-Four Chord

It is the bass, rather than the upper voices, that gives its name to the passing six-four chord. Here the bass is a passing tone between two tones a third apart, usually of the same harmony. The rhythmic value of the passing six-four chord is therefore weak. Its upper voices enter and leave by step, so that they may be explained contrapuntally in relation to the surrounding harmony, the sixth as neighbor, the fourth as harmony note, and the octave of the bass as passing tone. The passing V_4^6 between I and I^6 is identical in function to the passing VII^6 used in the same way (compare Example 6–34).

EXAMPLE 10–20

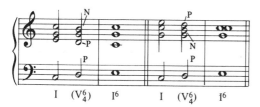

$$I \quad (V_4^6) \quad I^6 \qquad I \quad (V_4^6) \quad I^6$$

EXAMPLE 10–21: Mozart, *Sonata*, K. 330, II

Andante cantabile

$$F: \quad I^6 \quad V_4^6 \quad I \quad IV^6 \qquad I^6 \quad V \text{ of } V \quad I_4^6 \quad V$$
$$(I \underline{\qquad} \quad IV \underline{\qquad} \quad I \quad V \text{ of } V \quad V \underline{\qquad})$$

As in the case of the auxiliary six-four chord, there are abundant instances of chords which have the melodic form of the passing six-four but that are rhythmically strong with respect to the chords that surround them. The passing V_4^6 in the following example, despite its rhythmic stress, has little harmonic effect on the tonic function of the measure, compared with the much stronger dominant in the measure that follows.

EXAMPLE 10–22: Beethoven, *Sonata, Op. 13 ("Pathétique"), I*

The following should be analyzed carefully for the relative harmonic strength of the tonic and dominant chords.

EXAMPLE 10–23: Schubert, *Impromptu, Op. 90, No. 1*

The Arpeggiating Six-Four Chord and Other Forms

The bass may touch upon the fifth in the course of its melodic movement among the tones of the chord, without producing the dissonant effect of a six-four chord. It must be decided on rhythmic grounds whether or not the fifth is the real harmonic bass. Certainly in the example below, illustrating the *arpeggiating six-four chord*, the fifth in the bass is unimportant contrapuntally and is merely a tone in a broken chord.

See also Exx.
10–7, 13–1

EXAMPLE 10–24: Mozart, *String Quartet, K. 465, I*

In the most frequently encountered usage of this type, the lower fifth alternates with the root in the bass of tonic harmony. The fifth in the bass thus gives a suggestion of dominant feeling without an actual harmonic change, at the same time providing an alternate form of the tonic. The arpeggiating six-four is often seen in keyboard music as part of figurations such as Alberti basses, and in accompaniments of a certain textural character, as in waltzes and marches.

EXAMPLE 10–25: Schubert, *Sonata*, Op. 53, IV

In orchestral music the bass of the arpeggiating six-four is a favorite ostinato for the kettledrums, which are most often tuned to tonic and dominant.

In the following example the dominant pedal underlying the entire phrase is like a large upbeat (anacrusis) to the root-position tonic at the end. The same phrase begins and ends the piece.

EXAMPLE 10–26: Schubert, *Nachtviolen*

Besides the auxiliary and passing six-four chord forms, other types of six-four chords of contrapuntal origin are frequently found and can be understood as groupings of any of the nonharmonic tones. They are usually not of sufficient rhythmic importance to be looked on as chords, but rather should be regarded as combinations of melodic factors.

EXAMPLE 10–27

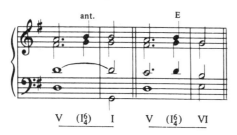

V (I$^6_4$) I   V (I$^6_4$) VI

Composers have occasionally been attracted by the feeling of suspense in the six-four chord and have specifically exploited the effect by means of uncharacteristic resolution. The following example is comparable in its voice leading to the nondissonant arpeggiating six-four of the type just shown, but its rhythmic placement shows it to be strongly cadential. The lack of the expected intervening dominant chord is dramatic; the appoggiatura leading tone on the downbeat of the third measure is the only dominant element present.

EXAMPLE 10–28: Beethoven, *Symphony No. 9*, I

Allegro ma non troppo, un poco maestoso

(tonic ped.)
d: V$^9_3$ of V   I$^6_4$ I($^5_3$)

These common formulae including six-four chords are to be played in all keys, and in as many different spacings as possible:

EXAMPLE 10–29

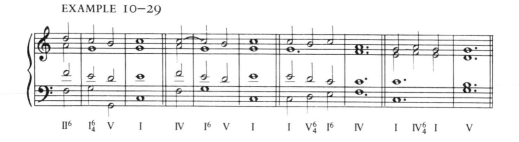

II^6 I$^6_4$ V I   IV I^6 V I   I V$^6_4$ I^6 IV   I IV$^6_4$ I V

EXERCISES

1. Write in four parts the following series of chords indicated by the symbols, choosing in each case an appropriate meter and rhythm.

a. A minor: $VI–II^6–I^6_4–V$
b. B♭ major: $II–I^6_4–V–I$
c. G minor: $V–VI–I^6_4–V$
d. E major: $V–I^6_4–V–VI$
e. C minor: $I–V^6_4–I^6–V$
f. D major: $IV^6_4–I–I^6_4–V$
g. B minor: $I–I^6_4–II^6–V$
h. F major: $I^6_4–III^6–IV–I$

2. Work out the following figured basses in four parts:

3. Harmonize the following soprano parts, introducing six-four chords where appropriate:

4. Harmonize the following unfigured basses, making use of six-four chords as appropriate:

c. **Siciliana**

d.

5. Find at least two examples of each of the following, drawn from a variety of styles and genres:

a. cadential tonic six-four
b. passing dominant six-four
c. auxiliary subdominant six-four
d. cadential tonic six-four with exceptional voice leading in the resolution (cf. Examples 10–12, 10–13, 10–14)
e. arpeggiating six-four
f. passing six-four on a root other than I or V

11

Cadences

There are no more important harmonic formulae than those used for phrase endings. They mark the breathing places in music, establish or confirm the tonality, and render coherent the formal structure.

It is remarkable that the convention of the cadential formulae could hold its validity and meaning throughout the entire common-practice period. The changes that took place in external manner and harmonic color did not disturb the fundamental cadence types, but seemed only to confirm their acceptance.

The Authentic Cadence

The harmonic formula V–I, the authentic cadence, can be extended to include the II or IV that customarily precedes it. We now also have the cadential six-four, the double appoggiatura over a dominant root, whose function is to announce the cadence. Thus a final cadence incorporating these preparatory elements in order, as II⁶–I$_4^6$–V–I or IV–I$_4^6$–V–I, will be harmonically very strong.

EXAMPLE 11–1: Bach, *Well-Tempered Clavier, II,* Fugue No. 9

"Rule, Britannia"?

The example above shows the authentic cadence in simple form. However, there are many ways of varying the arrangement of the formula, a few of which are explained below.

In the following example, II is replaced by its close relative, V of V, and instead of the tonic six-four, just the fourth above the bass appears as a suspension. (Compare Example 10–3c.)

EXAMPLE 11–2: Handel, *Suite No. 6*, Fugue

The final tonic chord may be ornamented by a suspension or an appoggiatura.

EXAMPLE 11–3: Chopin, *Fantasy*, Op. 49

The dominant chord may continue to sound over the final tonic in the bass, later resolving, or it may act as an appoggiatura to the tonic. (Compare Example 11–13.)

EXAMPLE 11–4: Beethoven, *Sonata*, Op. 28 ("Pastorale"), II

Cf. Exx. 8–13, 8–34

Perfect and Imperfect Cadences

The use of the authentic cadence is not restricted to final phrases. It is often employed elsewhere, but with less finality. The most conclusive arrangement, with dominant and tonic chords in root position and the tonic note in the soprano at the end, is generally called the *perfect cadence*, all other forms of the authentic cadence being termed *imperfect*, meaning less final.

The approach to the tonic by means of the first inversion of the dominant chord is generally considered a less conclusive cadential effect.

EXAMPLE 11–5: Mendelssohn, *Prelude*, Op. 25, No. 6

If the tonic chord is inverted the phrase will probably be extended so that the more final cadence comes later. Placing the third in the soprano also gives less feeling of finality than having the tonic in both outside voices. The following example by Beethoven shows an imperfect

EXAMPLE 11–6: Beethoven, *Symphony No. 8*, I

authentic cadence with the third in the soprano, balanced by a perfect cadence with the tonic in soprano and bass.

The Half Cadence

The *half cadence* (or *semicadence*) is any cadence that ends on the dominant chord. Where the authentic cadence is comparable to a full stop, the half cadence is more like a comma, indicating a partial stop in an unfinished statement.

EXAMPLE 11–7: Bach, Chorale No. 1, *Aus meines Herzens Grunde*

A characteristic use of the half cadence is at the end of the first of a pair of parallel phrases, when the second phrase will end with an authentic cadence. Example 11–21, below, is a good illustration.

Of equally common occurrence, however, is the pair of phrases ending in half and full cadences which do not have a precise thematic similarity.

EXAMPLE 11–8: Haydn, *Sonata No. 10*, I

As the preceding example shows, the cadential six-four chord may be employed to accentuate the half cadence. Some common formulae are given below.

EXAMPLE 11–9

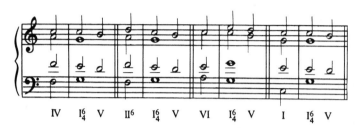

IV   I$^6_4$ V   II^6 I$^6_4$ V   VI   I$^6_4$ V   I   I$^6_4$ V

EXAMPLE 11–10: Mozart, *Sonata*, K. 576, II

A: I   V$^6_5$ I   IV   II^6 I$^6_4$ V

The tonic may be suspended into the dominant chord, without six-four, or it may appear as appoggiatura to the leading tone.

EXAMPLE 11–11: Franck, *Symphony*, II

B: V^7 of VI   VI   V$^4_3$ of IV   V$^0_9$ V$^4_3$ I^6 V$^6_5$ of V   V^7
                              of V

In many cases the chord before the dominant will contain a chromatically raised fourth degree, the leading tone to the dominant. This may have more melodic than harmonic significance, as illustrated by the reaching-tone G♯ in the example below.

EXAMPLE 11–12: Beethoven, *Sonata*, Op. 2, No. 2, II

More often the leading tone to the dominant will be an actual harmonic component of the dominant of the dominant, V of V, which in progression to the dominant forms an especially strong half cadence. The example below shows the V of V as a prepared appoggiatura over the dominant root.

EXAMPLE 11–13: Schubert, *Moments musicaux*, Op. 94, No. 6

It is not always necessary to differentiate between a half cadence containing the tonicizing V of V and an authentic cadence in the key of the dominant. When the phrase that follows is still in the tonic key, it seems unnecessary to declare that there is a modulation just because of one chord. On the other hand, if there is a strong series of chords in the dominant key leading up to the cadence, it would appear more logical to recognize an intermediate modulation in the analysis. This distinction will be explored more fully in Chapter 14.

The Plagal Cadence

The *plagal cadence* (IV–I) is most often used after an authentic cadence, as an added close to a movement. The subdominant chord seems tonally very satisfactory after the emphasis on dominant and tonic.

EXAMPLE 11–14: Chopin, *Etude*, Op. 25, No. 8

For a modern example, see Ex. 31–74

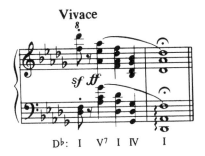

D♭: I   V⁷ I   IV   I

There are many instances of the plagal cadence as a phrase ending, without a preceding authentic cadence.

EXAMPLE 11–15: Handel, *Messiah*, Hallelujah Chorus

D: I⁶ IV I   I⁶ IV I   I⁶ IV I   I   IV   I

EXAMPLE 11–16: Schumann, *Symphonic Etudes*, Op. 13

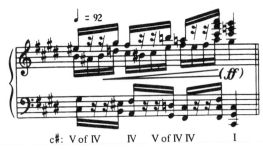

c♯: V of IV   IV   V of IV IV   I

The minor form of subdominant harmony is frequently used in the plagal cadence at the end of a movement in the major mode. It gives a particularly colorful ending.

EXAMPLE 11–17: Mendelssohn, Overture to *A Midsummer Night's Dream*

E: I   V   IV (min.)   I

The supertonic degree may be added to the subdominant chord without impairing the effect of plagal cadence. It may appear as a passing tone or it may be a chord tone in a seventh chord in first inversion. Used in this way, the II⁶₅ is regarded as a substitute for IV.

More on this in Chap. 23; see also Ex. 21–24

EXAMPLE 11–18

IV   I   IV(II)⁶₅   I

EXAMPLE 11–19: Dvořák, *Symphony No. 9* ("From the New World")

D♭: I   V⁶ VI   I⁶₄ IV(II)⁶₅   I   IV(II)⁶₅   I   IV(II)⁶₅   I

Downbeat and Upbeat Cadences

The final chord of a phrase may occur on a downbeat or on an upbeat. A cadence having its final chord on the downbeat is called a *downbeat cadence*, as illustrated below.

EXAMPLE 11–20: Beethoven, *Violin Concerto*, Op. 61, I

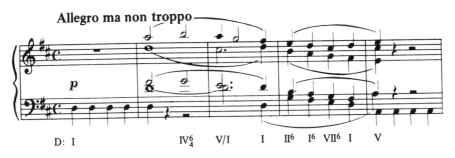

D: I   IV$^6_4$ V/I   I   II^6 I^6 VII^6 I   V

Example 11–1 shows the final tonic chord on the third beat of the measure, not the downbeat; but the dominant chord preceding it is rhythmically weaker, and therefore this cadence too is called a downbeat cadence.

See also Exx.
8–13, 8–27,
13–13

A cadence in which the two final chords convey a strong-to-weak, down-up, rhythmic progression is called an *upbeat cadence*.

EXAMPLE 11–21: Schumann, *Album for the Young*, Op. 68: No. 24, *Harvest Song*

A: I   V   I   IV   I   I$^6_4$ V   I   V   I   IV

I^6 V^7 of V   V^7 I

Any of the general types of harmonic cadences may be either downbeat or upbeat. In Example 11–6 the first authentic cadence is also an upbeat cadence, which emphasizes the continuation into the next phrase. The perfect cadence that follows four measures later is a downbeat cadence.

The definitions just given are offered in this book instead of *masculine cadence* and *feminine cadence* respectively, terms that are no longer used.

The Deceptive Cadence

The fourth general type of cadential formula is the *deceptive cadence*. It is similar to the authentic cadence except that some other chord is substituted for the final tonic. There are as many deceptive cadences as there are chords to which the dominant may progress. Needless to say, some are more deceptive than others and some will seem overworked.

The deceptive cadence is quite as good an indicator of the tonality as the other cadences—often even better. It is generally true that the key is established more strongly by the firm appearance of the dominant than by the chord to which the dominant ultimately resolves. Furthermore, as we saw in Chapter 5, some progressions involving the dominant, such as V–IV, can be heard unambiguously in only one key.

By far the most frequent alternative to V–I is V–VI. In the example below, the dominant chord appears as appoggiatura chord over the sixth degree.

EXAMPLE 11–22: Schubert, *Sonata*, Op. 120, I

See also Exs. 8–29, 14–7

If, at the end of a phrase that has been predominantly in the major mode, the major triad on the minor sixth degree is used, there is a particularly strong element of surprise in the resolution. Composers sometimes accentuate this effect, as in other deceptive cadences, by a sudden change of nuance or orchestration.

EXAMPLE 11–23: Schubert, *String Quartet*, Op. 29, I

A: V²   I⁶   IV   I⁶₄ V⁷   VI

F: I   V⁷   I   V²

Between the V and the VI, the dominant harmony of the sixth degree may be used as a passing chord. This does not change the main outline of the cadence or the tonality.

EXAMPLE 11–24: Beethoven, *Sonata*, Op. 101, I

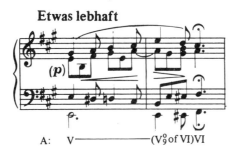

A: V————————(V⁰₉ of VI)VI

Upon the same bass as the V–VI cadence, the chord of resolution may be the subdominant triad in first inversion.

EXAMPLE 11–25: Schumann, *Wer machte dich so krank?*, Op. 35, No. 11

(ge)-sun-den,   sie las - sen mich nicht ruh'n.

A♭: V⁶₅ of V   V⁷   IV⁶ V⁶₅   I

In the following example the appoggiatura B♭ adds to the effectiveness of the deceptive cadence, which is here especially strong, as it has been led up to with every appearance of a conclusive ending to the entire prelude.

EXAMPLE 11–26: Bach, *Well-Tempered Clavier, I,* Prelude No. 8

Bach introduced still another kind of deceptive cadence later in the same piece. This time the dominant resolves to a tonic chord which has been altered to make it a dominant of the subdominant.

EXAMPLE 11–27: Bach, *Well-Tempered Clavier, I,* Prelude No. 8

The use of a deceptive cadence near the end of a piece helps to sustain or increase the musical interest at the moment when the final authentic cadence is expected. It also provides the composer with an opportunity to add another phrase or two in conclusion.

EXAMPLE 11–28: Bach, *Well-Tempered Clavier, I,* Fugue No. 4

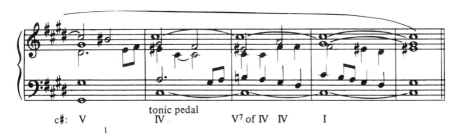

The Phrygian Cadence

The Phrygian cadence is a Baroque mannerism consisting of a IV⁶–V final cadence in the minor mode at the end of a slow movement or slow introduction. It implies that a fast movement is to follow without pause, generally in the same key. The Phrygian cadence is so called, not very accurately, because of the half-step relationship in the bass, supposedly a late survivor from the II–I cadence of the fifteenth century. The following example of Phrygian cadence precedes a final movement in G major.

EXAMPLE 11–29: Bach, *Brandenburg Concerto No. 4*, II

e: I⁶ II⁶ V   I   V⁶   IV⁶   V

See also Ex. 26–11

A particularly unusual Phrygian cadence in Bach's *Third Brandenburg Concerto* occupies a single Adagio measure of IV⁶–V in E minor between two fast movements in G major, and thus serves as the entire slow movement! Perhaps in Bach's time it was meant as a cue for keyboard improvisation, like a cadenza.

Exceptional Cadential Types

In the nineteenth century composers began to search for new harmonic bases for cadential formulae as a way of varying the forms that had been established for the better part of two centuries. The results of the search often appear most dramatically in the final cadence of a movement or a work, where it is particularly apparent that the harmony is set off from what has preceded it. Below are two examples from Chopin, one of the earliest and boldest experimenters with cadential harmony.

Both Examples 11–30 and 11–31 can be considered as variants of the plagal formula; in each case the chord used has two factors in common with the IV for which it substitutes.

EXAMPLE 11–30: Chopin, *Etude*, Op. 25, No. 4

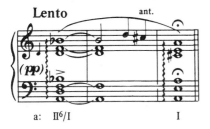

a: II⁶/I   I

EXAMPLE 11–31: Chopin, *Sonata*, Op. 58, III

B: I   ⁻VI⁶(mixed   I
                      min.)

The following celebrated example is an early instance of a dissonant harmony serving as the final chord of a piece. Some analysts have held that it summarizes the rather uncertain tonality of the entire song; in any case, the chord is held to have an implied, though irregular, resolution in the beginning of the next song. This explanation is somewhat easier to accept if one thinks of the end of the first song as a contrapuntally modified Phrygian cadence.

EXAMPLE 11–32: Schumann, *Dichterliebe*, Op. 48: No. 1, *Im wunderschönen Monat Mai*, and No. 2, *Aus meinen Tränen spriessen*

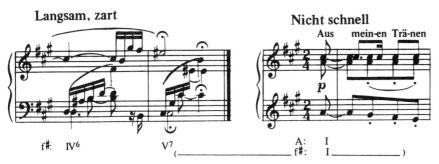

f♯:   IV⁶   V⁷   A: I
                         (f♯: I   )

Cadential formulae, to be played in all keys:

EXAMPLE 11-33

EXAMPLE 11-33

EXERCISES

1. Write the following series of chords in four parts. Each short phrase should be given rhythmic organization, with an appropriate meter.

    a. Eb major: VII⁶–I–I⁶–IV–I₄⁶–V–I
    b. D minor: I–VI–IV–II–V–I
    c. G major: I⁶–IV–V–VI–II–I₄⁶–V
    d. A minor: V⁶–I–IV–II–I₄⁶–V–VI
    e. D major: I–VII⁶–I⁶–IV–I₄⁶–V–I
    f. F# minor: II–V–VI–II–V–I–IV–I

2. Realize the following figured basses:

c.

d.

3. Harmonize the following unfigured basses:

a. **Moderato**

b. **Andante**

c. **Moderato**

4. Harmonize the following soprano parts:

a. **Andante**

b. **Allegretto**

c. **Lento**

5. *Analysis.* Analyze the following excerpt, indicating all nonharmonic tones. (Compare Example 5–14.)

Bach, Chorale No. 121, *Werde munter, mein Gemüte*

12

Harmonic Rhythm

It is helpful to review our conceptions of *meter* and *rhythm* in connection with our study of musical phrase structure. Meter is simply measurement, a means of regulating the passage of musical time by grouping pulses into countable units called measures or bars. Rhythm implies something more than meter, something that includes the possibility of unequal beats and unequal durations which contrast with pulses.

The metric organization of pulses into regular measures of equal length does not mean that all pulses within the measure have the same metric stress. The most useful convention, which has been referred to as the "tyranny of the barline," defines the first beat, with the barline placed immediately to the left of it, as the strongest beat in the measure, and the other beats as variously weak or weaker. Obviously, the first beat of a measure should be dynamically accented only when the music calls for it, and not because it happens to be the first beat.

Probably the most important concept in rhythm is the *agogic stress*, in which tones that are longer in duration are perceived as stressed with respect to those of shorter duration. The relative value of the agogic stress always depends on the musical context. A tone on the weak beat of a measure is unstressed relative to the measures; but the same tone can be perceived as stressed relative to a shorter tone that follows it within the beat. At the same time, we sense these agogic stresses on a background of countable, regular meter. Even if the rhythm is not regular, it nevertheless coincides with the meter at important points, and we can sense both rhythm and meter as contrasting with each other.

In our study of the structure of melody we recognized the importance of rhythm as an element of melodic shape, both in the motive

and in the phrase. We also saw that nonharmonic tones have rhythmic
values of their own, in that they are perceived as rhythmically strong
(appoggiatura) or weak (passing tone, neighbor note) relative to the
tones that precede or follow them. We will now consider rhythm and
meter more generally as elements of overall musical texture, and specifically as a component of harmony.

Rhythmic Texture of Music

In its total effect on the listener, the rhythm of music derives from two
main sources, melodic and harmonic. The following example shows
these two kinds of rhythm:

EXAMPLE 12–1: Beethoven, *Sonata*, Op. 31, No. 3, III

The combined melodic rhythms in this example may be indicated
thus:

EXAMPLE 12–2

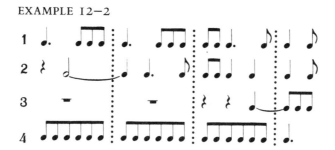

Clearly, the four patterns do not all have the same agogic stresses,
nor do they all coincide with the meter at the same points.

Using roman numerals to indicate the root changes in the phrase,
we can represent the pattern of the harmonic rhythm thus:

EXAMPLE 12–3

From this limited, quantitative notation of rhythm, two significant observations can be made:

a. The pattern of harmonic rhythm, although differing from each pattern of melodic rhythm, results from the combination of all of them. This is an excellent corroboration of the often-stated principle that chords are made by moving voices. It does not matter that the composer may have had a particular harmonic succession in mind in planning the melodic working-out of the phrase, because the harmonic and melodic coherence are interdependent.

b. The root changes, which provide the pattern of the harmonic rhythm, are not regular in time, nor are they of equal rhythmic value. Both of these aspects of harmonic rhythm, frequency of root change and the quality of that change, must receive attention in a study of common-practice harmony.

Harmonic Rhythm and Melodic Rhythm

There need not be as much diversity in patterns as that found in the Beethoven example above. It is true that rhythmic independence of melodic lines is the mark of good counterpoint, but music is not always notably contrapuntal, and the complexity of its texture varies widely.

Changes of harmony occurring at regular intervals, like a regular meter, are characteristic of much music of the eighteenth and nineteenth centuries.

EXAMPLE 12–4: Brahms, *Waltz*, Op. 39, No. 1

Andante sostenuto

In the example above, the harmonic changes, the rhythmic motive of the melody, and the accompanimental pattern all coincide with the regular meter, with a departure in the last two measures to allow a cadence.

The rhythmic outline of all the voices may coincide, in which case the resultant harmonic rhythm will be in agreement with the melodic rhythm, although not necessarily with the meter.

EXAMPLE 12–5: Beethoven, *Sonata*, Op. 53 ("Waldstein"), I

EXAMPLE 12–6: Schumann, *Symphony No. 1* ("Spring"), I

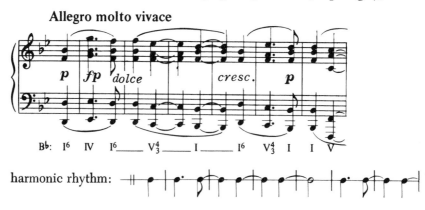

In all three preceding examples, the top voice is heard as a melody. These are good illustrations of homophonic texture, in which all the parts move together, as distinguished from polyphonic texture, in which the rhythmic independence of parts is particularly important.

When one melodic line predominates over everything else we have melody and accompaniment. The accompaniment is often lacking in rhythmic interest, to avoid diverting the listener's attention from the melody. The following is an example of flexibility in melodic rhythm combined with a perfectly regular harmonic rhythm.

EXAMPLE 12–7: Chopin, *Nocturne*, Op. 48, No. 1

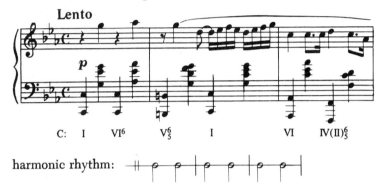

For vitality of rhythmic contrapuntal texture over a clear harmonic background, the works of J. S. Bach remain models of perfection.

EXAMPLE 12–8: Bach, *Well-Tempered Clavier, I,* Fugue No. 1

Frequency of Root Change

It is possible that a phrase may be constructed with little or no change in harmony. Below is an example of a phrase that serves as introduction to the main body of the piece, setting the stage for what is to come. The same phrase is used to close the piece.

EXAMPLE 12–9: Mendelssohn, *Songs Without Words*, Op. 62: No. 4, *Morning Song*

The opposite extreme is represented by a change of harmony on every pulse of the measure. This effect is very restless in fast tempo, but at a more moderate pace it allows the ear to focus on the maximum richness of harmonic variety.

EXAMPLE 12–10: Beethoven, *33 Variations on a Waltz by Diabelli*, Op. 120, No. 28

harmonic rhythm:

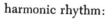

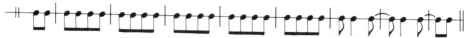

EXAMPLE 12–11: Schumann, *Album for the Young*, Op. 68: No.
41, *Northern Song*

Most phrases will show a more balanced harmonic rhythm. The
chord changes are designed to assist melodic movement and to provide
harmonic contrast without drawing too much attention to themselves.
No rule can be given, for every kind of variability in the amount of
harmonic change can be found between the two extremes.

Widely spaced changes of harmony give the impression of breadth
and relaxation.

EXAMPLE 12–12: Mozart, *Symphony No. 40*, K. 550, I

harmonic rhythm:

There are instances of complete absence of harmonic rhythm throughout whole sections of a composition. Static harmony, or absence of harmonic rhythm, is usually considered a defect, but in exceptional cases it can be very successfully used. A famous instance is the prelude to Wagner's music-drama *Das Rheingold*, where the chord of E♭ major provides the unchanging background of the entire prelude, 136 measures in moderate tempo. You will find it profitable to analyze this prelude from its beginning as a single pitch which is progressively expanded and elaborated.

Comparable to static harmony is the effect of a tonic or dominant pedal, particularly when it is in the bass, where it is strong enough to establish its own harmonic identity. The pedal in the bass tends to over-power the sense of harmonic progressions above it, and may cause them to be heard more as melodic tones above a single root. In the analysis of such a passage, it is customary to note the presence of the pedal function side by side with the harmonic functions.

EXAMPLE 12–13: Chopin, *Mazurka*, Op. 6, No. 4

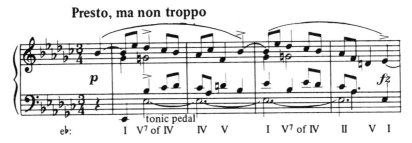

Strength of Harmonic Progressions

In Chapter 3, harmonic progressions were categorized as relatively strong or weak on the basis of their root motion: root motion by fourth or fifth as generally strong, by a third or sixth as generally weak, and stepwise root motion as strong in some cases and weak in others. Some of these qualities are easy enough to appreciate when the progression involves two triads in root position, but in actual music the strength of the progression invariably depends upon other criteria as well. A root-position triad, when in progression with a first-inversion triad, will generally be heard as the stronger component, but its harmonic strength may be offset by its metric placement in the measure.

EXAMPLE 12-14

I^6 IV I^6 IV I^6 III I^6 III III^6 I III^6 I

Other things being equal, chords on the tonal degrees (I, IV, V, and sometimes II) are generally harmonically stronger than those of the modal degrees (III, VI). This generalization does not include secondary dominants having these degrees as roots, as for instance V of II having the same root as VI, because these chords function as dominants and therefore have dominant strength.

As a rule, a chord that is rhythmically or metrically strong will also be harmonically strong. A weak harmony occurring on a strong beat, or agogically stressed, may tend to be heard more as a substitute for a stronger harmony, that is, it will have a nonharmonic component; we saw several examples in the discussion of III^6 and VI^6 in Chapter 6 (pages 78–82). By the same token, a weak harmony will naturally occur on a weak beat in the measure, or on the weak fraction of a strong beat; a chord that is harmonically strong but metrically or rhythmically weak may be perceived as a nonharmonic chord (see below).

To sum up, then, we can apply any or all of the following considerations to our perception of the relative strength of harmonic progressions:

a. Root progressions by fourth or fifth are stronger than those by third or sixth.
b. Chords in root position are stronger than those in inversion.
c. Chords that are agogically stressed are perceived as stronger harmonically than those that are agogically weak.
d. Chords situated on metrically strong beats are perceived as stronger harmonically than those on weak beats.

It cannot be too strongly emphasized, however, that in a given musical situation these different considerations will often contend with each other. One's perception of the harmonic strength of a given chord or a given passage will inevitably depend on a balance between different rhythmic, metric, and positional values of the chords as well as the root successions themselves.

EXAMPLE 12–15: Schubert, *Fantasy*, Op. 15 ("Wanderer")

In the example above, the rhythm of the harmonic changes is in distinct contrast to the perceived metric structure of the two three-measure phrases. The preponderance of dominant harmony, situated between two shorter durations of tonic harmony, is not felt as a defect. The two phrases are identical in length, rhythm, and melodic shape; the balanced phrase structure is further reinforced by the strong cadences. There is no real feeling of weak–strong or strong–weak in the harmonic rhythm because the tonic and dominant are really of equal strength, and because their progressions complement each other in the phrases.

Dynamic Indications

Directions for nuances of loud and soft, *crescendi* and *diminuendi*, accents, *sforzandi*, and the like, are of course not elements of harmonic rhythm. Ordinarily, they help to confirm and accentuate the natural rhythmic feeling already present in the music, although sometimes the composer may employ them in a contrary sense for a particular expressive purpose.

EXAMPLE 12–16: Beethoven, *Sonata*, Op. 31, No. 3, II

Cf. Ex. 6–27

In the example above, the second chord, although a dominant seventh chord, is in a metric position and in an inversion that would suggest its complete subordination to the tonic chord, the soprano and bass being passing tones and the alto a neighbor note. The accent indicated by Beethoven would probably never have occurred to the player if no dynamic signs had been given.

Nonharmonic Chords

The question raised by the Beethoven example (12–16), of whether a vertical combination of tones is an independent chord or just some melodic tones that happen to form a chord at the moment, is open to differing interpretations. Such problems will often be decided on the basis of rhythm and metric placement, that is, they will be aspects of harmonic rhythm, but one may also need to take into account the general pace and musical character of the piece.

In a slow tempo the ear has time to fix on every chord change and to hear its harmonic value, even in a passage like the following, where the parallel writing and the absence of root position give the impression of passing motion.

EXAMPLE 12–17: Haydn, *Sonata No. 29*, II

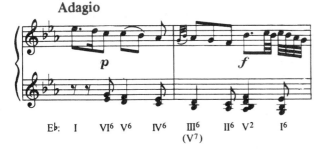

The example above is comparable in construction, but quite opposite in effect, to Example 6–12, from Beethoven's *Sonata*, Op. 2, No. 3. In that example the first-inversion chords between I and IV were transient and melodic, not harmonic. The difference between the two examples is in their harmonic perception, which in turn is due entirely to the great difference in tempo.

In the following example the speed of the music justifies a broader view of the harmony than would be indicated merely by the visible root changes.

EXAMPLE 12–18: Mozart, *Piano Concerto*, K. 271, III

In this example, although the dominant harmonies in the first three measures are all in root position, they are rhythmically weak with respect to the tonic; moreover, the upper part of the dominant harmony forms a double neighbor surrounding the tonic note. In the last four measures, the tonic and dominant functions are metrically the reverse of what they were in the first four. Thus with these considerations it seems reasonable to invoke a "harmonic meter" of one chord per four measures, or only two harmonies for the whole passage.

Here is another example, from a work written over a century later by a composer whose style is entirely different from Mozart's, which shows a comparable underlying harmonic basis.

EXAMPLE 12–19: Lalo, *Namouna*, Thème varié

The way we have interpreted these examples suggests that just as there are nonharmonic tones, there may also be nonharmonic chords, triadic sonorities that arise from combinations of nonharmonic-tone motions in simultaneous voices. We have already seen that it was possible to interpret certain dissonant chords in this way, such as VII[6] and the passing and auxiliary six-four chords. In those cases, the dissonant chords were assessed as having weak rhythmic value, and now we have done the same for consonant triads, even those in root position. In the Mozart example above, the root of the root-position V is not considered as a nonharmonic tone like a passing tone or neighbor note, but rather as an arpeggiated tone extending or anticipating the tonic harmony.

EXERCISES

1. Construct phrases in four parts, having the following patterns of harmonic rhythm and employing the harmonies indicated by the given numerals. Use root position or first inversion except where otherwise specified. Write two versions of each pattern, one in moderate tempo with no note-values shorter than an eighth note in the added parts, and the other in slow tempo, including sixteenth notes in the added parts.

2. Write phrases in four parts, having the following patterns of harmonic rhythm and employing optional harmonies:

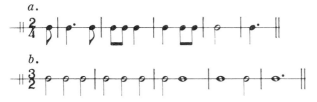

3. Work out the following figured basses in four parts:

4. Harmonize the following unfigured basses:

5. Harmonize the following soprano parts:

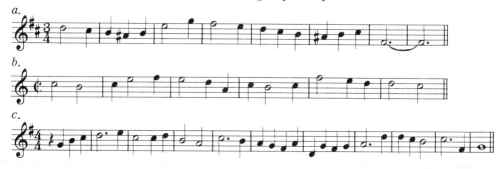

6. *Analysis.* Find examples of phrases and parts of phrases:

a. in which only tonic and dominant harmonies are used;
b. in which the melodic structures are similar between phrases, but the tonic role of one is taken over by the dominant in the other, and vice versa;
c. in which tonic, dominant, and only one other harmony are used
d. in which the tonic and dominant functions within the phrase are precisely balanced;
e. in which the tonic function within the phrase is all out of proportion to the dominant, and vice versa.

13

Harmonic Structure
of the Phrase

Unity and Variety

The principles governing the selection and distribution of chords within the phrase are unity and variety, conditioned by any special purpose for which the phrase is written. Such a purpose is illustrated by Example 12–13, in which the static harmony was appropriate to the fanfarelike introductory function of the phrase. Another appropriate reason would be transition, in which the phrase is moving from one place to another, tonally speaking. Still another would be the presentation of a phrase previously heard, but in a new form, with varied harmony, or with thematic development.

Before such aspects are investigated, it is is important to understand the harmonic structure of normal phrases having no special functions, whose role is simply that of presentation or exposition of the musical thought.

Harmonically, a phrase consists of a series of progressions designed to make clear and maintain the tonality, while confirming and enhancing the harmonic implications in the melodic line. These are principles of unity. The harmony alone will often seem to possess too much unity, with many repetitions of the same root progressions. This is balanced by other significant elements in the phrase. (See Example 13–1.)

Ordinarily, however, it will be found that a great deal of attention has been paid to the matter of balance between unity and variety, both in the choice of roots and in their rhythmic distribution. An elucidation of this balance, and an appreciation of its harmonic and rhythmic details, is an important goal of harmonic analysis.

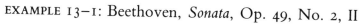

EXAMPLE 13–1: Beethoven, *Sonata*, Op. 49, No. 2, II

Number of Measures in the Phrase

A phrase of music seldom contains as many changes of harmony as the average harmony exercises. It may be argued that the purpose of the harmony exercise is to teach the manipulation of chords, and that the more chords it contains, the more practice the student will have. Nevertheless we should never forget the objective of our study, which is to understand how composers have used harmony in their works. Harmonized hymn-tunes and part-songs, with harmony changing more or less regularly on every beat, represent only a small part of the music of the eighteenth and nineteenth centuries. However admirable and appropriate to their purpose they may be, they are only partially representative of the common practice of the period.

During the period of common practice, most composers sought general regularity in rhythm and meter, allowing at the same time for much freedom and variety. These same qualities are dependable aspects of phrase structure. Since we are concerned primarily with norms, we shall deal with four- and eight-measure phrases for the most part. There is often, however, an added musical interest in the phrases which do not agree with the standard. The majority of them were originally four or eight measures long in conception, but were lengthened by one or more technical means such as deceptive cadence, sequence, or prolongation by repetition of part of the phrase.

EXAMPLE 13–2: Haydn, *Sonata No. [2]*, III

EXAMPLE 13–3: Schubert, *Winterreise*: No. 11, *Frühlingstraum*

Many instances, however, can be found where the phrase is actually conceived with an odd number of measures.

See also Ex. 12–15

EXAMPLE 13–4: Brahms, *Ballade*, Op. 118, No. 3

EXAMPLE 13–5: Dvořák, *Slavonic Dance*, Op. 72, No. 3

The Phrase Beginning

Phrases do not necessarily begin with the tonic chord, nor do they necessarily begin on the first beat of the measure. Rhythmically, they may start either with an *anacrusis* (upbeat) or with a *thesis* (downbeat). Harmonically, it is customary to establish the tonality within the first two or three chords. As we already learned in Chapter 5, this does not require the presence of the tonic chord.

EXAMPLE 13–6: Mozart, *Sonata*, K. 281, III

Here the first chord is actually the dominant of C, but, since the key is B♭ and C is the second degree, the chord is properly called V of II.

Connection of Phrases

As we have already seen in Chapter 11, the cadence of a phrase has both a rhythmic and a harmonic function, which serve to make the phrase ending as final or unfinal as the moment requires. At the end of a piece, there will of course be a final cadence. Within the piece, the progress of the music may require continuity from phrase to phrase, or it may demand a perfect cadence at the end of one section before another begins, even if there is no feeling of pause.

A phrase whose cadence is harmonically and rhythmically complete may nevertheless be connected melodically to the next phrase. The following example is a good illustration of the use of connective melody (Chapter 7) for this purpose. The melodic movement during the last chord in the cadence serves as anacrusis to the first downbeat in the second phrase. This often happens in half cadences.

EXAMPLE 13–7: Mozart, *Rondo*, K. 485

Another very common kind of connection is illustrated by the bass motion in the fourth measure of the following example, which adds rhythmic interest and movement to an otherwise static harmonic rhythm.

EXAMPLE 13–8: Beethoven, *Symphony No. 3* ("Eroica"), II

A different situation exists with *overlapping phrases*. Phrases overlap when the second phrase begins on the last chord of the first phrase, as in the sudden *forte* tonic chord in the following example:

EXAMPLE 13–9: Mozart, *Symphony No. 40*, K. 550, I

Overlapping of phrases is very often the result of a deceptive cadence. The following shows the deceptive cadence to the submediant triad of the opposite mode (see also Example 11–23).

EXAMPLE 13–10: Schubert, *Symphony No. 5*, I

Sequence

When a harmonic progression is immediately restated, starting on another degree of the scale, the result is a *harmonic sequence*. This common procedure is an important means of obtaining harmonic variety and extension. Many different types of sequence can be found in music even in the twentieth century, and the most important of these will be discussed in Chapter 20. For the present, you should learn to recognize the characteristic features of the sequence: systematic transposition of a harmonic pattern and its concomitant melodic and rhythmic patterns.

EXAMPLE 13–11: Schubert, *Waltz*, Op. 9, No. 3

Ab: I   IV   II   V

In the above example, the harmonic progression of the third and fourth measures, II–V, is in the same intervallic relationship to that of the first and second measures, I–IV, an upward motion of a perfect fourth. The interval of transposition between the two patterns is a step (I to II, IV to V). The only difference between the patterns is that some melodic or harmonic intervals are changed from major to minor or vice versa; these adjustments keep both patterns within the Ab-major scale, and no accidentals are involved.

EXAMPLE 13–12: Beethoven, *Sonata*, Op. 2, No. 3, I

Allegro con brio

(*f*)

C: I   V⁶   VI   III⁶   IV   I⁶   II   VI⁶   VII   VII⁶   V   II⁶   (III) V⁴₃   I   V⁶   I
                                                of V   I⁶

The sequential procedure would seem to indicate that the harmonic progression itself is motivic, and therefore is an organizer of musical time. This is especially true in a *regular sequence,* when not just the root succession, but all the harmonic factors and their associated melodic motions and rhythm, are transposed without substantive change. (See Example 13–12.)

A sequence may occupy any length within the phrase, or it may require an entire phrase for a single statement, in which case sequential phrases will result. When one statement of a pattern and one sequential restatement add up to half a phrase, and the remainder of the phrase does not continue the sequence, we have what is called a *half sequence* (Example 13–6).

Phrase and Period; Antecedent and Consequent

The terms *antecedent* and *consequent* were introduced in Chapter 7 to designate the respective components of a matched pair of phrases, or the first and second halves of a single phrase. What is implied by these two terms is the idea of a beginning followed by a result, a balanced "before" and "after," the musical action of the second phrase complementing or fulfilling that of the first phrase. Not all phrases have an antecedent–consequent structure, for many show an essentially unitary organization, or appear to be made up of several segments of different lengths.

Where a balanced division can be felt, the antecedent–consequent

Exs. 7–16, 7–19

Cf. the cadences of this example and Ex. 7–16

EXAMPLE 13–13: Mozart, *Piano Concerto,* K. 488, I

relationship preserves the metric unity of the phrase. In most cases, this will be apparent first of all in the organization of the principal melody. If there are motives, the commonest procedure will be to organize the harmonic changes to coincide with them, especially when they are metrically regular. (See Example 13–13.)

A balanced pair of phrases is called a *period*. To some writers this is a phrase pair whose two parts resemble each other closely. Such a period is illustrated by the following example, in which only the cadences show important differences, the second being the more final.

EXAMPLE 13–14: Mozart, *Sonata*, K. 333, III

A balanced pair of periods forms a *double period*. In the following example, the first period ends with an "authentic half cadence," that is, a cadence on the dominant preceded by V of V. The second period balances the dominant harmony of the first period, with a complete contrast in melodic character.

EXAMPLE 13–15: Beethoven, *Symphony No. 1*, IV

Form of the Short Piece

When we consider phrases in combination, in such groupings as period and double period, we are already dealing with important elements of musical form. You are already familiar with hymns and songs containing no more than four phrases or two periods, sometimes even only one period. The same is true of many short pieces for the piano, and many longer pieces show a sectional layout in which a regular grouping of phrases is the most prominent formal feature. Art songs and dances, often matched to texts in rhymed verse or to regular patterns of dance steps, provide the models for most sectional pieces, with regular rhythmic patterns and phrase lengths, balanced melodic organization, and strong cadences. Such short sectional pieces are said to be examples of *closed form*.

A wide variety of closed forms appear in the literature, but the most familiar are *binary forms*, involving two balanced sections, and *ternary forms*, involving three. Many examples of theme and variations typically demonstrate binary form in their individual variations, often with each section marked by a repeat sign. This is also true of individual numbers in dance sets, such as Schubert's waltzes and ländler. In ternary forms the three sections may all be essentially different, or the third section may be a repeat of the first (*da capo*, Italian, "from the head"). The minuet with trio is a typical da capo form; many examples of this form can be found which show a regular sectional structure (Mozart, *Eine kleine Nachtmusik*, K. 525, III), although just as many demonstrate irregularities of phrase length resulting from added development (Mozart, *Symphony No. 40*, K. 550, III).

Open forms are those in which the element of thematic development is most prominent. Combined with the possibility of modulation, or change of key, thematic development permits great freedom for sectional expansion and extension over a long period of musical time. The most important forms are those that came to full flower during the period of Viennese Classicism, especially the sonata and rondo forms, which are typical components of multimovement genres such as the symphony and string quartet.

Analysis of Short Pieces

You will not be called upon to carry out harmonic and formal analysis of the longer forms until much later in the study of harmony. However, many of the typical problems in the analysis of a sonata or a symphony will already be familiar from your examination of shorter works. If only for that reason, regular scrutiny of short pieces such as songs and dances is strongly encouraged. Facility in score reading and skill in harmonic analysis developed at an early stage will be of great value in advanced study.

It is always important, in approaching the analysis of a work, to determine what elements of the piece to focus upon, and then to examine them individually and systematically. It may be helpful to prepare a short outline of observations, including such aspects as the variety of chord functions, rhythmic and melodic motives, harmonic rhythm, regularity or irregularity of the phrase, and individual details of particular interest.

An example of a short dance by Schubert is given on page 215. Schubert wrote over 300 of these delightful pieces, which afford fertile material for individual and comparative analysis.

The melody involves a careful blend of motives. One of these consists of an upper dotted quarter (usually an appoggiatura), followed by an eighth and a quarter which are both the same pitch (mm. 1, 5, 9, 10, 13); another is the half note followed by a quarter, a rhythmic figure usually preceded by three undotted quarters (mm. 3–4, 7, 15). Three of the four semiphrases, the first, second, and fourth, have the same rhythm, giving a subtle intensity to the third semiphrase, which is more heavily dotted, and which also includes the dynamic maximum of the piece. The harmony of the first half of the piece alternates dominant

EXAMPLE 13–16: Schubert, *German Dance*, Op. 33, No. 7

and tonic in two-measure groups, with the second half including a greater variety of functions and different tonicizations (V of IV to IV, V of II to II) and a generally faster harmonic rhythm, some of which is underlined by accent marks. The relative monotony of the lower bass notes on the downbeats is subtly relieved by the passing motion in the bass in m. 12.

Considered as moving voices, the Schubert dance shows a largely homophonic texture of five or six, sometimes even seven parts, many of which are doubling voices in a chordal distribution such as can easily be played by two hands. (The Fs in the right thumb, mm. 1–7, and on the offbeats in the left hand, are a good example of such chordal doublings.) The true bass is formed entirely by the left-hand downbeat notes, except in m. 12; during the first half of the piece, the upper melody is paralleled by a collateral part a third below it. All the other parts show relatively little motion, as we should expect of smoothly connected inner voices.

It was stated near the beginning of the chapter that a typical harmony exercise will contain more chord changes than would normally be found in a typical piece of music of comparable length. Our analysis of the Schubert waltz reveals that there are only a few harmonic progressions, but they support the melody in two balanced phrases adding up to sixteen measures; in a sense, it is like a harmony exercise writ large. In our written work and practice, we attempt to experience at a very simple level some of the same basic thought processes that Schubert had in constructing a piece like this waltz, even if we do not expect to emulate the subtlety of his imagination. At this stage in our study of harmony, mastery of harmonic progression and an understanding of the harmonic structure of the phrase are complementary goals.

Application

The more obvious principles of harmonic variety, such as change of key (modulation), use of secondary dominants, and chromatic alteration of chords, will all be extensively treated later in this book. At this point we will concentrate on the different kinds of musical variety that may be obtained by variation of melody and texture. Our basic procedure will consist of the following steps:

   a. analysis of a given phrase, deriving a rhythmic pattern of root progressions, shown by roman numerals;
   b. construction of a four-part harmonic scheme showing the reduction of the original texture to these terms;
   c. composition of several new phrases unlike the given phrase, but using the root successions obtained in the first step, together with their rhythmic pattern, as a basis.

Here is an illustration of the application of each of these steps.

EXAMPLE 13–17: Mozart, *Violin Concerto*, K. 268, II

   a. The pattern of root changes is as follows:

EXAMPLE 13–18

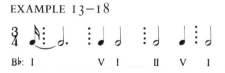

The initial upbeat is so comparatively short as to give the impression of anticipating the downbeat with I on the first beat of the first full measure. The I occupies the whole measure. In the second measure the harmonic rhythm of V–I is a short–long, down–up, whereas the third measure gives II–V as long–short proceeding to I on the next downbeat, making an authentic downbeat cadence.

b. The original texture can be expressed as the following four-part harmonic scheme:

EXAMPLE 13–19

Bb: I   V   I   II   V   I

c. Taking advantage of the slow tempo to gain variety in the melodic lines by arpeggiation among the chord tones, a version like the one below can be created, using triads in root position and first inversion to allow more melodic freedom in the bass line. Note also the organization of the melodic rhythms.

EXAMPLE 13–20

Bb: I   V   I   II   V   I

Another version introduces one more elaborating element, passing tones. It is better not to write more than two notes against one in the basic pulse, unless they are chord tones or passing tones. Rhythmic motives may be introduced as an element of interest.

EXAMPLE 13–21

It is also instructive to write versions in three parts or even two, so as to gain experience in melodic writing. At first a version using only chord tones should be made, with the bass adhering fairly closely to the basic root succession.

EXAMPLE 13–22

Tempo di menuetto

Passing tones and neighbor notes will increase the flexibility of the melodic line.

EXAMPLE 13–23

When composition of more elaborate versions is attempted, other elements of variation may be introduced, such as change of mode, change of meter, or substitution of one or two different harmonies for chords of comparable tonal strength (IV substituted for II⁶, for example).

EXERCISES

1. Treat the phrases given below, following the three steps as in the example above.

   a. Derive the rhythmic pattern of the roots.
   b. Construct the four–part harmonic scheme.
   c. Construct new phrases from the derived harmonic basis.

Beethoven, *Variations on a Theme by Salieri,* WoO 73, Theme

Couperin, *Harpsichord Pieces, Book III:* Sixteenth Order, *L'Hymen-Amour*

Other phrases, chosen from among the examples in this book, may be used additionally.

2. Construct original phrases, four measures in length:

a. starting with an upbeat and ending with an upbeat cadence;
b. starting with a downbeat and ending with a downbeat cadence;
c. with a minimum of harmonic activity contrasted with much melodic movement;
d. with a maximum of harmonic activity and little melodic movement.

3. Construct phrases according to the following patterns.

a. A♭ major, $\frac{2}{4}$, slow:

|I   V |I   V |I V VI II |V |

(Compare Beethoven, *Sonata*, Op. 13, II.)

b. D major, $\frac{3}{4}$, fast:

V | I | V | I | I | V | I   II | V |

(Compare Beethoven, *Sonata*, Op. 10, No. 3, III.)

c. A major, $\frac{2}{4}$, slow:

V | I   II | V | I   IV II | V |

(Compare Schumann, *Album for the Young*, Op. 68, No. 28, *Remembrance*.)

d. A♭ minor, $\frac{6}{8}$, moderately fast:

|I |I |V |V |III |V of III |III   I |V   I |

(Compare Schubert, *Auf dem Wasser zu singen*, Op. 72.)

4. *Analysis.* Find examples of phrases containing:

a. only tonic and dominant harmony
b. only tonic, dominant, and one other harmony
c. other than four or eight measures
d. balanced antecedent and consequent, with close similarity of melodic and harmonic structure

e. balanced antecedent and consequent without such close similarity
f. regular sequence
g. antecedent and consequent with two authentic cadences
h. antecedent and consequent with upbeat and downbeat cadences

5. *Analysis.* Analyze the following short piece:

Schubert, *Ländler*, No. 11, from Op. 18

14

Modulation

Psychological Necessity for Change of Key

Tonality, like the natural world, encompasses both static and dynamic states. The static state of tonality is represented by music that never departs from a fixed diatonic collection of pitch-classes from which its notes are drawn. A good deal of sixteenth-century music sounds this way to our twentieth-century ears, and a number of examples can also be found in later periods, for instance in many of Schubert's waltzes. Even where chromatic nonharmonic tones are added to a diatonic texture, the sense of key may remain firmly fixed, fully defined by the tonic triad, by its reinforcing dominant, and by a limited number of possibilities for other harmonies that support the structure of the individual phrases.

Part of our conception of tonality is the notion that a tonal piece is "in" a particular key, implying that the particular key defines just one tonic for the piece. Nevertheless, composers in the common-practice era seem to have agreed that it was aesthetically undesirable for a piece of music to remain in only one key, unless it was quite short. Compositions of any substantial length invariably include tones from outside the underlying diatonic scale and at least one change of key, meaning the adoption of a different tonal center to which all the other tones are to be related.

The process involved in changing from one tonal center to another is called *modulation*. Modulation represents the dynamic state of tonality. The word implies that there is a key in which a piece of music begins, a different key into which it progresses, and a process of getting there.

Modulation is therefore an aspect of musical form. It is an element of variety, but also of unity, when the balance of keys in support of a main tonality is used to advantage. Beethoven's *Third Symphony* is said to be "in E♭ major," and while it is obvious that the first movement begins and ends on the E♭-major triad and maintains the three-flat key signature throughout its nearly 700 measures, it is also obvious that a large portion of this twenty-minute-long movement is occupied with music that does not use the E♭-major scale at all. Thus in some sense E♭ major is the defining background tonality of the movement, within which all of the other keys that appear are somehow embraced, whether these are closely related keys like B♭ major or A♭ major or relatively remote keys like E minor. The listener perceives that these different keys are related compositionally, because they are part of a unified composition; the analyst can establish the relationships according to their intrinsic properties, as well as according to Beethoven's purposeful use of them.

E.g., Ex. 26–21

Elementary Relationships: Three Stages

There are three stages in the process of bringing about a modulation. First of all, a tonality must already be clear to the hearer. Second, the music at some point must change its tonal center. Third, the hearer is made aware of the change, and the new tonal center is confirmed.

In the first stage, the establishment of the first key, the principles described in Chapter 5 on tonality should be observed. It is not essential that the tonic chord appear, but the dominant must be made to sound as such. Overuse of triads on the modal degrees may result in the whole phrase being heard in the second key, especially if the second key is then strongly established.

The second stage of the modulation involves the choice of a chord which will serve as a tonal vantage point for both keys. In other words, it will be a chord common to both keys, which we will call the *pivot chord*, and to which we will give a double analysis.

For example, the C-major triad could be employed as a pivot chord in a modulation from C to G, indicated thus:

EXAMPLE 14–1

C: I
G: IV

The most logical pivot chord will be one that has a simple function in both keys. This means that the pivot chord should not be the dominant of the second key, because that chord would normally not be a fundamental chord in the first key. (Modulation to the subdominant key, as from C to F, is an exception to this caveat.) In the second stage we are still at the point where only the composer need be aware that a modulation is to take place. The sounding of the dominant chord of the new key belongs to a later stage, where the new tonality is to be confirmed for the listener.

The following scheme represents a modulation effected by means of the pivot chord shown above:

EXAMPLE 14–2

$$\text{C: IV II V } \begin{cases} \text{C: I} \\ \text{G: IV II V I} \end{cases}$$

The third stage, establishment of a new key, is accomplished by means of the cadence that ends the phrase, although there may occur strong progressions in the key before the cadence. The cadence may be any of the types studied in Chapter 11.

Examples of Modulating Phrases

EXAMPLE 14–3: Mozart, *Eine kleine Nachtmusik*, K. 525, I

The lengthy example above is a typical passage preparing the second theme in a sonata form, a process that normally takes a fair amount of musical time. It shows a modulation up a perfect fifth, or from a given key to the key of its dominant. The key of G major is well established by tonic and dominant harmony, with the tonic root maintained as a pedal for three measures. I of G major is identical with IV of D major, so it is taken as the pivot chord, and it introduces the incomplete dominant seventh, VII^6, of the new key, making the strong tonal progression IV–VII^6–I in D. The new tonic is confirmed strongly by a prolonged half cadence in mm. 9 and 10, preceded by the dominant of the dominant in D.

EXAMPLE 14–4: Bach, Chorale No. 320, *Gott sei uns gnädig*

This phrase modulates down a minor third, from a major key to its relative minor. After the strong tonic and dominant chords of A major, the key previously established, the supertonic triad is used as a pivot chord, the subdominant of F♯ minor. As such it introduces the cadential six-four chord in the fourth measure. The authentic cadence in F♯ is made more conclusive by the plagal cadence, which extends the final tonic. The major third in the tonic chord is a Picardy third (see Example 5–30).

EXAMPLE 14–5: Bach, *French Suite No. 3*, Minuet

Here the modulation is up a minor third, from a minor key to its relative major. The only accidental signs belong to the leading tone of B minor, which disappears in the new key. The pivot chord is IV, which translates into II of D, proceeding to V.

EXAMPLE 14–6: Beethoven, *String Quartet*, Op. 18, No. 3, III

A modulation up a major third. The progression IV–V–I confirms the key of D. The pivot chord is VI of the major mode, taken to be the equivalent of IV in F♯, minor mode. Then the strong progression IV–V–I follows in the new key.

EXAMPLE 14–7: Bach, Chorale No. 200, *Christus ist erstanden*

In this excerpt modulating up a major second, the first phrase is shown with its strong cadence in F major. Therefore the first chord of m. 3 may be taken as V, and at the same time as subdominant of G minor, with a major third, sixth degree of the ascending minor scale. The new key is here confirmed by a deceptive cadence.

Levels of Tonality:
Tonicization and Intermediate Modulation

The examples of modulations just shown are taken out of context, the assumption being that the second key is well established as a new key. Presumably the new key is established as firmly as the old key, and in the same way—by the appearance and reappearance of tonic harmony and its reinforcement by the dominant. If we look at numerous modulations, however, we will see that the establishment of the new key is not necessarily that simple. In most cases, musical time is an essential consideration in modulation. The first key has a special tonal advantage for its having been first. The new key must compensate for this; if it does not project the new tonic sufficiently strongly, or over a long enough time, the ear will retain the memory of the first key, and a return to the first key by reverse modulation will make it appear that no real modulation has taken place.

Example 14–8 contains all the necessary ingredients for a modulation and is analyzed as modulating from D major to A major. On the other hand, the authentic cadence on A is followed immediately by a return to D major, both before and after the repeat. The A-major

EXAMPLE 14–8: Mozart, *Fantasy*, K. 397

tonic cadence is certainly strong, and is heralded in the phrase by more than just its dominant; nevertheless, its appearance is only momentary relative to the surrounding D major. Rather than a real modulation, the A major here is a tonicization that has been prolonged. It has more tonal weight than the tonicization of III in Example 5–31, where we first encountered the concept of tonicization by means of a secondary dominant; in that example, the III was tonicized only by a single V of III, whereas in the Mozart example above, the A-major tonic is strengthened by an entire consequent semiphrase interpretable in A major.

A comparable illustration is given below. No more definite immediate appearance of D major could be imagined; yet the composer shows at once that it is not meant to last.

EXAMPLE 14–9: Schubert, *Sonata in C minor*, Op. posth., II

The tonal strength of a tonicization is in direct proportion to its duration. In the Mozart example the tonicization of A first appeared in the sixth measure, the remaining measures serving as a prolongation. The continuation of A major throughout the length of the next phrase ought to be sufficient to confirm the new key and to establish that a

modulation has indeed occurred; but in this case, with D major returning immediately in the next phrase, it would be more accurate to say
that the A major is only an *intermediate modulation*, or "false modulation," as the phenomenon has also been called. Similarly, in the Schubert example, the departure from A major begins in the second half of
the phrase with a secondary dominant tonicizing F♯ minor, and the
appearance of D major is strengthened by a prolongation of the tonic
by reference to the minor subdominant, as a plagal cadence.

In this way we may define tonicization of a secondary tonic as
something that occurs within a short length of musical time, the reappearance of the original tonic occurring within the same phrase; intermediate modulation extends long enough to delay the return to the
original tonic until the next phrase. The distinction is arbitrary, but it
will nevertheless be useful in most cases where a distinction is to be
made.

What these examples show is that the ear is capable of compre-
hending different tonalities at different structural levels. On a chord-
to-chord basis the ear can perceive these progressions as modulating,
without knowing for certain that the original key will reappear until it
actually does so. On a phrase-to-phrase basis, with a longer time scale,
the overall tonal scheme is that of a single key, with the apparent modulations actually existing as temporary tonal emphases on nontonic harmonies, assisted momentarily by harmonies drawn from outside the
key.

At a more remote level we could employ a still longer time scale,
for instance extending on a section-to-section basis throughout the length
of a sonata-form movement. At this level, modulations occur between
subsections of considerable length, as for instance between the tonic
first theme and the dominant second theme in a major-mode exposition. The ear is satisfied to relinquish the first key in favor of the second, without a feeling of certainty as to when the original key would
return. Nevertheless, the eventual return of the first key, even after
several different modulations, is a vindication of the principle of tonal
unity in common-practice harmony. In this most fundamental sense,
modulations can be only secondary tonal events in a piece beginning
and ending in the same key. Certainly this is plain enough in shorter
pieces employing only one or two keys different from the main key; it
is revealed by analysis in larger works as well, even when there are
many modulations.

The Modulation Chain

When the modulation from the main key is not followed by a return but by another modulation to a third key we have a *modulation chain*. The ear's memory of the original key is progressively weakened by continued modulations to other keys, only to be reaffirmed when the original key finally reappears.

Modulation chains are a resource of musical development. They are regularly found in the development sections of sonata-form movements or in episodic sections of fugues, where six or seven different keys or even more may be traversed before the original tonic returns. Sequential modulations are very common in such passages; these will be discussed more fully in Chapter 20, although one example is seen later in this chapter (Example 14–15). The extreme tendencies of modulatory practice are represented by continuous chromatic modulation, which came to be favored by composers in the latter part of the nineteenth century.

The individual time elements in the modulation chain may be quite long, in which case the appearance of new keys may be relatively stable, or they may be short, with only fleeting appearances of new tonics until the end of the chain. Successive modulations that lack strong confirming cadences are sometimes called *passing* or *transient modulations*. Some modulating sequences, as will be seen in later chapters, proceed by dominants alone, allowing for no stable tonics, even temporarily, until the sequence ends.

Related Keys

All keys are related. It is only a question of the degree of relationship. The common expression "related keys" always means those most closely related, measured by nearness on the circle of fifths or by key signature. Thus it is plain that the keys C major and G major are closely related, since they differ only in the F and F♯. By this measure, the keys of nearest relationship to a given key are those having one sharp (or flat) more, or less, in the signature.

EXAMPLE 14–10: Major Mode

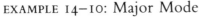
C maj.   A min.   G maj.   E min.   F maj.   D min.

It will be noted that the keynotes in the example above comprise the steps of the scale of C major, with the exception of VII, and that the modes of the keys, as indicated by their tonic chords, are in agreement with the triads on the scale degrees of C major. The family of keys in the illustration above can be described in this way: tonic (major); dominant; subdominant; and the relative minors of all three.

EXAMPLE 14–11: Minor Mode

A min.   C maj.   E min.   G maj.   D min.   F maj.

The family of keys having one sharp (or flat) more or less than a given minor key shows two important differences from the scheme just described. The triad on the second degree does not appear. It will be remembered that II in the minor mode is a diminished triad and could not serve as a tonic chord. The seventh degree, however, is present, not in its form as the leading-tone triad but as a major triad on the seventh degree found in the descending melodic scale. Its relationship is that of relative major of the dominant, or dominant of the relative major. This family of keys may be described thus: tonic (minor); dominant; subdominant; and the relative majors of these.

Interchange of Modes

It is important to recognize that a change of mode is not the same thing as a modulation, because parallel major and minor modes have the same kinds of harmonic functions and the same tonal degrees. The tonic triads of parallel major and minor modes are major and minor respectively, built on the same root, and the dominant functions are identical in both modes. We have already seen how a change of mode within the same key, from phrase to phrase, is a familiar coloristic resource (Examples 5–28, 5–29).

At first glance the keys of C major and C minor would appear to be rather distantly related, since there is a difference of three flats in the signature. But because of the similarity of their harmonic functions, these two keys could be considered as identical in many ways, since they have the same tonal degrees and really differ only in the third degree. Common practice in the nineteenth century, and much individual practice in the eighteenth, regarded the two modes as simply two different aspects of one tonality. The family of related keys under the two modes is thereby greatly enlarged, because the major mode has all the related keys of its relative minor available, and the parallel minor mode has all the related keys of its relative major.

The change of the tonic triad from major to minor or vice versa is the signal of an actual mode change. On the other hand, it is also possible for the progression itself to include chords from both modes even when the opposite tonic triad does not appear. Such a progression illustrates what is called *modal mixture*, or simply mixed modes. The commonest instance involves a prevailing major-mode context in which IV or II is borrowed from the minor. The coloristic use of the sixth degree of the minor mode in the midst of chords in the major mode, as in the example below, is frequently found.

EXAMPLE 14–12: Mendelssohn, *Songs without Words*, Op. 102: No. 2, *Retrospection*

See also Exx.
11–17, 19–4

*But see also Ex.
11–31*

The major triads on the minor third degree and the minor sixth degree can occasionally be found in works from later in the period. Because these triads include the minor third degree, they imply some kind of actual change of mode when used in conjunction with the major tonic.

EXAMPLE 14–13: Beethoven, *Choral Fantasy*, Op. 80

EXAMPLE 14–14: Schubert, *Symphony No. 4*, IV

C: I   VI⁶   I   VI⁶
(tonic pedal)

Progressions involving modal mixture do not necessarily signal a modulation, and many examples like those above can be found where the sense of tonality is not affected. It is apparent, however, that such progressions increase the number of pivot chords available for modulation, especially to keys that are relatively remotely related. Some of these are discussed under Abrupt Modulations, later in this chapter.

A few examples of such relationships within the C family would be these:

> D major is related to C minor as the dominant of the dominant.
>
> A♭ major is related to C major as the submediant of the parallel minor, or as the subdominant of the relative major of the parallel minor.
>
> G minor is related to C major as dominant minor, or as subdominant of the second degree, or as supertonic of the subdominant.

Cf. Ex. 11–23

The logic of modal interchange is governed in modulation by the same principles developed first in Chapter 5, wherein we saw that the change of mode is favored by some progressions but not by others. IV or VI in the minor can readily be followed by I in the major, for instance, but IV or VI in the major is seldom followed by I in the minor; the major V proceeds to either a major or a minor tonic with equal ease regardless of the mode that has preceded it; and so forth.

In the following modulation sequence, the apparent remoteness of the keys involved is accounted for by the resolution of each successive dominant to the minor tonic, which in turn serves as the mediant in the major mode of the next key; in other words, each modulation also brings about a mode change. The pattern of keys (A♭ minor–E minor–

C minor–A♭ major) travels all the way around the circle of fifths, and thus an enharmonic change (see below) occurs as well.

EXAMPLE 14–15: Schubert, *Symphony No. 9*, I

Exploration of Means

The steps given earlier show how the composer modulates by adopting a new tonal center for a given chord. The problem is slightly different when two tonalities are given and the pivot chord has to be found. Here, as in all branches of theoretical study, it is urged that no steps be omitted. It is tempting to take advantage of the first good pivot chord that comes to mind, and it may happen that none better could be found. Nevertheless you should try to find all the possible pivot chords between two given keys, and then to select the one likely to be the most effective.

Since we are still limiting ourselves to triads while we establish fundamental principles, the total number of pivot chords between two keys is not very large. In order to discover them, it is necessary to interpret all the chords of the first key in terms of the second key.

Using the two keys of C and B♭ for demonstration purposes, we first write all the forms of the triads we know in C and note those for which we find a correspondence in the key of B♭.

EXAMPLE 14–16

Looking at these possibilities, we can say at once that the V in B♭ is not very good, since it is preferable to locate the pivot chord in advance of the dominant in the new key. The B♭ II would be excellent for the second key, but, as it is the minor form of I in C, it would be convenient only if we wished to leave the impression of the minor mode in the first key. The B♭ I is not without objection; the note B♭ would have to appear in C as part of the descending melodic minor scale, and to make that clear it would have to proceed next to A♭, a note we do not particularly welcome in B♭. These considerations leave the two remaining possibilities, III and IV of B♭. Since IV contains the troublesome note B♭, that leaves III of B♭, or in other words II of C, as the best choice for the pivot chord.

Enharmonic Changes

In modulations between flat keys and sharp keys it will be necessary to invoke an enharmonic reading in one of the keys at some point. In Example 14–15 above, the pivot chord, I in A♭ minor (seven flats) is also III in F♭ major (eight flats), whose dominant is given as V_5^6 in E major (four sharps). If the dominant were to be notationally consistent with the preceding key it would have to be notated C♭, E♭, G♭, B♭♭. Common practice shows no great consistency in the employment of enharmonic notation for the sake of ease of reading, double sharps and double flats being freely used.

Abrupt Modulations

Modulation means change of key; hence there cannot be a change of key without modulation. Some modulations sound sudden and unexpected, and sometimes one feels that the composer did not intend an overlapping transition between the two keys, as though there were no pivot chord. Nevertheless it is always possible to define a pivot chord, even if only with difficulty. Because all keys are related, and every chord has a function, any chord may be heard in any key. By this means the harmonic progression at the point of modulation is accurately described, and the degree of suddenness brought to light.

A modulation will seem sudden for rhythmic reasons when it appears at some unexpected point in the phrase, as by deceptive cadence; just as often, the reason for the suddenness will be remoteness of the tonal relationship. The more distant the relationship to either key, the more abrupt will be the modulation.

EXAMPLE 14–17: Schubert, *Sonata in B♭*, Op. posth., I

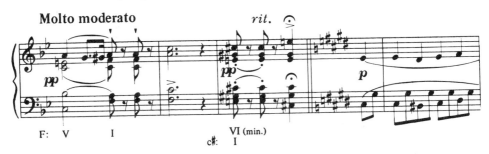

The above example shows a modulation from F major to D♭ minor (enharmonic). This very unusual relationship involves two modal interchanges, first from F major to F minor to obtain the flat submediant triad, which is then itself changed to minor. The contiguous relationships of C and D♭ (C♯) and of A and A♭ (G♯) are strong enough to associate the chord as a submediant despite the remote connection between F and F♭ (E).

In the following example a pivot-chord relationship may be defined, but one could hardly say that it is easily heard if it is even heard at all, despite the common tone B.

EXAMPLE 14–18: Haydn, *Sonata No. 1*, I

The long-held cadential chord, the abrupt change of register, and the different textures all help to obliterate the sense of transition between the two keys. There is no modulating process; there is only a modulated state. A pivot chord might theoretically be defined, but it cannot really be heard. Such special modulations may be described by the term *shift*, and their analyses given without a pivot chord.

A fairly common type of shift in the nineteenth century is the chromatic shift to a key a semitone higher. In many cases the shift takes place in a single voice, to avoid the appearance of parallel triads.

EXAMPLE 14–19: Schubert, *Symphony No. 9*, I

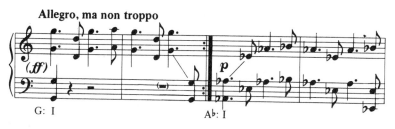

The analysis of the passage above indicates a direct shift between the two keys, without a pivot chord.

Semitonal modulations using pivot chords are more common; generally these employ chromatically altered chords and are treated in later chapters of this book. Some semitonal modulations make use of simpler relationships. In the following example, the modulation to the key a semitone lower uses a pivot chord which is the dominant of the first key and the submediant of the second key.

E.g., Ex. 27–23

EXAMPLE 14–20: Schubert, *Winterreise*: No. 7, *Auf dem Flusse*

The reverse of the above relationship is seen in the following example.

EXAMPLE 14–21: Beethoven, *Symphony No. 3* ("Eroica"), I

Pivot Tones

When the modulation is brought about through a single-voice texture substituting for the pivot chord, we have a *pivot tone*. A single tone will stand for a triad, often a tonic triad which has just been stated. Such a process obviates the need for a full triad or for proper voice leading to the triad of the new key. In the following example, the change of texture from a single part to three parts, the bass far below the other two voices, heightens the surprise of the modulation. It is not that the ear retains no memory of the full F-major triad of two measures earlier; certainly some of that feeling will be perceived; but what connects the two remotely related keys is the dual value of the single pitch F, the root of one triad and the third of the other.

EXAMPLE 14–22: Beethoven, *Andante in F* ("Andante favori"), WoO 57

In the following longer example, the pivot tone C is especially ambiguous because it is not a factor of the tonic triad just heard; it might even be momentarily perceived as B♯, the leading tone to the major sixth degree, rather than as the minor sixth degree itself, which would require one to imagine a mode change from E major to E minor. As the third of the A♭-major triad it enables an abrupt modulation to the major mediant (enharmonic) of E major. Similarly, the C♭ is the third degree of A♭ major changed to minor, and the fifth (enharmonic) of the tonic triad in E major.

EXAMPLE 14–23: Schubert, *Symphony No. 8* ("Unfinished"), II

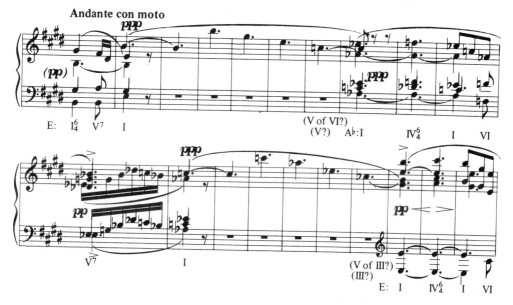

EXERCISES

1. Interpret the triad below in as many ways as possible, using roman numerals.

2. Label the triad below as a pivot chord in as many modulations as possible.

3. Work out the following figured basses:

4. Using as models the phrases by Schumann and Schubert given below, carry out the following steps:

    a. Analyze the phrase and write out the pattern of harmonic rhythm.
    b. Construct the four-part harmonic scheme.
    c. Using this harmonic pattern, construct a new phrase different from the original.

Schumann, *Album for the Young,* Op. 68: No. 17, *The Little Morning Wanderer*

Schubert, *Last Waltzes,* Op. 127, No. 15

5. Show by roman numerals the relationship of all chords in A major to the tonality of C♯ minor.

6. Write in four parts the following phrases:

    a. C minor, $\frac{2}{2}$: VI | IV II | V I
                         III | IV II | V | I ||

    b. E major, $\frac{3}{4}$: | I V I | IV II | VI
                         IV I IV | V | I ||

    c. B♭ major, $\frac{4}{4}$: | V VI II | V I | VI
                           II VI IV | V I ||

7. *Road maps.* Using only triads, construct phrases according to each of the following specifications:

    a. The pivot chord is II of the second key.
    b. The pivot chord is V of the first key.
    c. The pivot chord is III of the first key and II of the second key.
    d. The pivot chord is VI of the first key and IV of the second key.

8. *Road maps.* Construct musical sentences in two phrases, each beginning with the progression VI–II–V–I in the key of C major, modulating, and concluding with:

    a. II–I$_4^6$–V–I in D♭ major
    b. IV–V–VI–V–I in A major
    c. IV–I^6–II^6–V–I in G♯ minor
    d. V–VI–II–V–I in E♭ minor

9. Harmonize the two chorale phrases given below, modulating from B minor to D major:

Herzliebster Jesu

10. *Analysis.* Examine twenty pieces or movements of similar form, for instance minuet and trio, drawn from the piano sonatas and string quartets of Haydn and Mozart. In each of these works identify a mod-

ulation, noting the type of cadence preparing the modulation, the duration of the new key, and whether there is another modulation before the return to the original key. Show the results of your investigation in tabular form.

11. *Analysis.* Analyze the following excerpt, noting pivot chords and keys:

Schubert, *Waltz*, Op. 9, No. 4

15

The Dominant Seventh Chord

Origin of the Harmonic Dissonance

Although seventh chords may be built by superposing an interval of a third upon a triad, these chords did not originate by that process. Chords, let us repeat, are made by moving voices. The seventh, the factor that gives its name to the seventh chord, first appeared as a melodic, non-harmonic tone, and is often seen in this capacity.

EXAMPLE 15–1

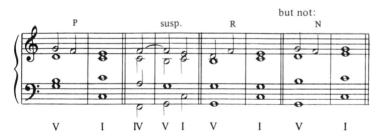

EXAMPLE 15–2: Handel, *Suite No. 8:* IV, Courante

Eventually, the major triad on V, plus the seventh above the root, became part of the harmonic vocabulary: the combination we call the dominant seventh chord, or V^7. Its complete figuring is V^7_3. In common practice, the seventh above the dominant root continued to be used as a nonharmonic tone as just shown, but it also appeared without preparation, that is by skip from above or below.

EXAMPLE 15-3

| IV | V^7 | I | II | V^7 | I | II | V^6_5 | I | I^6 | V^4_3 | I |

The adoption of V^7 as an independent chord brings to the vocabulary the first unequivocal harmonic dissonance. With three exceptions, all dissonances thus far have been nonharmonic or contrapuntal tones foreign to the chords with which they are sounded. The seventh of V^7 adds a dissonant element to the chord itself, so it is a harmonic dissonance.

The three exceptions referred to above are the dissonant diminished triads VII and II (in minor) and the augmented triad III (in minor). The leading-tone triad may be disposed of at once by declaring it to be an incomplete dominant seventh. Certainly it sounds and acts like a dominant; the resolutions and voice-leading characteristics of V^7 in general apply equally to VII.

II of the minor mode is used chiefly in first inversion, with the second degree standing as a nonharmonic tone for the tonic note in a chord of the subdominant. Likewise, though it is much less often seen, the third degree in III of the minor mode, also in first inversion, is described as an appoggiatura in a dominant chord.

EXAMPLE 15-4

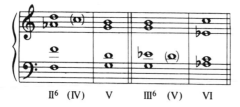

| II^6 | (IV) | V | III^6 | (V) | VI |

The dominant seventh contains two dissonant intervals: the diminished fifth between third and seventh, and the minor seventh between root and seventh. It has been common practice to resolve these dissonances. Harmonically, the dissonant intervals are followed in resolution by consonant intervals. Melodically, or contrapuntally, the tendency tones set up by the dissonant intervals move in the direction of their tendencies to a point where they are no longer dissonant and no longer have the tendency to move.

The tendency of the diminished fifth is to contract to a third, major or minor, both voices moving inward by step. If the lower of the two voices, the leading tone, alone moved, the resultant interval would still be dissonant, a perfect fourth.

In the case of the seventh, it would be possible for the upper voice alone to move, downward by step according to its tendency. This would leave an imperfect consonance, the major or minor sixth. When the lower note, the dominant, moves up to the tonic by skip, a more satisfactory interval, the third, is reached.

EXAMPLE 15-5

5   4   5   3   7   6   7   3

Inversion of these two dissonant intervals gives an augmented fourth and a major second, or ninth if the voices are further apart. The tendencies of the tones remain the same, so that the augmented fourth will expand to a sixth and the major second will become a third.

EXAMPLE 15-6

4   6   2   3

If we disregard the tendency of the seventh to descend, the following would result:

EXAMPLE 15-7

5   5   7   5   2   1   9   8   5   6

The two fifths (*a*) should not be referred to as parallel fifths. Strictly speaking, the voices are not parallel, one fifth being smaller than the other. The characteristics of this motion are, first, the improper resolution of the tendency of the two voices in the dissonant interval, and, second, the prominence of the perfect fifth approached by similar motion. The same comment applies to the resolution of the seventh by similar motion to the fifth (*b*). These motions are generally avoided, though a common exception permitting *a* is shown below (Example 15–18); they are always avoided, however, between soprano and bass.

The resolution of the second into the unison (*c*) is used only when it is a minor second, and the upper voice is a nonharmonic anticipation.

EXAMPLE 15–8

"Corelli clash,"
see Ex. 8–17

EXAMPLE 15–9: Bach, Chorale No. 153, *Alle Menschen müssen*
                        sterben

An interval of a ninth is followed by an octave (*d*) only when it is the upper voice that moves.

EXAMPLE 15–10

The motion shown in *e* above is found only when the dominant seventh chord changes position or spacing, as in *a* in the example below, where the seventh reappears in some other voice. The seventh is not used as a neighbor note (*b* below) unless an ornamental resolution is to follow it (*c*).

EXAMPLE 15–11

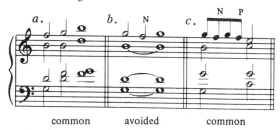

common   avoided   common

It is a generally valid principle that the seventh of V⁷, once introduced, must have a stepwise resolution outside the chord. Examples like *a* below are rarely found in common practice; typical postponements by arpeggiation, with transfer of the seventh to another voice, are shown in *b* and *c,*

EXAMPLE 15–12

See Exx. 6–14, 7–19

Regular Resolution

All dissonant chords in common practice have a regular resolution. Harmonically, this is the chord to which the dissonant chord usually progresses. It is best expressed in terms of root progression.

The regular resolution of V⁷ to I is probably the most fundamental and the commonest harmonic progression in music. It seems to be felt as a natural musical word even by an unmusical person. The presence of the fourth degree, subdominant, supplies the only important tonal factor that was missing in V–I; hence the progression contains all the elements necessary for the strongest possible definition of the key.

In the resolution, the seventh descends one degree. The third ascends to the tonic, and the fifth of the chord, having no tendency, moves down to the tonic instead of doubling the modal third degree. This results in an incomplete chord of resolution. Nevertheless, the tonal balance of three roots and one third is generally preferred to that of two roots and two thirds. The principle of doubling tonal degrees in preference to modal degrees is thus confirmed.

EXAMPLE 15–13

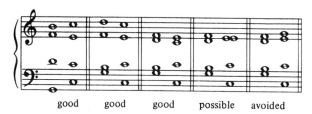

good   good   good   possible   avoided

EXAMPLE 15–14: Mozart, *Symphony No. 41*, K. 551 ("Jupiter"), III

The second degree, fifth of the chord, is not essential to the satisfactory sonority of the dominant seventh chord, and is frequently omitted. The consequent doubling of the root gives a convenient common tone between the two chords, and the repetition of this common tone supplies the missing fifth of the tonic chord.

EXAMPLE 15–15

The third is less often omitted, but there are occasions when the melodic line brings about such a disposition.

EXAMPLE 15–16: Chopin, *Prelude*, Op. 28, No. 21

In order for the tonic chord to include the fifth, as for instance in the final chord of a movement, the leading tone must descend to the dominant—only, however, when it is in the alto or tenor voice. Here harmonic considerations take precedence over melodic ones. The leading tone thus treated proceeds by skip, that is, without an interpolated passing tone, which would draw too much attention to this internal motion.

EXAMPLE 15–17

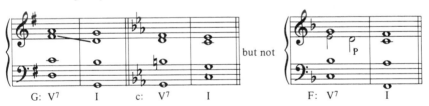

When the dominant seventh chord resolves to I^6, the bass may be said to have taken over the resolution of the seventh. The seventh may not resolve as usual because of the direct octave with the bass that would result. It therefore must resolve upward, and the diminished fifth between

EXAMPLE 15–18

the seventh and leading tone resolves to a perfect fifth by direct motion (*a* in Example 15–18). If the seventh is below the leading tone, the direct motion to a perfect fifth is avoided (*b*).

This is an example of *irregular resolution*, about which more will be said in Chapter 17.

The First Inversion

The first inversion of the dominant seventh chord is commonly called the *dominant six-five*, its complete figuring being $V^6_5{}_3$.

Factors are rarely omitted from inversions of seventh chords. The root, since it is an inside voice, will be repeated in the next chord so that the tonic chord of resolution will be complete. The dominant six-five is most effective when the original seventh of the chord is in the soprano, the resolution producing strong contrary motion in the outer voices. Observe that the tendency tones move just as they did in the root-position resolution.

EXAMPLE 15–19

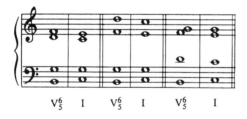

$$V^6_5 \quad I \quad V^6_5 \quad I \quad V^6_5 \quad I$$

EXAMPLE 15–20: Haydn, *Symphony No. 94* ("Surprise"), II

See also Exx.
4–9, 5–32,
11–5, 11–10,
11–13, 12–7,
14–8, 26–6

$$\text{C: } V^6_5 \quad I \quad V \qquad V^{(9)} \quad I \quad V$$

This inversion is useful in constructing a melodic bass and also as a contrast to the weightiness of the root-position progression.

The Second Inversion

The inversion with the fifth in the bass is called the *dominant four-three* chord, V^6_4 with complete figuring. The four-three inversion is thus equivalent to the dominant six-four with the seventh present, and like the dominant six-four has a somewhat restricted usage. It is generally considered weaker rhythmically than the other inversions, and it is very often used as a passing chord between I and I^6, the bass being treated as a passing tone between the tonic and the third degree, moving either up or down. The other voices follow their normal tendencies, except when the bass moves up to the third of I^6; then the seventh resolves upward in the same way and with the same contrapuntal results as in the progression V^7–I^6 (compare Example 15–18).

EXAMPLE 15–21

See also Exx. 6–15, 6–27, 10–7, 12–5, 12–16, 19–20, 20–3, 24–15, 26–9, 27–26

EXAMPLE 15–22: Beethoven, *Sonata*, Op. 31, No. 3, III

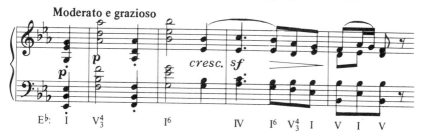

EXAMPLE 15–23: Haydn, *String Quartet*, Op. 76, No. 4, II

In Example 15–23, the V⁴₃ chord is a neighbor chord, the bass being melodically a neighbor note. In the example below, the V⁴₃ is used for its characteristic sound, as an important chord in the phrase.

EXAMPLE 15–24: Schubert, *String Quartet*, Op. 29, II

C: I   I⁶   V⁴₃   V⁶₅   I   V⁴₃ I⁶   V⁶₄ V⁷ of V V

The Third Inversion

The third inversion, with the seventh in the bass, is a strong chord. Its full figuring is V⁶₄₂, usually abbreviated to V², or V⁴₂. The bass is the lower note of two dissonant intervals, the augmented fourth and the major second, and thus must resolve downward by step.

The other voices move as usual, with one occasional exception, when the soprano moves from supertonic up a fourth to dominant, doubling the fifth in I⁶.

EXAMPLE 15–25

See also Exx. 6–15, 6–29, 14–6, 17–12, 17–16, 20–3, 23–14, 25–5, 25–19

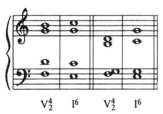

V⁴₂   I⁶   V⁴₂   I⁶

EXAMPLE 15–26: Beethoven, *Sonata*, Op. 13 ("Pathétique"), II

Ab: I   V²   I⁶   V⁶₅   I   V⁶ VI V⁴₃ of V V

The following example, showing a pair of phrases employing only tonic and dominant seventh harmony, is a good illustration of the melodic and contrapuntal possibilities of the dominant seventh chord in several positions.

EXAMPLE 15–27: Schubert, *Impromptu*, Op. 142, No. 2

Formulae, to be played in all keys:

EXAMPLE 15–28

EXERCISES

1. Work out in four parts the following figured basses:

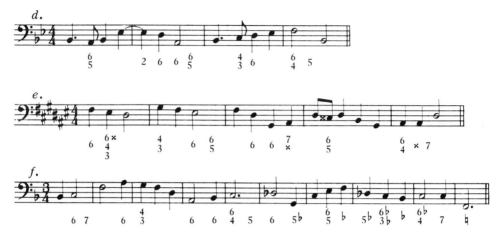

2. *Road map.* Construct a musical sentence of two phrases according to the following specifications:

 a. The first phrase begins in G major and ends with an authentic cadence in E minor.
 b. The second phrase returns to G major by means of a pivot chord which is the supertonic triad in G.
 c. One example of each of the three inversions of the dominant seventh chord is introduced appropriately.

3. *Road map.* Construct a musical sentence of two phrases according to the following specifications:

 a. The first phase ends with a deceptive cadence, without modulation.
 b. The first phase shows the resolution of V^7 to I^6.
 c. The second phrase shows two uses of the V^2 chord—with the seventh prepared and with the seventh unprepared.

4. Harmonize the following basses, introducing dominant seventh chords and inversions:

c. **Moderato**

d. **Allegretto**

5. Harmonize the following soprano melodies, employing dominant seventh chords, in root position or inversion as appropriate, at the places indicated by the asterisks:

a.

b.

6. Harmonize the following soprano melodies.

a.

b.

c. **Allegro**

d. **Andantino**

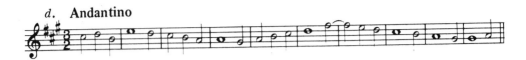

7. *Analysis.* Analyze and compare the following two excerpts:

Beethoven, *String Quartet*, Op. 131, IV

Beethoven, *Sonata*, Op. 110, I

16

Secondary Dominants

Importance and Definition of
the Secondary Dominant Function

Almost any page of music we look at shows numerous accidentals—
sharps, flats, and naturals. These indicate chromatic alterations of the
tones of the diatonic scale. We know that these chromatic signs do not
necessarily indicate that a modulation has taken place. Some of them
are required to notate the major sixth and seventh degrees in the harmonic minor mode. Others are chromatic nonharmonic tones, like a
passing tone between two diatonic scale degrees, or a neighbor note
acting as a temporary leading tone beneath a principal note.

Many accidental signs result from composers' preference for the
sound of dominant harmony to that of nondominant function, a preference that prevailed until late in the nineteenth century. Next to the
dominant function in the main key itself, the secondary dominant principle, first introduced in Chapter 5, is the most important generator of
dominant harmony. The principle expanded the range of harmonic color

EXAMPLE 16–1: Mozart, *Sonata*, K. 283, III

Cf. Ex. 20–11

by the addition of new notes and thereby new chords; moreover it increased the sense of direction and movement in harmonic progression. In its most extended form it produced a sequential harmonic scheme in which each chord became the dominant of the next. (See Example 16–1.)

From observation of this practice the following rule emerges: any degree of the scale may be preceded by its own dominant harmony without weakening the fundamental tonality.

These temporary dominant chords have been referred to variously as *attendant chords, parenthesis chords, borrowed chords,* etc. The designation *secondary dominants* in this book reflects the belief that the term is fully descriptive of their function. The chords for which they serve as secondary dominants may be called *secondary tonics;* the function itself is thus one of *tonicization.*

Far from weakening the tonality, the secondary dominants can be a means of strengthening it. If we imagine a tonal center, supported on either side by subdominant and dominant, it is easy to see that if these two important tonal degrees are supported by their respective dominants the whole tonal edifice is reinforced. This is essentially the scheme Beethoven used in the opening measures of his *Symphony No. 1.* The actual tonic chord is delayed in its arrival, but it is made the more inevitable by the strong secondary tonics established beforehand.

EXAMPLE 16–2: Beethoven, *Symphony No. 1,* I

I⁶

The secondary dominants have not only a functional value but are an important source of harmonic color as well. Composers of the eighteenth and nineteenth centuries were interested in the expressive advantages of new notes which could logically be included in the tonality. The harmonic vocabulary was greatly enriched through the introduction of these chords. In the following example, within the space of just ten measures of moderate tempo, all twelve pitches of the chromatic scale appear as harmonic factors.

EXAMPLE 16–3: Schubert, *Waltz*, Op. 18, No. 2

All the forms in which the regular dominant of the key may appear are also employed as secondary dominants. That means, at the present stage, major triads, dominant seventh chords, and the dominant seventh without root (leading tone triad), with all inversions. For example, V of V in the key of C may have these forms:

EXAMPLE 16–4

The normal triads of the major and minor modes in C are shown below; where applicable, their associated secondary-dominant functions are also given. Four dominant sevenths, derived from major triads, are included in parentheses because their parent triads cannot readily be understood as having a secondary-dominant function unless the seventh is present. Note that the diminished-triad forms of II and VI in the minor mode can be interpreted as incomplete secondary dominants, just as VII in its diminished form may be understood as an incomplete V^7. None of these incomplete sevenths, however, can serve as secondary tonics, and their dominants are not available. The major triad on VI in the minor mode is sometimes used, as well as its seventh chord, as the dominant of the chromatically lowered supertonic, or Neapolitan sixth (Chapter 26).

EXAMPLE 16–5

I V^7 of IV   II (VII of III)   II   V of V   III (V of VI) V^7 of VI   III   V of VI   IV (V of VII)

V^7 of VII   V   VI (V of ⁻II) VI (VII of VII) VI   V of II   VII (V of III) V^7 of III   VII   V of III

Resolution

The principles of resolution in the dominant-to-tonic progression apply equally to the resolution of secondary dominants. The secondary dominant and its tonic are taken as a unit of two chords for purposes of voice leading. Thus, in Example 16–4, the F♯ is for the moment not the subdominant of C but the leading tone of G, and so it is not doubled. The D is temporarily the tonal degree in the chord.

An important principle of chromatic alteration will be seen in the treatment of secondary dominants: a note chromatically raised has a tendency to resolve upward, and, conversely, a note chromatically lowered has a tendency to proceed downward.

EXAMPLE 16–6

Using the Secondary Dominants

The simplest and most natural way to introduce a secondary dominant is to precede it with a chord that may be interpreted as a normal triad in the key of the secondary tonic. In this case the group of three chords (the secondary dominant as the second chord of the group) could be regarded as in the temporary tonality, but the first and third chords would still be strong members of the primary tonality.

EXAMPLE 16–7

C: VI V of V V
G: II   V   I

    Such a duality of tonal meaning facilitates the chord connection and guarantees the logical sound of the harmonic progression. (More will be said about dual-function chords in Chapter 19.)

    Often, however, the preceding chord cannot be simply analyzed in the temporary key. This will ordinarily mean that a chromatic relationship exists between the two chords. A tone of one will appear in chromatically altered form in the other.

Cross-Relation

When this chromatic relationship is found between two different voices it is called *cross-relation*.

EXAMPLE 16–8

cross-relation

A cross-relation normally occurs when the two tones involved are treated as scale degrees of the melodic and harmonic minor modes. In the example above, the cross-relation would be acceptable if the key were G minor, with F♮ as descending seventh degree. A passing tone E♭

E.g., Ex. 8–28

would either be written or implied between F and D; the F♯ is, of course, the ascending leading tone.

In C major, however, no such logic exists and this cross-relation would likely be avoided. The chords would be arranged in a manner allowing the chromatic progression to take place in a single voice.

EXAMPLE 16–9

C: IV V of V V

A succession of V^7 of V to V^7 would generally be arranged in like manner, even though keeping the chromatic succession in the same voice means that the leading tone of the secondary dominant, and sometimes the seventh as well, resolve contrary to their normal tendencies. This is therefore an irregular resolution, but one that shows smooth stepwise or common-tone connection. The formulae given below are different forms of the "barber-shop" progression.

EXAMPLE 16–10

C: V VII⁶ of V V⁶₅   I   I⁶ V⁷ of V V⁶₅   I   I⁶ V⁷ of V V⁷   I

In working out your exercises, you should connect such chords at first without cross-relation, but also experiment with the sound of other arrangements and look for examples of cross-relation in the literature. The following examples include cross-relations formed between inflected scale degrees and nonharmonic tones.

EXAMPLE 16–11: Bach, *Well-Tempered Clavier, II*, Prelude No. 12

f: V⁷ of IV   IV⁹   V⁷ of III   III⁹

EXAMPLE 16–12: Bach, *St. Matthew Passion*, No. 1

e: IV⁶   II⁷   V⁷

EXAMPLE 16–13: Schumann, *Liederkreis*, Op. 39: No. 5,
            Mondnacht

Zart, heimlich

Es war als hätt____ der Him - mel

(p)

E: V⁶₅ of II   II   V⁶₅

See also Exx.
24–16, 31–61

V of II

See also Exx.
13–6, 15–23,
16–13, 17–16,
19–5, 24–26,
24–40

The dominant of the second degree has as its root the sixth degree of the major scale. It is not used in the minor mode, since in that mode the supertonic is a diminished triad and hence never acts as a tonic. The tonic note is chromatically raised to make it the leading tone of II.

The following examples both illustrate the use of V of II as a reinforcement to the supertonic harmony preceding a cadence.

EXAMPLE 16–14: Schumann, *Novellette*, Op. 21, No. 1

EXAMPLE 16–15: Liszt, *A Faust Symphony*, II

V of III

As there are two third degrees, major and minor, so there will be two dominants available, a semitone apart in pitch. Needless to say, the dominant of the third degree of the minor mode does not progress to the third degree of the major mode, and vice versa.

See also Exx.
19–6, 19–7

In the major mode two alterations are necessary. The second degree is raised to become the leading tone of the third, and the fourth degree is raised to form a perfect fifth with the seventh-degree root.

EXAMPLE 16–16: Schubert, *Symphony No. 8* ("Unfinished"), II

In the following instance, the chord V of III is given the rhythmic prominence of the final chord in a cadence, as though there were a half cadence in C♯ minor. The entire chorale is, however, clearly in A, so that a change of key so soon hardly seems logical.

EXAMPLE 16–17: Bach, Chorale No. 216, *Es ist genug*

If the minor third degree is employed, its dominant will be found on the lowered seventh degree, and the two chords will sound like a V–I progression in the relative major key. This extremely common relationship was discussed at length in Chapter 5.

Exx. 5–31, 5–32

EXAMPLE 16–18: Beethoven, *Sonata*, Op. 2, No. 1, IV

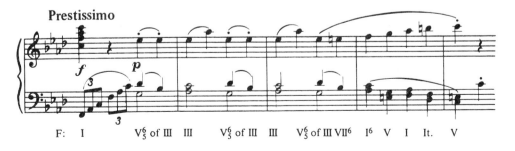

See also Exx.
4–9, 7–8,
8–42, 8–46,
11–16, 11–27,
11–28, 12–13,
14–4, 17–17,
19–8, 19–10,
21–19, 21–20,
24–29, 25–19
28–5

V of IV

The major tonic triad may be interpreted as V of IV, provided a minor seventh is added to clarify this relationship to the hearer. V of IV is one of the commonest of the secondary dominants and is often used toward the end of a movement, where emphasis on the subdominant balances previous dominant modulations.

EXAMPLE 16–19: Brahms, *A German Requiem*, No. 5

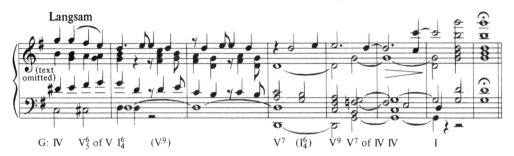

The same kind of subdominant emphasis may be found at the beginning of a work, as in Example 16–2 and the following:

EXAMPLE 16–20: Mozart, *Sonata*, K. 332, I

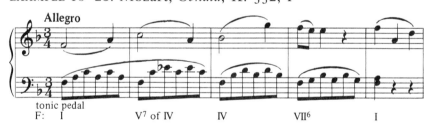

In an established minor mode it is necessary to raise the third degree chromatically to create the leading tone to the subdominant.

EXAMPLE 16–21: Mozart, *Piano Concerto*, K. 466, III

V of V

The dominant of the dominant has already been mentioned in connection with its use in half cadences (see Example 11–13). The following is a typical case in which a modulation to the dominant would not be called for in the analysis. The seventh in the final chord of the half cadence provides an element of continuity, implying the resolution to the tonic at the beginning of the next phrase.

*See also Exx.
15–26, 6–15,
6–35, 8–7,
13–4, 11–2,
11–25, 17–7,
17–13, 19–7*

EXAMPLE 16–22: Schumann, *Album Leaves*, Op. 124: No. 16,
                Slumber Song

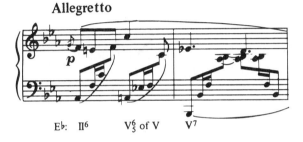

In the following example there is a cross-relation between the A♯, leading tone of V, and the A♮ in the bass of the chord of resolution. In this type of cross-relation the first of the two notes is a leading tone, which follows its tendency upward, while the A♮ enters as a strong appoggiatura-like dissonance, with downward tendency, in the bass of a V$^4_2$ chord.

EXAMPLE 16–23: Wagner, Overture to *Tannhäuser*

V of VI

Like the mediant, the submediant is minor in the major mode and major in the minor mode, and thus there are different forms of the dominant

See also Exx.
8–16, 8–27,
13–5, 10–10,
12–5, 14–9,
17–10, 20–4

for each. In the major mode, the dominant note is chromatically raised to form the leading tone in V of VI.

EXAMPLE 16–24: Schubert, *Piano Quintet*, Op. 114 ("Trout"), III

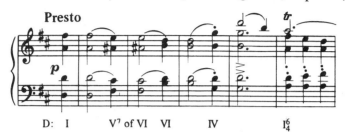

In the minor mode, the dominant note is not altered in V of VI, but its function changes from that of tonal degree to leading tone. If the chord contains a seventh, a new tone—the chromatically lowered second degree—is introduced into the key.

EXAMPLE 16–25: Bruckner, *Symphony No. 7*, II

Unlike the mediant, the submediant of the minor mode is fairly common in the context of the major mode, even though its dominant seems rather remote from the major scale, as shown in Example 16–26.

V of VII

See also Ex.
20–13

The leading tone is not considered a possible temporary tonic, so that its dominant is not employed. The lowered melodic seventh degree of the minor scale can, however, be found preceded by dominant harmony. Used in connection with an established major mode, as in the following example, it demonstrates the coloristic possibilities of modal mixture.

EXAMPLE 16–26: Bizet, *L'Arlésienne*, Suite No. 2: I, *Pastorale*

The sequential pattern of this example is noteworthy; the modulating sequence of a descending cycle of fifths is a common device in the eighteenth and nineteenth centuries.

Formulae, to be played in all keys:

EXAMPLE 16–27

EXERCISES

1. Work out the following figured basses:

2. Realize the following figured bass in three or four parts, with continuous eighth notes in the soprano except at the half cadence and the final cadence. Some nonharmonic tones are indicated by figures; others may be included as desired.

Allegretto grazioso

3. *Road map.* Construct a musical sentence of two phrases according to the following specifications:

  a. The prevailing mode is minor; the meter is $\frac{3}{4}$; the rhythmic texture contains eighth notes.
  b. The first phrase modulates to the subdominant of the relative major.
  c. The second phrase starts in that key and modulates to the original tonality.
  d. The sentence ends with a plagal cadence introduced by V of IV and finishing with a Picardy third.

4. Harmonize the following unfigured basses:

a.

b.

c.

d. **Moderato**

5. Harmonize the following soprano melodies:

6. *Analysis.* Analyze the Schubert *Waltz,* Op. 9, No. 4, given on page 242, without invoking a modulation, but instead including secondary dominants.

17

Irregular Resolutions

Definitions of Irregularities

The regular resolution of the dominant seventh chord is to the tonic triad; by definition, then, all other resolutions are irregular. Two aspects of irregular resolution must be clearly understood before generalizations regarding their use in common practice can be made. The irregularity may consist in a departure from the customary practice in voice leading, or it may be a purely harmonic matter of root progression.

In the example below, the harmonic progression is typical of the regular resolution of a dominant seventh chord. V_5^6 of V proceeds to its goal, V. On the other hand, the voice leading contains two unusual skips.

EXAMPLE 17–1: Schubert, *String Quartet*, Op. 29, II

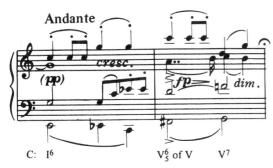

In the next example, the progression V[7]–VI is properly regarded as an irregular resolution, but the voice leading quite typically illustrates the rules for this progression, differing from V[7]–I only in the motion of the root.

EXAMPLE 17–2: Mendelssohn, *Andante con variazioni*, Op. 82

See also Exx.
7–24, 8–29,
11–23, 1 –26,
16–2

Eb: II⁶   I⁶ V⁷ VI IV   I⁶₄ (III⁶)V⁷   I

The leading tone rises to the tonic to emphasize the key. The second degree also moves to the tonic, because if it rose to F it would form parallel fifths with the bass. The seventh of the chord resolves down, according to its tendency; it could not skip up to the sixth degree, C, as that would make a poor direct octave on the resolution of a dissonance. One observes that the voice leading of this progression, as shown, is essentially no different from that of the V–VI progression without the seventh.

The examples show that a regular root progression may occur with extreme irregularity of melodic movement, whereas an irregular resolution of V⁷ may show strict voice leading. From a harmonic standpoint, the details of contrapuntal variants are less important, because contiguity, or smoothness of connection, remains a valid principle even in irregular resolution. The chord of resolution may receive a particular emphasis because the natural voice leading of the dominant seventh has been contravened; yet in the majority of cases it will be found that the chord of resolution has at least one note in common with the expected chord, and often two notes; with or without common tones between the chords, a stepwise voice leading will usually be present.

Such connections are illustrated by the resolution of V⁷ to V⁷ of IV. The minor seventh above the tonic is in a chromatic relationship

EXAMPLE 17–3

V⁷ V⁷ of IV   V⁷ V² of IV

with the leading tone, so that the latter usually descends (*a* in Example 17–3), although the cross-relation is sometimes used when the lowered tone is in the bass (*b*).

We have here a dissonant chord resolving to another dissonant chord, a frequent occurrence. When the progression includes a seventh chord in inversion, it will be arranged so as to allow the inverted chord to contain all four factors.

Variety of Irregular Resolutions

The following irregular resolutions of the dominant seventh chord include some of the types most frequently encountered, but it is not suggested that these constitute an exhaustive list. All should be tried out in various positions and spacings for an appreciation of their particular qualities.

EXAMPLE 17–4   *Cf. Ex. 11–27*

The resolutions to the submediant (*a, b* above) and to the subdominant in first inversion (*c, d*) are already familiar in their pure-triad forms as deceptive cadences, discussed in Chapter 11. In the resolution to IV the seventh does not resolve but is repeated or tied over into the doubled root of the second chord. When both chords are in root position, the leading tone is customarily placed in an inside voice.

EXAMPLE 17–5: Chopin, *Prelude*, Op. 28, No. 17

A♭:   IV   V⁷   IV

More often the subdominant is found in first inversion, allowing a choice of doubling either tonic or fourth degree. In the Mozart example below, the dynamic change and the sudden leap in the upper melody add to the surprise of the irregular resolution.

See also Ex. 11–25

EXAMPLE 17–6: Mozart, *Sonata*, K. 279, II

F: II⁶   I⁶₄   V⁷   IV⁶   V⁶₅   I

The progression shown in Example 17–4e, with the leading tone in the soprano voice in V⁷–IV, has a peculiar kind of sound, appearing to emphasize the tritone relationship between the soprano of the V and the bass of the IV; in common practice, this progression is unusual even with pure triads, although it was of common use in the sixteenth cen-

EXAMPLE 17–7: Schubert, *Symphony No. 9*, II

a: III of V of V of V of   V⁷ of V   I   V⁷   IV   I⁶₄   V
    III   V of III III V of V

tury. Example 17–7 shows V^7 of V resolving irregularly to I, followed by V^7 to IV, in both cases with the leading tone in the soprano, so that the tritone relationship is not avoided; rather it is deliberately stressed for dramatic effect.

With two factors in common with the dominant seventh, the supertonic triad makes a weak resolution (Example 17–4f); it is similar to a dominant ninth without root and third. The alteration of II to V of V (Example 17–4g) gives a more satisfactory chord of resolution, the seventh proceeding chromatically upward to give a new color. In the following example, a junction of phrases, the omission of the root D from V of V eliminates another common tone.

EXAMPLE 17–8: Mozart, *Sonata*, K. 533, I

Chords on the third degree (Example 17–4h, i, j) are also not very satisfactory, since they tend to be absorbed into the dominant harmony. The major third sounds more like a nonharmonic melodic tone than like a real resolution of the seventh. The resolution to the major triad on the minor third degree is seldom found.

EXAMPLE 17–9: Schubert, *Symphony No. 9*, I

Comparatively common as a chord of resolution, however, is the form of III which is V of VI (Example 17–4k). Here again there is a chromatic relationship involved.

EXAMPLE 17–10: Beethoven, *String Quartet*, Op. 18, No. 1, I

F: V⁷   V⁷ of VI   VI

You are urged to experiment with resolutions of V^7, in root position and inversion, to all the known chords within a single tonality.
E.g., Ex. Not all resolutions will prove to be satisfactory, but let your ear be
25–5 your guide, and experience will show the extent to which the various
chords are practicable.

Irregular Resolutions of the Secondary Dominants

Irregular resolutions may occur with the secondary dominants, although
there are somewhat fewer possibilities within a single key. These chords
are generally identified by resolution to their temporary tonic. When
such progression is lacking it may be that a modulation has taken place,
or that the chord appears as an enharmonic notation of a chord of quite
different harmonic significance, as for instance an augmented sixth chord.
If, however, the resolution is to a chord unquestionably of the original
key, the secondary dominant is plainly understood as such, without
weakening the tonality. The best example of this principle is the progression V^7 of VI to IV, which is as strong as the regular resolution
because of the tonal strength of IV.

EXAMPLE 17–11

Cf. Exx. 10–5,
12–5, 24–15

V⁷ of VI IV   II   V   I
        (VI of VI)

EXAMPLE 17–12: Bach, Chorale No. 268, *Nun lob', mein' Seel',
den Herren*

C: V⁶₅ of VI   IV⁶   I   V⁷   VI   I⁶₄   V⁷   I

The same relationship is found between V⁷ of III and its irregular
resolution to I, or in V⁷ of V to III. The latter is shown in the following
example.

EXAMPLE 17–13: Chopin, *Mazurka*, Op. 7, No. 4

F: V   I   V⁷ of V   III   V   I

Another common irregular resolution is V⁷ of V to I, particularly
when I is in the six-four position in a cadence. The principle of the tonic
six-four substituting for a dominant is confirmed by this strong progression.

Cf. Ex. 10–21

EXAMPLE 17–14: Schumann, *Dichterliebe*, Op. 48: No. 4, *Wenn
ich in deine Augen seh'*

so muss ich   wei-nen bit   -   ter - lich.

G: II V⁴₃ of II II⁶   V⁶₅ of V   I⁶₄   V   (7)   I   V⁶₅ of IV   IV   I

The dominant of the supertonic progresses quite naturally to V^7, the altered tonic following its tendency as a leading tone of the second degree.

EXAMPLE 17–15: Franck, *Symphony*, III

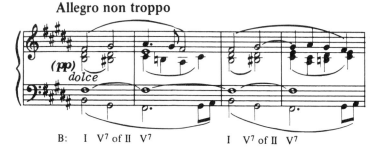

With the resolution of a secondary dominant to another secondary dominant, the validity of harmonic functions in tonality is demonstrated. The chords as dominants represent degrees of the key, but each contains at least one note foreign to the scale. It will be readily appreciated that even in irregular resolution the secondary dominants may provide much harmonic enrichment and a remarkable extension of the unity of a single tonal center. The following are two examples out of numerous possibilities.

EXAMPLE 17–16: Schubert, *String Quintet*, Op. 163, III

EXAMPLE 17–17: Franck, *Prelude, Aria, and Finale*

In these examples the tonal unity of the phrase is assured by the reappearance of the tonic. The following example shows a succession of two irregular resolutions, the second to a secondary dominant of a different key, becoming the pivot chord in a modulation. This is a typical instance of the use of common tones and stepwise motion to provide smooth connection between harmonies that are distantly related, a resource of increasingly common occurrence in the nineteenth century.

EXAMPLE 17–18: Bach, *Magnificat*: No. 5, *Et misericordia*

Consecutive secondary dominants may be used sequentially in modulation, each chord appearing as the dominant of the next, with tonal stability not being reached until the sequence is broken off. (See Example 17–4*l*, and the formulae below.) We will have a fuller treatment of this topic in Chapter 20.

The irregular resolutions vary widely in their frequency of use. At the same time, individual examples are often encountered, and familiarity shows them to be usefully and sensitively employed by composers. In addition to noting the various types found by analysis, you will want to try resolving the secondary dominants to the various chords in a given key, translating the progressions into terms of the tonality of the secondary dominant to clarify the voice leading.

Formulae, to be played in all keys:

EXAMPLE 17–19

V^7 IV^6 V^2 III   VI V^7 V^7 of II II^6 V^7 V^7 of V V V^2 V^7 of VI IV

I V^7 V^6_5 of IV V^6_5 of V I^6_4 V^7 I

EXERCISES

1. Write four irregular resolutions of each of the following chords:

    E♭ V^7 F major V^7 of VI

    E♭ minor V^7 of IV   C minor V^7 of V

    2. Choosing appropriate meter and rhythm, write single phrases according to the following harmonic schemes, employing chords in root position and inversions.

    a. D major: I–V^7 of IV–IV–I–V^7 of II–V^7–I

    b. E minor: V^7–V^7 of IV–IV–I–V^7 of V–V^7–I

    c. A♭ major: I–V^7–IV–V^7 of VI–VI–V^7 of V–I–V^7–I

    d. G major: I–V^7 of III–V^7 of VI–V^7 of II–V^7 of V–V^7–I

3. Work out the following figured basses:

a.

    $^4_2$ ♯   6♮   7   7

b.

    $^6_5$ 7   6 $^6_4$ $^{4♯}_2$ 6   7 $^6_4$ ♯
            ♯   ♯

c.

6   7   7   6   #   7   7
        ♮

d.

3   ♮   6   6   6   6   6   5   7   7   ♮
        4   6   5   5   4   ♮___   ♮
                ♮

e. **Andante cantabile**

6   6   6   7# 8, 6♮ 4# 5♮ 6   6# 6   6   6   6   4   6# 6   6   7
   5♮   5   4   3# 4   2   4   4   5   6   5♮ 5   6   3♮ 4   6   4♮   6-5
                    3   #   3

4. Harmonize the following soprano melodies:

a.

b.

c.

5. Harmonize the following unfigured basses:

a.

b.

18

Musical Texture

Musical texture results from the synthesis of individual parts in a composition. We describe a texture as having one or more elements (such as melody and accompaniment), as being in two or more parts, as homophonic, polyphonic, light, dense, complex, transparent, or other more or less precise attributes. We may also speak of vocal or instrumental texture, of orchestral or keyboard texture, terms that reflect performance media.

In the early exercises in this book it was convenient to deal with block triads in root position, a very simple texture. The four constituents of each chord are usually three triadic factors and a doubled tone, and these are connected from chord to chord in linear successions which we call voices. The four voices are different on paper, and each sounds different when sung; yet in the successive chords the four voices all move at the same time. We are speaking then of a pure *homophonic texture*, with no rhythmic differentiation between any of the voices. In such a homophonic texture, the ear is drawn mainly to the uppermost part, the soprano line, the bass being perceived in a subsidiary and supporting role. The still lesser function of the two inner parts is to supply triadic elements not included in the outer parts, or to provide a doubling voice, or both. Yet the rhythmic unity of all the parts sustains a uniform texture in which the soprano line is, texturally speaking, only the first among equals.

Vocal and Instrumental Texture

Only a small portion of music throughout history is as purely homophonic in texture as a beginning harmony exercise. The early Protestant hymns come closest, showing as they do a spare homophony with limited motion in each of the voices; these pieces were designed for congregational singing rather than performance by trained choirs. Examples like the following show how successfully the restricted genre could be employed by composers of skill. The homophony is governed by the rules of sixteenth-century counterpoint; all the same, works of this type are among the earliest in which functional harmony can be said to exist.

EXAMPLE 18–1: Goudimel, Psalm 127, *On a beau sa maison bastir* (1565)

EXAMPLE 18–2: Osiander, *Nun komm, der Heiden Heiland* (1586)

The chorales of J. S. Bach are widely considered the finest examples of Protestant hymnody. As examples of four-part texture, they show a superlative balance of homophony and polyphony. Nonharmonic tones are used imaginatively and the melodic lines in all parts are elegantly shaped. At the same time, the texture is still basically chordal, with regular harmonic rhythm and a new syllable of text on each chord change.

EXAMPLE 18–3: Bach, Chorale No. 170, *Nun komm, der Heiden Heiland*

Polyphony means, literally, "many sounds," i.e., many voices, as opposed to monophony such as Gregorian chant; more specifically, polyphony is different from homophony in that the individual voices in a polyphonic texture are well differentiated from each other. We see this in another four-voice piece by Bach:

EXAMPLE 18–4: Bach, Motet No. 6, *Lobet den Herrn, alle Heiden*

In this vigorously contrapuntal texture the voices are as intervalli-cally and rhythmically different from each other as possible, that is, they are independent; yet they are also interdependent, because each voice is part of the texture of the whole. In the sacred styles of sixteenth-century music, this sort of texture is the norm, but regulated by the rules of strict counterpoint.

Historically speaking, it is proper to regard *a capella* counterpoint like the above, in which unity and variety are maximally balanced, as representing rather a kind of ideal texture. In the music of the late fif-teenth to the beginning of the seventeenth century, this ideal prevailed regardless of whether the music was sung or played on instruments. Music written for voices was often played by whatever instruments were available, with little or no change necessary to make it playable. Not until the Baroque era did it become customary to specify instru-ments, because it was not until the seventeenth century that well-defined instrumental idioms came into being. Both of the Bach examples above, though representing very different kinds of polyphony, reflect sacred vocal styles that had already been in existence for two centuries and more.

In the period of common practice, most music shows a texture of three or four parts, with every imaginable balance between homo-phonic and polyphonic elements, and every kind of doubling element. Examples of texture of more than four truly independent parts are relatively rare.★ It is plain that as the number of parts increases, so must the necessity for doubling of triadic factors in any given harmony, with a resultant increase in parallel motion of parts and a decrease in independent motion.

Instrumental music composed for ensembles may be chamber music, from two or three instruments to eight or occasionally more, or it may be for a much larger group, up to the size of a full orchestra. A symphony by Brahms, for instance, may call for an orchestra of seventy or eighty players in which at least fifteen different kinds of instruments are represented. Obviously these do not all play all of the music all of the time, in a four-part texture with everything doubled; no duller sound could be imagined. After all, the heart and soul of the orchestral sound lies in the variety of instrumental timbres and registers, and the different combinations of these. The overall sound reflects the ensemble texture, which in turn depends on the ways in which the different instrumental roles and their individual sound characteristics relate to each other at any given moment. Such matters are proper to the study of orchestration, and we will not discuss them here. But without laying undue stress upon instrumental idioms, we can learn much from some elementary considerations of texture which will assist our ongoing study of harmony and our analysis of masterworks.

Examples of Homophonic Texture

EXAMPLE 18–5: Schubert, *Schwanengesang*: No. 4, *Ständchen*

This familiar passage is a typical example of *melody and accompaniment*. This texture is comparable to the four-part hymns of Examples

★Familiar examples of five-part counterpoint include Bach, *Well-Tempered Clavier*, Book I, Fugues Nos. 4 and 22; *Prelude and Fugue in E♭ major* for organ ("St. Anne"); *Mass in B minor*, Kyrie I and Confiteor; and Mozart, *Symphony No. 41* ("Jupiter"), IV. Six-part counterpoint is exemplified by the great Ricercar in Bach's *Musical Offering;* and the Credo in his *B-minor Mass* begins with a fugue in which as many as eight simultaneous independent parts may be found.

18–1 and 18–2, in that the melody is the upper and prominent part. But here the melody is differentiated from the accompaniment both melodically and rhythmically, and because it is sung by a voice while the accompaniment is played on a piano. The accompaniment itself, Schubert's pianistic approximation of a serenader's guitar, shows two elements, bass and upper parts, which are distinct in register and rhythm. The bass is doubled at the octave, a phenomenon familiar in keyboard music. It is perhaps not immediately obvious how many parts are played by the pianist's right hand. Our understanding is aided by an *analytical reduction*, in which repetitions of tones are eliminated and harmonic factors are, so to speak, dis-arpeggiated, that is, represented as tones of like value. (Stemless black notes are used in the reduction to remove any rhythmic attribution; at the same time they are written vertically as chords, to show that they are considered together.)

EXAMPLE 18–6: Analytical Reduction of the Accompaniment

In the reduction, the voice leading becomes more visible. The E in the second measure is really a neighbor note to the D (see Chapter 23, on neighbor-note harmony). The G in the same measure prepares the seventh of the dominant chord in the next measure.

If the bass is considered one part and the solo voice another, are there really three and then four internal parts, making five and then six in all? If this seems unlikely, then perhaps there is a simpler interpretation. First of all, we might notice that the voice is doubled in the accompaniment on the downbeat of every measure:

EXAMPLE 18–7

(bass omitted)

Seen thus on paper, these doublings have the appearance of forbidden parallel octaves; but the ear does not perceive them that way. They are heard as one part, not as two mutually independent parts. In the third and fourth measures the appearance of a fourth right-hand part is the result of suspension of the G and its subsequent resolution; the A is the doubled root of V, and does not clutter the texture.

The foregoing illustrates a homophonic texture because its voices all move from one harmony to the next at the same time, and because even though there are different rhythmic elements, these too are regular from measure to measure. It is an excellent example of voice-leading practice in instrumental accompaniment, and others like it can be found everywhere in the literature. The important lesson to be drawn is in comparison with a four-part choral texture and its melodic character. In such a comparison, one asks how many real parts are present in the Schubert example, whether these change, and what parts are doubling at any given moment.

A waltz accompaniment is an example of another very familiar kind of homophonic texture.

EXAMPLE 18–8: Chopin, *Waltz*, Op. 69, No. 2

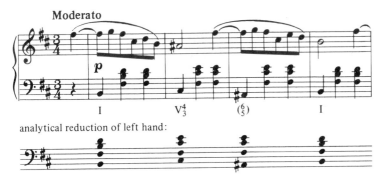

analytical reduction of left hand:

Considered by itself, the left-hand part of the example above is a four-voice texture, even though not all four voices sound together at precisely the same instant. It is not a texture of one voice on the first beat abruptly changing to three voices on the second beat, and all over again from measure to measure; the harmony does not begin with a single note changing to an unstable six-four chord, even though this is what is plainly seen in the score from beat to beat. The textural integrity of the four voices is guaranteed by the motivic shape (so familiar that it is often called "oom-pah-pah"), by the regular repetition of the shape, by the registral separation (the "ooms" are lower than the "pah-pahs"), and above all by musical memory, which allows the ear to retain the presence of the bass even after it has ceased to sound. (It is true that Chopin calls for the damper pedal to be used throughout the duration of each measure, but the ear does not depend on that. We would hear this as a uniform texture even without any use of the pedal.)

The following is another typically pianistic texture, using a four-note figuration. The harmonic rhythm is basically the half measure (*alla breve* meter); the texture of two notes at a time is really six voices, with two of these (except in the first measure) octave doublings, the inner-most voices in the thumbs doubling the outermost. (Compare Example 7–20.)

EXAMPLE 18–9: Beethoven, *Sonata*, Op. 13 ("Pathétique"), I

The keyboard is well suited to textures involving arpeggiation and figuration over a wide range. Certain types of music may particularly demonstrate these capabilities, such as song accompaniments and dance forms, studies using particular patterns and motives, and works in variation form. The piano, with the widest range of any instrument except the organ, and with the sustaining power of the damper pedal, has inspired numerous examples of every kind of harmonic texture. One can easily imagine the big sound of the Lizst excerpt, without in any way being in doubt about its essential tonic–dominant progression or voice leading. (See Example 18–10.)

Despite the many notes and different registers, this is basically a harmony in three parts, as the reduction shows when adjustments for octave equivalence and doubling are made.

The examples chosen thus far illustrate textures that remain fairly consistent, for the most part with the same numbers of voices from harmony to harmony. But it is characteristic of keyboard music that

EXAMPLE 18–10: Liszt, *Grand Etudes after Paganini*, No. 6

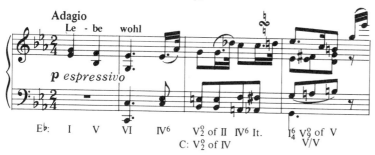

texture need not be uniformly maintained from phrase to phrase or even within the phrase; examples such as the following, showing several apparent changes of texture within the space of a few measures, occur frequently.

EXAMPLE 18–11: Beethoven, *Sonata*, Op. 81a ("Das Lebewohl"), I

The piano's sound in this varying texture is aided by the damper pedal. Such a resource would not be available on the harpsichord, for which the following, with its more obviously accumulating texture, was written.

EXAMPLE 18–12: Bach, *Partita No. 1, Präludium*

tonic pedal
Bb: I   V² of IV IV   V⁴₃ of IV IV   I   V² of IV IV V⁰₂   I   (6)   II⁶   V   I
                                                              (V of IV)

Bach's distribution of voices, which is at least partly indicated by
the beams, rests, and directions of the stems, is especially to be noted
as the most obvious indication of how the composer conceived of the
texture. Another aspect of the texture is shown by the uppermost part,
a compound line in which the Bb is a fixed element until near the end.

Changes of texture occurring freely are also idiomatic in music for
the guitar and lute. The nature of these instruments and their playing
technique makes it difficult to maintain independent voices of any great
range or complexity; at the same time, they are well suited to chords
and single melodic lines.

EXAMPLE 18–13: Sor, *Grand Sonata*, Op. 22, III

In this example, one might ask how strongly the bass line is felt,
and how consistent is the texture of strummed chords.

Ensemble Texture

Any melodic or harmonic element may be doubled in a given texture.
Doubling at the octave of the upper or lower melodic elements is an
everyday occurrence in practically all piano and ensemble music. As
the following example shows, it is not unthinkable to space the doubling voices so widely that they completely surround the harmony
within.

EXAMPLE 18–14: Beethoven, *Violin Sonata*, Op. 47 ("Kreutzer"), I

The true bass (note the arrows in the example) is not a prominent element in this texture, but it is sufficient to distinguish it from the piano doubling, three octaves below, of the violin melody.

In the following example, the melody in the first violins and flute, with strings accompanying, has already been heard without the piano.

EXAMPLE 18–15: Beethoven, *Piano Concerto*, Op. 58, I

The notes in the piano's upper part form an ornate melody, recognizably organized around the violin melody sounding with it. The contrapuntal differentiation between the two melodies is slight, because one senses that they are really the same even while they are different. If the violin melody were not present in the accompaniment, the piano melody itself would be called a melodic variation of the melody already heard (see Chapter 7); when the two appear together, the piano melody is what is called a *heterophonic doubling* (Greek *heteros*, "other"). In this case the composer appears to have wanted the piano's sound to be the principal element heard, with the violin in a secondary but by no means negligible role. A balance is struck between making the solo dependent on, and independent from, the rest of the ensemble texture. This balance bespeaks a kind of spatial counterpoint, the solo instrument against the ensemble, that is at the heart of the concerto principle.

The texture of an instrumental ensemble can demonstrate endless variety and is inextricably bound up with the overall sound. Much more is involved than just the number of players or the number of parts visible in the score.

EXAMPLE 18–16: Mozart, *Piano Concerto*, K. 453, III

In this example, the upper melody in the first violins and flute is melodically and rhythmically well differentiated from the bass (violas, cellos, and contrabasses in three octaves). The inner part, a polyphonic melody for second violins, is typical of instrumental ensemble writing; sometimes it parallels the upper melody closely (collateral part), while at other times it adds harmonic factors by arpeggiation, but its equally important function is to energize the ensemble sound by steady eighth-note motion. The example shows how, in ensemble music, a particular voice in a texture may simultaneously have melodic, harmonic, and purely instrumental functions that cannot readily be separated.

The following is another illustration of how a melody relates to its accompaniment:

EXAMPLE 18–17: Borodin, *String Quartet No. 2*, III, *Nocturne*

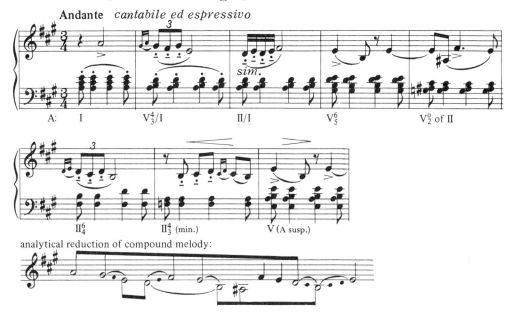

analytical reduction of compound melody:

We may analyze the expansive upper melody as a compound line of two basically descending components, shown in the analytical reduction in white notes with upward or downward stems. The lower melodic element includes notes that are duplicated in the accompaniment. The melody reaches into the accompaniment, so to speak, and pulls out tones from different parts of the close texture. The Chopin waltz (Example 18–8) may serve as a comparison: in what ways, for instance, is the upper melody of the waltz a compound line? What parts of it double the accompaniment? What parts of the accompaniment move so as to avoid doubling, or to accommodate the upper melody?

The Orchestra

An orchestral texture always will have important elements of timbre, or tone color, and these may be very complex; yet as a rule, in the period of music that we are studying, timbral considerations are separate from and subordinate to such textural considerations as numbers of real parts and their proper voice leading. From Haydn to Brahms, the elements of orchestral writing are governed by essential aspects of part writing such as we have already studied. The complexities of texture that turn up in the analysis of orchestral works are most often seen to be aspects of doubling, tone-weight, octave placement, and idiomatic writing for instruments.

EXAMPLE 18–18: Beethoven, *Symphony No. 7*, I

In this familiar example of an orchestral *tutti*, the main melody, in the first violins, has already been stated; placed at the top of the string group it will not fail to be the most prominent element. It is doubled an octave below by the first horn in a high and brilliant register; the second horn and the bassoons share partial doublings and collateral parts. The other woodwinds (flutes, oboes, clarinets) reinforce the overall sound by doubling various factors of the harmony, for the most part in registers where they will sound particularly bright; their notes are smoothly connected, sometimes briefly doubling the melody itself, but generally in this passage the melodic interest of the upper woodwinds is secondary. The same is true of the second violins and violas, which reinforce the harmony with a particularly massive sound. The only other element present is the rhythmic tonic pedal, in four different octaves, with the second trumpet the weakest of these. In short, we observe that all the instruments have different roles, but that they are all well conceived and necessary in a large texture.

Reduction of Textures

We have already demonstrated reductions for analytical purposes, but reductions for performance are also widely used in music. Arrangements of orchestral scores for smaller forces, or simply for a rehearsal piano, are familiar to everyone. (Composers have often arranged their own works or those of others; Beethoven, for example, arranged his own *Second Symphony*, Op. 36, for piano, violin, and cello.) Arrangements can involve no reduction at all, but only transcription, as for instance condensing a choral score to two staves so that a pianist can read it easily. More usually, reduction of a larger score to a smaller requires a careful understanding of the texture. In arranging, say, a Beethoven symphony for piano four hands, the arranger is constantly confronted with questions of what can be omitted and what must be included, and of what elements must be emphasized so as to recreate faithfully as much of the original as is practical.

Answers to these questions are to be had from analysis of the texture, by identifying the textural elements and comparing them. The simplest doublings are the first to be determined, and perhaps eliminated from the reduction. Other elements, such as figurations which are primarily harmonic in character, can often be simplified so that their constituent factors and proper voice leading are retained in slower-moving note values. The practical playability of the reduction is a secondary but important consideration, and may stimulate reexamination of the relative importance of the elements of the ensemble.

Inevitably, a practical reduction will entail some recomposition, some actual redistribution of notes and changes of octave position, as well as systematic deletion, and all of these will involve some subjective judgments. Proper respect for the original demands that changes be made carefully and discreetly.

Practical considerations in carrying out a reduction are never entirely separate from the theoretical, and for this reason the student should consider the preparation of a reduction as a useful analytical tool. The kind of reduction illustrated in Examples 18–6 and 18–7 should be carried out mentally, or where the texture is complex, written out in one or more successive steps. An appreciation of the problems of voice leading and doubling that are to be gained in this way will later be valuable for advanced studies in counterpoint and orchestration.

EXERCISES

1. Prepare a harmonic reduction in four parts of the first four measures of Beethoven's *Sonata quasi una fantasia*, Op. 27, No. 2.

2. Prepare a harmonic reduction in six parts of the first four measures of Schubert's *Impromptu* in G♭ major, Op. 90, No. 3; where possible, reduce this further to four parts.

3. Prepare a harmonic reduction in five or six parts of the first eight measures of Chopin's *Etude* in C major, Op. 10, No. 1. Reduce this further to four parts if possible, keeping all of the upper parts in one register.

4. Make reductions of the following excerpts:

Schubert, *Impromptu*, Op. 90, No. 4

Beethoven, *Alla ingharese, Quasi un Capriccio* (The Rage Over a Lost Penny), Op. 129

5. Select one or two phrases from a *tutti* passage in an orchestral work from the Classical period, such as a symphony by Haydn, Mozart, Beethoven, or Schubert, choosing a work in which several different instrumental types are represented. From this excerpt prepare a score like Example 18–18, in which all the instruments are shown at actual pitch, with the higher instruments at the top and the lower at the bottom. Next, make a reduction with all the doublings removed. Finally, make a practical reduction, which can be easily played on the piano by two or four hands. What kind of changes did you have to make in the music itself, if any, in order to make it easily playable?

19

Problems in Harmonic Analysis

Purpose of Analysis

One may well ask what the purpose of musical analysis is. The specific answer to this question must address the specific composition. One applies analytical skills to a particular piece in order to understand it better. "Understanding" in this sense means uncovering the musical structure in both the large outlines and the small details, and this kind of understanding leads to more meaningful hearing. The general answer addresses more than the composition itself; analysis aims at an appreciation of the composer's style, and even to a stylistic comparison of works by different composers.

In the compositional process, melody, rhythm, harmony, counterpoint, and form are considered more or less simultaneously. The composer's technique and imagination permit all of these to be held together in the mind's ear, even though they may not all be realizable without a laborious sketching process. The finished product displays these elements as a unified whole; it does not appear as though, for example, the successive pitches in the melody were chosen first, then a rhythm applied to them, and after that a harmonization fitted to the composite. The analyst knows that any separation of the whole into its elements is bound to be an artificial act, one that does not retrace the composer's steps in reverse.

You are already aware that although this book is about harmony, it does not treat the subject as an isolated component of musical thought. Considerations of melody, rhythm, and counterpoint always influence one's analysis of the harmonic element. "Pure" harmony is a creature of theory, useful for demonstrating relationships in the abstract; but when we analyze the harmonic relationships of a particular piece of music, that is no longer theory but practice, and must be considered in relation to other musical elements.

In the practical analysis of compositions so far, you have concentrated on the identification of particular chord successions (musical words), their relationship to each other and within the larger structure of the phrase, the extent to which chords reinforce or weaken the prevailing tonality, and the musical meaning of various applications of nonharmonic tones. This chapter will attempt to give some of these aspects a somewhat broader view and to suggest ways of dealing with a few of the problems that sometimes arise.

Extension of the Secondary Dominant Principle: Dual-Function Chords

The secondary dominant principle, as we have seen, presents what appears to be a paradox: the secondary dominant supports a secondary tonic, not the actual tonic of the key, and thus would seem in some way to actually change the key momentarily. Nevertheless, the returning tonic is actually strengthened by virtue of its associated harmonies having been given temporary tonic value. It would seem that the stronger the emphasis on the secondary tonic, and the more remote the secondary tonic from the main key, the greater is the satisfaction of the return to the main tonic.

The idea of a secondary dominant applied to a secondary tonic, creating as it were a miniature tonal region of its own within the larger context of a surrounding tonality, is analogous to a modulation, though on a smaller scale. It should be conceptually possible, then, to extend the secondary dominant principle to other degrees of the scale. If, for instance, there can be V of V progressing to V, then it should be possible to precede the V of V with II of V, just as in the progression II–V–I, but applied to V. This is exactly like what happens in an ordinary modulation to the dominant key where the pivot chord is VI in the first key; the difference is that a modulation is not deemed to have taken place. The examples at the top of page 301 show how the extended principle operates.

In *a* and *b* the phrases are identical except for their endings, in *a* an authentic cadence in C major and in *b* an authentic cadence in G major. We already know that our perception of modulation depends on more than the immediate successions of chords. On the time scale of only two measures, only a brushstroke (the F♮) must be added to *b* to place

EXAMPLE 19–1

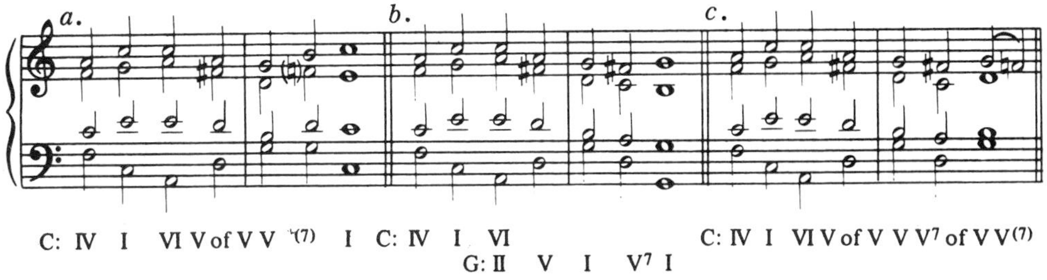
a.
b.
c.
C: IV I VI V of V V (7) I
C: IV I VI
G: II V I V7 I
C: IV I VI V of V V V7 of V V(7)

the whole phrase definitely in C major (*c*). Whether a modulation to G has taken place has to be determined by what happens afterward.

In *a* above, the third chord is seen in the analysis as a *chord of dual function* (compare Chapter 16, Example 16–7); with respect to I it is VI, but with respect to V it is II. We define a chord of dual function as one that serves as a pivot chord without an actual modulation. In *b*, the third chord is the actual pivot chord. In neither case does the meaning of the chord become clear until the remainder of the phrase has either confirmed the initial key or established a new key. The extension of the secondary dominant principle permits the theoretical existence of these dual-function chords, allowing the hearer to perceive within one key a wide variety of tonal relationships from outside it, borrowed as it were for the duration, without upsetting the main perception of tonality.

EXAMPLE 19–2: Beethoven, *Violin Sonata*, Op. 47 ("Kreutzer"), I

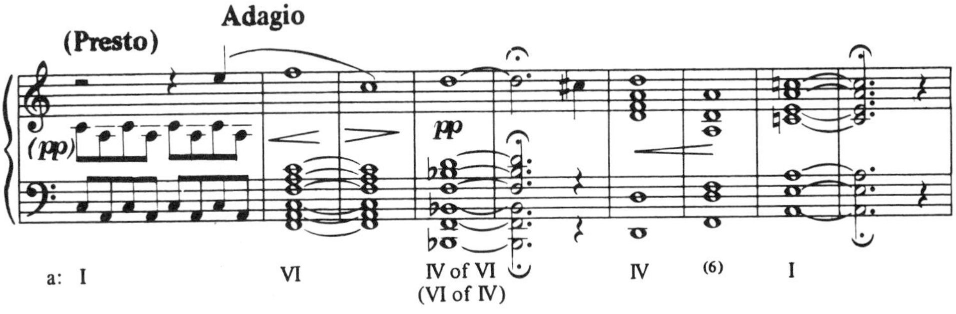
Adagio
(Presto)
(pp)
pp
a: I
VI
IV of VI
(VI of IV)
IV
(6)
I

In the example above, the IV of VI shows the relationship of the chord to what has already been heard, whereas the VI of IV shows the relationship to what is about to be heard. The relationship of the B♭ triad to F major and to D minor is closer in both cases than the relationship to A minor, in which the B♭ triad would be the chromatically lowered supertonic, the Neapolitan sixth (Chapter 26).

The borrowed chord need not have a clear function in both keys, but what must be clear is the relationship to either the preceding or the succeeding harmony, preferably the latter. In the following example the direct relationship of the G-minor triad to A (as minor VII) or to III of A (as minor V) is in neither case very satisfactory, but is entirely convincing with respect to D minor, relating secondarily to A minor as IV of IV.

EXAMPLE 19–3: Brahms, *String Quartet*, Op. 51, No. 2, I

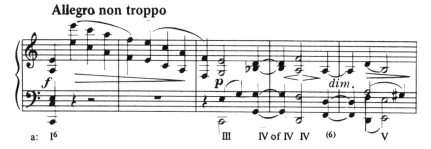

The minor triad on the fifth degree is quite lacking in dominant feeling. When it stands in subdominant relationship to the supertonic it may be called IV of II, as below.

EXAMPLE 19–4: Beethoven, *Symphony No. 9*, III

The diminished triad on D exists in B♭ as incomplete V of IV, but as used in Example 19–5, its function in sequential harmony is better described as II of II. To invoke a modulation to C minor because of this one triad would exaggerate its importance.

Mendelssohn's *Wedding March* begins with the formula IV–V–I as of E minor, but, as everyone knows, the piece is in C major. The first

EXAMPLE 19–5: Krebs, *Minuet*

chord is, then, properly designated as IV of III rather than $V^{\circ 6}_{5}$ of V in C.

EXAMPLE 19–6: Mendelssohn, *A Midsummer Night's Dream,*
Wedding March

The analysis of the next example goes a step further, in suggesting that the second chord, VI of E, is part of a group of four chords in G♯ minor, which is III of E.

EXAMPLE 19–7: Bach, Chorale No. 278, *Wie schön leuchtet der*
Morgenstern

See also Exx.
12–11, 17–7

In another Bach chorale three such groups are shown, centering about III, VI, and IV of Bb major. The last chord in the second measure, F minor, is obviously II of IV here rather than V of Bb, so that its dominant has been given the designation V of II of IV.

EXAMPLE 19–8: Bach, Chorale No. 279, *Ach Gott und Herr*

Bb: V⁶₅ IV⁶₅ of III V⁶₅ of III (V⁶ of IV) III VI of VI V⁰₉ of VI VI V of II II of IV V of IV IV   I
                                                                                    of IV

Four alternative analyses of the next example are presented for your consideration.

EXAMPLE 19–9: Bach, *Well-Tempered Clavier, I, Fugue No. 4*

a. as modulating:

c♯: I {c♯: VI | {e: I | {b: I | {f♯: I |
       {e: IV V {b: IV V {f♯: IV V {c♯: IV V I |

b. literal roots in C♯:

c♯: I   VI | VII   III | IV   VII | I   IV | V I |

c. with secondary dominants:

c♯: I   VI | VofIII   III | VofVII   VII | VofIV IV | V I |

d. functions in one key, by extension of the secondary dominant
   principle:

    ⟶   ⟶   ⟶   ⟶

```
        ⎧ I   IVof    │    IVof     │    IVof    │  IV(of) │ I
        ⎪
c#:   ⎨ I   IVofIVofIV│ VofIVofIV   │   VofIV    │ VofIV IV│ V I
        ⎪      ofIV    │   ofIV      │   ofIV     │
        ⎩             │   IVofIV    │  IVofIV    │
                       │    ofIV     │
```

Each analysis is correct on its own terms, and a preference for one
should not mean a rejection of what the others may offer. The modulating sequence in *a* is immediately clear, although one feels that the
changes of tonal center happen too quickly, and that each key noted
does not remain long enough to justify the analysis as a modulation.
The pattern is not readily discernible in *b*, whereas *c* tells more about
the grouping of the harmonies in the sequence. In *d* the organization of
the passage is set forth as a step back from the tonic to a thrice-removed
subdominant, in order to return symmetrically by means of four IV–I
progressions, with intervening dominants.

The extension of the secondary dominant principle to include other
secondary tonal functions is an analytical construction, but it reflects an
important observation: the feeling of modulation is received by the
experienced ear with a certain inertia, together with a tendency to interpret foreign harmonies in terms of a key already established. Secondary
dominants naturally point to secondary tonics, and this process of tonicization is a means of emphasizing the tonal strength of particular functions within one key; but modulation, as we have seen, requires more
than that, including not only the establishment of the new key but a
confirmation of it, by a cadence in the new key and maintenance of it
beyond any ambiguity to the ear.

The following example shows a modulating passage from a subsidiary section, beginning in F major, of a movement whose main tonality
is A minor. The passage is analyzed with two changes of key, subsidiary analyses being given in parentheses for dual-function progressions.
Some listeners might hear more changes of tonal center than the given
analysis indicates; others might hear fewer. What is brought out by the
alternate analyses is the large amount of plagal motion, IV–I being the
intervallic equivalent of I–V.

EXAMPLE 19–10: Schubert, *Symphony No. 9*, II

Rules of Voice Leading: Some Exceptional Circumstances

In Chapter 3 we learned that certain kinds of voice leading have always been systematically avoided by composers in the common-practice period, whenever they wrote in a texture of independent voices. Certainly the avoidance of parallel perfect octaves and fifths is one of the most frequently stated rules of all theorists. In your own exercises you doubtless found it hard and frustrating at first to follow these rules carefully.

Yet it is plain that composers, even though most of them were once students who had to learn the rules and do exercises, have written music with their imagination, and not by applying rules. Avoidance of parallel fifths and octaves was part of their practiced instinct as educated musicians. Nevertheless, in harmonic analysis of masterworks, you will sometimes encounter departures from the strict rules of voice leading. There is often a simple explanation for these departures; sometimes a good reason will be harder to find, or will not be found at all.

One of the commonest sources of parallel octaves is doubling, and the ubiquitous practice of melodic doubling in octaves was extensively discussed in Chapter 18. Some types of doubling are, to be sure, more frequent than others, but all types and dispositions may be seen in orchestral textures, even a melodic line doubled in three or four octaves with only a relatively narrow harmonic layer in between. Such doublings are a matter of instrumentation rather than of harmony, and do not disturb the ear unless the part writing is unclear.

E.g., Ex. 22–7

The following example of irregular doubling may be puzzling at first. The texture seems to shift back and forth between melodic doubling (in the "tenor") and an independent four-voice texture with occasional additional voices.

EXAMPLE 19–11: Schubert, *Sonata*, Op. 53, II

Certainly there is a textural ambiguity here, but nevertheless such seemingly casual changes, with one voice or another appearing to drop out or to shift from independent line to doubling, are found everywhere in instrumental music.

Another apparent violation, particularly of the parallel-fifth prohibition, arises from contrapuntal writing. Even in such a simple progression as the following, the combination of passing tone and anticipation produces this parallel motion.

EXAMPLE 19–12: Bach, Chorale No. 121, *Werde munter, mein Gemüte*

See also Exx.
15–2, 15–9,
16–25, 6–24

This type of motion was prohibited in the strict counterpoint of the sixteenth century, but it occurs frequently in the works of Bach and his contemporaries. The anticipation and the passing tone are both rhythmically weak with respect to the harmonic rhythm, and are avoided on the strong part of the beat.

The appoggiatura in the following example forms parallel fifths with the bass on the strong part of the beat, but is of such short duration that it is hardly noticed.

EXAMPLE 19–13: Mozart, Overture to *The Magic Flute*, K. 620

Parallel perfect fifths or octaves between successive offbeats are freely permitted over short distances. Between successive strong beats, with melodic motion intervening, they are best treated cautiously in contrapuntal writing. In the following sequence, the suspensions effectively offset the parallel fifths.

EXAMPLE 19–14: Bach, *Prelude and Fugue in A minor for Organ*

See also Ex. 8–4

Parallel fifths, but not octaves, may sometimes occur as a result of ornamental resolution, or in the combination of melodic tones with accompanimental patterns.

EXAMPLE 19–15: Chopin, *Etude*, Op. 10, No. 3

Lento ma non troppo

E: V⁷ of IV IV   II⁶

*See also Ex.
15–24*

A fairly common type of consecutive octave pattern between the outer voices is found in V–I cadential patterns, particularly final cadences where the cadential harmonies are repeated several times, or otherwise detached from the phrase. In such cases the octaves will generally be in contrary motion. Examples such as the following can be justified as cadential mannerisms, where the dominant note followed by the tonic note in the soprano makes for greater finality. The octaves are thus doubling octaves in a sense, and are not really considered independent voices.

EXAMPLE 19–16: Mozart, *Sonata*, K. 332, I

Allegro

F: I⁶   V⁷   I   V⁷   I   V⁷   I

*See also Ex.
5–32*

Parallel fifths are used with greater freedom in Chopin's works than anywhere else until the late nineteenth century, actually becoming a minor aspect of his style. Sometimes he seems to have chosen them for their open-string–like bass sound, such as in the mazurkas and other pieces suggesting the style of folk music. The following remarkable passage is unique for its time in its systematic chromatic succession with fifths in the outer voices.

EXAMPLE 19–17: Chopin, *Mazurka*, Op. 30, No. 4

Elsewhere one can find fifths in the outer parts occurring seemingly as intrusions in an otherwise independent texture, not to be readily accounted for other than as part of the melodic continuity.

Cf. Ex. 30–20

EXAMPLE 19–18: Chopin, *Scherzo*, Op. 39

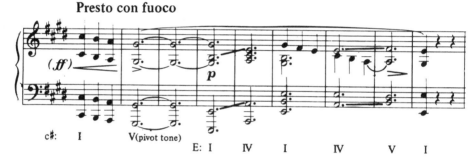

By the end of the nineteenth century parallel fifths became integrated into several post–common-practice styles, which will be studied in detail in Part Two of this book. At the same time, even composers whose techniques were essentially rooted in common practice began to accept occasional parallel fifths as a normal component of tonal part writing. The subtle use of fifths in the cadence of Example 19–19 makes a fine effect.

EXAMPLE 19–19: Mahler, *Ich atmet' einen linden Duft*

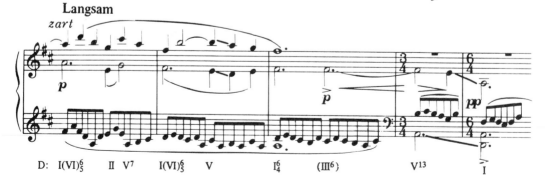

Finally there are examples of parallel fifths that can probably be attributed to inadvertence. One such instance is seen in Example 14–4, a four-part chorale by Bach; another is this often-cited passage by Beethoven.

EXAMPLE 19–20: Beethoven, *Symphony No. 6* ("Pastorale"), I

Allegro ma non troppo

F: I   V$^4_3$ I   IV   I   V

Below are two examples of V–I progressions in which the leading tone in the upper voice resolves downward by skip to the fifth degree.

EXAMPLE 19–21: Bizet, *L'Arlésienne*, Suite No. 1: No. 2, Minuet

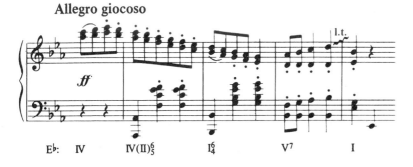

Allegro giocoso

E♭:   IV   IV(II)$^6_5$ I$^6_4$ V^7 I

EXAMPLE 19–22: Brahms, *A German Requiem*, II

Etwas bewegter (Langsam)

So seid nun ge - dul - dig, lie - ben Brü - der, bis auf die Zu - (kunft)

G♭:   I   V   I   V   I   V   IV   VII^6 I

In the long run, it is hard to say that any of these examples represents an actual defect for which we cannot find an explanation. Certainly in every case they represent sounds that were satisfactory to the composer. It is only in the work of lesser composers that the violations reveal themselves as defects, when they will actually seem to be thoughtless inhomogeneities of style or flaws in technique.

Score Reading

You should make an effort to acquire a familiarity with orchestral scores as early as possible. In an orchestration course you will do this in order to gain knowledge of instrumental techniques and orchestral styles, but there is much benefit in score reading in the study of harmony as well. The principles of harmony become visible in the most realistic way possible when they are seen at work in orchestral music, where their action is distributed between a variety of instrumental types and textures and over long stretches of musical time. Choral music and piano music have prepared you for this by demonstrating a great variety of textural types, but they include only a portion of the total repertory of Western music; ensemble music, from chamber music to the largest orchestral works, forms a very significant part of the music of more than three centuries.

Orchestral works of the period of Haydn, Mozart, and Beethoven, including full scores of operas, should be studied first, beginning with pieces in which the complement of woodwind and brass instruments is relatively small. In this way you will learn to become easily familiar with the layout of instruments in the score, even when those instruments are not labeled on every page. The most difficult problem at first in reading scores will be the transposing instruments. Various ways of deciphering these have been devised, such as clef equivalents, but all require constant practice. One infallible rule of transposing instruments may be stated here: for any instrument "in X," the note C appearing in the part sounds X. The note D will sound a major second above X, E will sound a major third above X, and so forth, although the proper octave may have to be determined separately.

Another essential part of fluent score reading is a working knowledge of the alto clef, the clef regularly used by the viola. The tenor clef is also often seen in upper-register writing for instruments normally using the bass clef (cello, double bass, bassoon, etc.). Fluency in the use of these clefs is best acquired through sight singing and sight reading, but listening to orchestral music while following the score is also valuable here, as it is generally.

You will notice that in most orchestral music up until Beethoven's time the main harmonic and melodic materials are most often entrusted to the strings. In part this is because the strings provide a remarkable homogeneity of sound quality and strength over virtually the entire orchestral range; another reason is that the woodwind and brass instruments, particularly the horns and trumpets, had not been perfected in their design and playing technique, and consequently could not be used as freely or over as wide a range as later became possible. Recognition of this reality becomes of practical value in reading orchestral scores at the piano.

In all types of analysis, you will sooner or later come to experience the sometimes bewildering and sometimes exciting feeling of discovery, when as many questions are raised as are answered by dint of thorough work. It is the authors' conviction that this sense of discovery, though not to be fully satisfied in a lifetime of effort, is one of the chief pleasures of musical study.

PROJECTS IN ANALYSIS

1. Analyze the minuet (really a scherzo) movement of Beethoven's *Symphony No. 1* and make a chart showing the modulatory scheme.

2. Analyze the tonal scheme of the exposition of the first movement of Mozart's *Symphony No. 40*, K. 550. Then analyze that of the recapitulation, and compare the two.

3. Compare and contrast the tonal organization, sectional structure, cadential types, and modulatory schemes if any, of ten or more different minuet movements chosen from the symphonies, piano sonatas, and string quartets of Haydn and Mozart. Show the results of this investigation in tabular form.

4. Examine the passage in the first movement of Schubert's *String Quintet in C major*, Op. 163, where the second theme is stated (mm. 60–99). As a rule in sonata form of this period, the second theme is in the dominant key, and in fact this theme is preceded by a full cadence in G major. How does one account for this theme's beginning in E♭ major? In what ways can you analyze the tonal emphases within the melody itself?

5. Explain why the first movement of Schubert's *Symphony No. 5* and the first movement of his *"Trout" Quintet*, Op. 114, are said to have subdominant recapitulations, and why these are unconventional. What advantage is there to such a tonal plan?

6. It was stated in Chapter 5 that relative minor and major are an association of special importance in tonal composition in the minor mode. One work that shows this association with particular intensity is Chopin's *Scherzo*, Op. 31, usually called the *Scherzo in B♭ minor* although it ends in D♭ major. Trace the course of these two keys and compare their relative importance throughout the work.

7. Chabrier's *España* for orchestra has a simple overall tonal plan, involving only a single modulation and return. Determine the larger tonal outlines of the piece and the proportion of tonic–dominant harmony relative to other types. (The more complex harmonic types may be ignored.)

8. The second movement, Andante poco moto, of Schubert's *Sonata*, Op. 42, is a theme with variations, the theme being in two sections of 8 and 16 measures, each repeated. A comparison of the theme with the first variation shows that the second half of this variation, with twelve measures, is apparently four measures too short; the second variation, with sixteen measures in the second half, confirms this deduction. Determine by analysis where the measures are missing, and what sort of harmonic structure they might be expected to have. As an additional exercise, compose four measures to fill the gap, making them as close as possible stylistically to the context. (Schubert's autograph of this sonata has not been found. All published editions follow the first edition, which was printed in 1825 or 1826, during Schubert's lifetime; but it is not known whether he corrected the mistake or even noticed it. It seems very unlikely that Schubert deliberately left the measures out, but he habitually composed at incredible speed and it is not unthinkable that he may simply have forgotten to compose them.)

20

The Sequence

The harmonic sequence, the systematic transposition of a melodic, rhythmic, and harmonic pattern, is a resource of development in music. The change of pitch level adds the element of variety to the unity of repetition. On close analysis the sequence is often discovered to be the basis for passages that do not at first seem sequential, notably in the fugue and in symphonic developments and transitional sections.

We are here concerned primarily with the harmonic background of the various kinds of sequence and will give our attention to those sequences whose fundamental structure is clear. By way of introduction to this chapter, you will find it helpful to review the material on sequences given in Chapters 13 and 14.

The Initial Pattern

The pattern chosen for transposition in the sequence may vary from a short motive on a single chord to a whole phrase. Although it is pos-

EXAMPLE 20–1: Beethoven, *Piano Trio*, Op. 1, No. 3, IV

sible to construct a musically significant pattern with but one chord as a basis, this kind of pattern is less interesting harmonically and the sequence is mainly dependent for its effect on the contrapuntal arrangement. (See Ex. 20–1)

Most often the pattern contains two chords. In the following example they are simple triads with roots a fourth apart, the commonest strong progression.

EXAMPLE 20–2: Mozart, *Sonata for Two Pianos*, K. 448, II

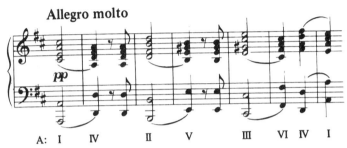

If the pattern is much longer, it is less recognizable as sequential than a shorter group, which can be heard as a unit. A short phrase may be successfully used as a pattern in a sequence.

EXAMPLE 20–3: Beethoven, *Sonata*, Op. 10, No. 1, I

Example 25–20 shows a pattern twenty measures long, with five chord changes, and even longer patterns have been used successfully.

Harmonic Rhythm

The harmonic formula upon which the pattern is based has its own particular rhythmic shape, arising from the choice of root progressions, time values, and other contributing elements. A strong harmonic progression at the beginning or ending of the pattern will result in a sequence whose patterns are well marked metrically. If the rhythmic pattern begins with an anacrusis a more fluent sequence will result.

EXAMPLE 20–4: Beethoven, *Sonata*, Op. 106 ("Hammerklavier"), II

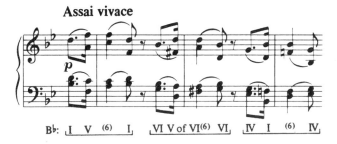

Length of the Sequence

It is generally agreed that a single transposition of a pattern does not constitute a full sequence, the systematic transposition not having been established until the third appearance of the initial group; in other words, three separate appearances, involving two transpositions, are necessary to show that the transposition interval is consistent. Certainly there are many examples of what can be called *half sequences*, with only a single transposition, the two patterns being antecedent and consequent in a phrase and not continuing sequentially (Examples 13–6, 13–11, 16–3). On the other hand, it is remarkable that composers seldom allow the symmetry to extend beyond the third appearance of the pattern without breaking it up by variation or abandoning it altogether. Exceptions to this rule may of course be found, and in certain types of musical expression, such as virtuoso cadenzas and compositions intended for technical study or display, sequences are sometimes written to extend by numerous repetitions throughout the entire range of the instrument.

Degree of Transposition

The pattern may be transposed by any interval, up or down. The interval of transposition chosen depends upon two factors, the desired harmonic destination of the passage and the feasibility of connecting the transposed patterns to each other. Construction of a sequence necessitates consideration of both of these problems. Often the looping of the pattern will be seen as a problem in the elementary contrapuntal relationships of melody and bass. A two-part reduction, showing the principal melodic motions and intervallic relationships between the outer parts, is usually helpful.

The Nonmodulating Sequence

The sequence is either a *modulating sequence*, changing the tonal center with each transposition of the pattern, or a *nonmodulating sequence*, sometimes called a *tonal sequence*, with one tonal center throughout.

In the nonmodulating sequence the transpositions are made to the scale degrees of the key. This causes some variation in the pattern, since the intervals between the scale degrees are not always the same. For instance, in Example 20–2 the harmonic background is I–IV, II–V, III–VI. The initial pattern consists of two major triads, the second of a minor and a major triad, and the third of two minor triads. Note that the transposition is upward by step, while the root progression at the junction between the patterns is down a minor third.

The nonmodulating sequence is also likely to contain variation in the transposition interval. In Example 20–4 the first transposition is down a minor third, while the second is down a major third, resulting from the intervals between I, VI, and IV in the major scale.

Both of these variations are present in the sequence descending by seconds, shown below. The root progressions are by fourths throughout the entire passage, all perfect fourths except from VI to II.

EXAMPLE 20–5: Paradisi, *Sonata in A major*, II

Secondary Dominants in the Sequence

The employment of secondary dominants in the nonmodulating sequence adds the harmonic color of tones foreign to the scale of the main tonality and emphasizes the unity of the group of chords making up the pattern.

See also Exx. 8–33, 16–11

EXAMPLE 20–6: Beethoven, *Sonata*, Op. 7, I

EXAMPLE 20–7: Schubert, *Symphony No. 5*, III

EXAMPLE 20–8: Berwald, *Symphony No. 5* ("Sinfonie Singulière"), II

In the next example, the secondary dominants with their resolutions divide the harmonic rhythm into a meter of two-four against the prevailing three-four meter.

EXAMPLE 20–9: Beethoven, *Symphony No. 3* ("Eroica"), I

In the following sequence the secondary dominant is not used on the third appearance of the pattern because the supertonic triad in minor, being a diminished triad, does not act as a temporary tonic.

EXAMPLE 20–10: Haydn, *String Quartet*, Op. 76, No. 4, III

Cf. Ex. 22–13

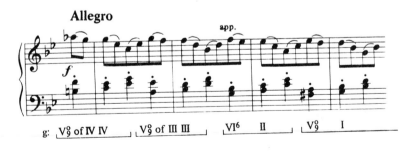

Sequences in which each harmony is a dominant of the next are of
uncertain tonality and may or may not be heard in a single key. The   *Cf. Exx. 16–1,*
commonest sequence of this type is the cycle-of-fourths sequence,   *16–26*
moving by successive subdominants, with alternating rising fourths and
falling fifths in the bass.

EXAMPLE 20–11: A. Scarlatti, *Fugue in F minor*

EXAMPLE 20–12: Chopin, *Mazurka*, Op. 59, No. 3

When the temporary tonics are themselves unsatisfactory chords
of the main tonality, there is a feeling of modulation, although in many
cases these modulations are so fleeting that even a far-fetched explanation of the chord function in the main key is preferable. In the following example two analyses are offered. The first is nonmodulating, but
necessitates reference to the minor triad on the dominant and the triad
on the lowered seventh degree as temporary tonics. The second, on the
other hand, shows four changes of tonal center in as many measures of
rapid tempo, only to return to the original key of C. You are advised
to make similar alternative analyses in other such cases, weighing for
yourself their advantages and disadvantages as descriptions of the harmonic effect.

EXAMPLE 20–13: Weber, Overture to *Der Freischütz*

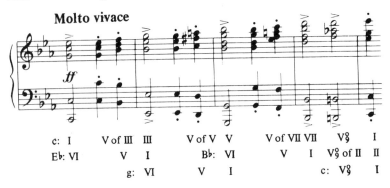

The Modulating Sequence

The commonest form of modulating sequence embraces three keys—an initial key modulating to a second key, and a modulation by the same interval to a third key. There is no return to the tonality of the initial pattern. The modulation does not take place within the pattern, but the final chord of the pattern is the pivot chord. The modulation to the second key is called a *passing* or *transient modulation* since there is no permanence to the key. It represents a stage in the modulation to the third, or ultimate, key. Passing modulations are not necessarily sequential, as we have already learned in Chapter 14, but the modulating sequence does contain a passing modulation in its most common form.

Cf. Ex. 19–9

EXAMPLE 20–14: Bach, *Well-Tempered Clavier, I,* Fugue No. 18

In this example the modulation to E is a passing modulation. The suspension in the inside voice is helpful in avoiding the cadential effect at each final chord of the pattern. The first transposition moves down a major third and the second down a minor third, since it is impossible to divide the interval of a perfect fifth (from the initial key, G♯, to the desired destination, C♯) into two equal parts. Moreover, there is a change of mode in the second key. The E-minor triad is a poor chord in both keys, so E major is chosen.

The pattern used in a modulating sequence is usually constructed on a clearly tonal harmonic basis. This does not mean that the tonic chord must be included. In the example below, the progression II–V serves very well to establish the tonal centers of three keys not closely related.

EXAMPLE 20–15: Brahms, *Symphony No. 2*, I

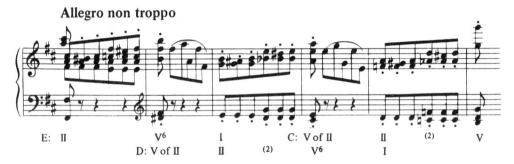

The modulating sequence offers more possibilities for transposition than the sequence with one tonal center. The following example shows a chromatic relationship between the keys.

EXAMPLE 20–16: Wagner, *Die Walküre*, Act I, Scene 1

The Sequence in Harmonization

A sequence in the melody is not always accompanied by sequences in the other voices or in the harmony. It is nevertheless advisable to treat sequences in given parts as harmonic sequences, until facility in arranging these sequences is acquired. Above all, sequential treatment should not be avoided because you have failed to notice the suggestion in the given part. For the purposes of instruction, you should assume that melodic sequences in the exercises of this book are to be treated as harmonic sequences.

Keyboard Practice

The sequence is an extremely useful device for practicing harmonic progressions at the keyboard. You should try to make sequences of all the harmonic formulae at your disposal, playing them all the way up or down the keyboard. The first problem will be to make a smooth connection between the pattern and its transposition. While there are some cases in which no really satisfactory connection can be made, you may assume that a solution exists and can be found by searching. Weak progressions can be used if they are properly placed in the rhythmic scheme. Lengthening of the time values facilitates change of position of the voices.

　　You are strongly urged not to write out the sequence. Two appearances of the pattern are enough to show the scheme. The continuance of the sequence will then be a mental exercise rather than a rote reading or memorizing. As in all keyboard exercises, rhythmic playing (meaning rhythmic thinking) is essential, and a steady beat should be adhered to at all times, even though it may be very slow at first.

　　The literal extension of a nonmodulating sequential pattern throughout all its possible transpositions will often bring about one or two progressions that would not otherwise be employed, as for instance IV–VII, with its tritone relationship and use of root-position VII with doubled leading tone. Such progressions are considered justified by the logic of the symmetrical melodic movement of the voices.

EXAMPLE 20–17

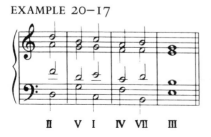

II　　V　I　　IV　VII　　III

EXAMPLE 20–18: Berlioz, *Symphonie fantastique*, III, *Scene in the Fields*

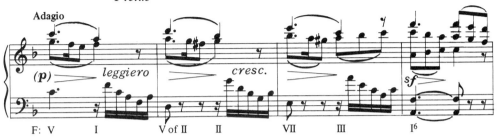

The following are a few examples of beginnings of sequences, to be played the length of the keyboard, and in all keys.

EXAMPLE 20–19

EXERCISES

1. Work out the following figured basses:

2. Construct different sequences on the same harmonic backgrounds as those in Examples 20–2, 20–3, 20–11, and 20–14. Vary the rhythm and the general melodic texture.

3. *Road maps*. Construct phrases containing sequences fulfilling the following requirements:

   a. a nonmodulating sequence in which the pattern contains three different chords and the transposition is upward by intervals of a third;

   b. a modulating sequence in which the final chord of the pattern is V of V in the second key;

   c. a modulating sequence that starts in the key of D and ends in the key of A♭;

d. a nonmodulating sequence that employs secondary dominant seventh chords.

4. Harmonize the following unfigured basses:

a.

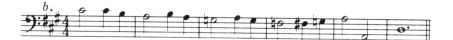

b.

c.

d.

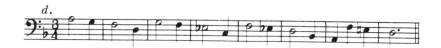

5. Harmonize the following melodies:

a.

b.

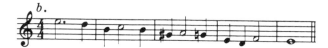

c.

d.

21

The Diminished
Seventh Chord

Definitions

With the superposition of another third upon the dominant seventh chord, the group of chords known as dominant harmony is extended to include two dominant ninth chords, major and minor.

EXAMPLE 21–1

The dominant ninth chords are most often found with root omitted, their dominant implication being sufficiently strong without the actual fifth degree present. Composers have shown a distinct preference for the incomplete forms of these chords over the more dissonant and heavy effect of the ninth chord with root.

Dominant harmony consists, then, of the following group of chords:

EXAMPLE 21–2

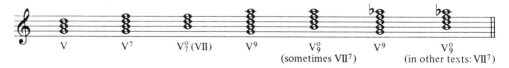

V   V⁷   V⁹₇ (VII)   V⁹   V⁰₉   V⁹   V⁰₉
                                 (sometimes VII⁷)   (in other texts: VII⁷)

By far the commonest of the dominant ninths is the last shown in the example, the *incomplete dominant minor ninth*, known as the *dimin-*

ished seventh chord. The factors of the incomplete dominant minor are identified by their intervallic relationships with the absent root, so that the minor sixth degree of the scale is the ninth of the chord, the fourth degree is the seventh, and the leading tone is the third. The second degree, which is the fifth of the chord, forms with the sixth degree a diminished fifth, so that all the factors of this chord are involved in dissonant relationships.

EXAMPLE 21-3

A chord made up entirely of tendency tones would seem to have very definite tonal significance, but, paradoxically, the diminished seventh is the most ambiguous of chords. The thirds are all minor thirds, and the inversion of the diminished seventh, the augmented second, is the enharmonic equivalent of the minor third in our tempered scale system. The diminished fifth interval has likewise an equivalent sound in its inversion, the augmented fourth. In consequence the ear cannot distinguish between the factors of a diminished seventh chord until its resolution shows which is the leading tone. The chord and all its inversions have the same sound.

EXAMPLE 21-4

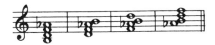

Enharmonic Equivalents

By application of the enharmonic principle, the same diminished seventh can be written in four different ways, taking each note in turn as leading tone.

EXAMPLE 21-5

The leading tone is readily found in each case by arranging the chord in a stack of thirds, when it will emerge as the lowest tone.

Such changes in notation, by designation of the leading tone, mean change of tonality and also change of root of the chord. The omitted root is found a major third below the leading tone. It is interesting to observe that the four real roots of one enharmonically respelled diminished seventh chord form in themselves the notes of another diminished seventh chord.

EXAMPLE 21–6

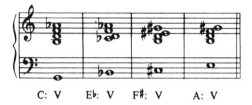

C: V   Eb: V   F#: V   A: V

String instrumentalists know that such different interpretations of one chord involve an actual change of pitch. The note Ab with destination G is perceptibly lower than the leading tone G# with destination A. It is likewise the experience of many musicians that the pitch of the notes seems actually to change when the different roots are struck in the bass against a diminished seventh chord sustained on the piano.

EXAMPLE 21–7

Resolution

The regular resolution of the diminished seventh chord is to the tonic triad. It is customary to resolve the two intervals of the diminished fifth, contracting each to a third, without regard for the doubling that results. If the diminished fifth is inverted, the augmented fourth will, of course, expand to a sixth. The diminished seventh chord resolves with equal ease to a major or a minor tonic. Resolving to the tonic triad in a prevailing major mode, the diminished seventh, by virtue of the minor sixth degree, is thus involved in mixed modes, such as we first discussed in Chapter 14; this is one of the commonest modal mixtures.

EXAMPLE 21-8

When the second degree is above the minor sixth degree (an augmented fourth), it may resolve downward, the upper three voices then moving in parallel motion. If it is below the minor sixth degree, downward resolution results in a diminished fifth resolving to a perfect fifth; this procedure is somewhat less often followed.

EXAMPLE 21-9

EXAMPLE 21-10: Bach, Chorale No. 4, *Es ist das Heil uns kommen her*

Nonharmonic resolution often occurs with the diminished seventh. The ninth resolves internally as a melodic tone without change of root. (See also Example 21-19.)

See also Exx. 26-9, 26-20

EXAMPLE 21–11

V_9^0 $\binom{6}{5}$

Inversions

As shown in Example 21–4, all positions of the diminished seventh chord sound alike. They vary contrapuntally in the orientation of factors, the bass being especially important; but this is realized by the hearer only through the manner of resolution.

Strictly speaking, there can be no root position, since the root of the chord is not present, although the grouping in which the leading tone is the lowest tone is often called root position. Many textbooks use the symbol VII[7] for this position, but we will use the symbol V_9^0, indicating the ninth above the absent root. For the inversions the V^0 will also be used, and the arabic numbers will show the intervals formed between the actual bass and the upper voices.

EXAMPLE 21–12

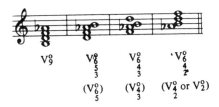

V_9^0 $\quad$ $V_6^0{}_5{}_3$ $\quad$ $V_6^0{}_4{}_3$ $\quad$ $\cdot V_6^0{}_4{}_2$

$\quad\quad\quad\quad (V_6^0{}_5)$ $\quad$ $(V_4^0{}_3)$ $\quad$ $(V_4^0{}_2$ or $V_2^0)$

In a literal sense, the ninth of these chords, wherever situated, should be indicated by a flat sign or other appropriate accidental next to the arabic numeral, as in Example 21–2. Elsewhere, however, we will not use this indication, since the distinction between major and minor ninth is easy enough to make by reference to the score itself, and omission of the accidental makes for less fussiness in the analysis.

The inversions resolve in the same way as the root position. When the second degree is in the bass it often resolves to the third degree to avoid a direct fifth on the resolution of the diminished fifth.

EXAMPLE 21–13

more usual   less usual

See Ex. 6–16

The six-four-three inversion, with the fourth degree in the bass, ordinarily resolves to the first inversion of the tonic triad, but it may also resolve to the root position.

EXAMPLE 21–14

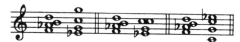

When the second inversion resolves to the root position, the fourth degree and minor sixth degree, by their resolution, have a strongly subdominant feeling. The leading tone and second degree, on the other hand, still have their characteristic dominant values. The diminished seventh chord in this position, therefore, seems to combine dominant and subdominant functions into a single sonority. The following example shows a perfectly prepared cadence of this type:

EXAMPLE 21–15: Schumann, *Toccata*, Op. 7

See also Ex. 30–1

When the lowest tone is the ninth, or submediant, the natural resolution is to the tonic six-four, which means dominant followed by a dominant substitute, a rhythmically weak progression. Furthermore, the disposition of the voices will be likely to produce a doubling of the sixth or the fourth in the chord of resolution, rather than the customary bass. This inversion is, therefore, less useful than the others.

EXAMPLE 21–16

As a rule, in four-part writing no factor of a diminished seventh chord is omitted in any position. Occasionally the third or fifth may be omitted in contrapuntal passages, though in such cases the omitted factor will often appear soon after, in melodic succession.

EXAMPLE 21–17: Bach, Chorale Prelude, *Meine Seele erhebt den Herren*

The Secondary Dominants

The diminished seventh chord is employed as a secondary dominant wherever such chords are used, whether the secondary tonic is major or minor.

EXAMPLE 21–18: Haydn, *String Quartet*, Op. 76, No. 1, II

See also Exx.
4–9, 8–32,
10–26, 10–28,
11–22, 12–10,
20–8

C: I   V°₉ of VI   VI   V°₃ of II   II⁶   VII⁶ of II   II   VI⁶   V⁶   V⁶₅   I   V

EXAMPLE 21–19: Bach, *Mass in B minor*, Kyrie I

b: I   V°₉₅   V°₉ of IV   IV   V⁶₅   I   V⁶ IV⁶   II⁴₃   V

EXAMPLE 21–20: Schumann, *Piano Concerto*, Op. 54, I

G: I   V°₉ of V   V   V°₉ of IV   IV   V°₉   I

Irregular Resolution

Since it is the resolution that establishes the tonal identity of the diminished seventh chord, most apparently irregular resolutions will be discovered to be regular when the notation of the diminished seventh chord is revised. Composers have never been overscrupulous as to the grammatical notation of this chord, especially in writing for keyboard instruments, so that it is necessary to evaluate the chord by what it does rather than what it looks like.

The following is cited in a harmonic treatise as an instance of irregular resolution of a diminished seventh chord:

EXAMPLE 21–21

In this case the B♮ does not function as a leading tone. If it were written C♭ the true nature of the two chords would be clear. They are both derived from the same root, B♭, the ninth C♭ resolving into the B♭, so there is no harmonic resolution.

EXAMPLE 21–22

E♭: V——————

Although detailed study will have to wait until Chapter 25, it is necessary to call attention to two diminished seventh chords that do not fall into the category of dominants. They are II⁷ and VI⁷ with root and third chromatically raised, acting as appoggiatura chords to I and V⁷ respectively.

EXAMPLE 21–23

+II⁷   I⁶   +VI⁷   V⁶₅
(not V⁰₉ of III) (not V⁰₉ of V of III)

Like other diminished sevenths these two chords are identified by their resolutions. They are mentioned here to avoid confusion with irregular resolutions and incorrect notations of other chords.

The diminished seventh chord will seldom be found without either the dominant relationship to its chord of resolution, or a relationship such as the two shown above. Only if these are lacking can the resolution be called irregular in terms of root progression. The seventh chord on II in the example below is a substitute for a V_9^0, differing from it only in the replacement of E by D♯.

EXAMPLE 21–24: Mendelssohn, *A Midsummer Night's Dream,* Nocturne

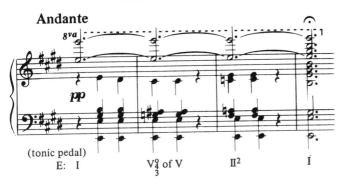

Often the chord preceding the diminished seventh, or the general sense of the tonality, will give it a meaning other than that defined by the resolution; that is, the diminished seventh will be a chord of dual function. The effect may be explained as irregular resolution, or as enharmonic change in the chord.

Cf. Ex. 23–21

EXAMPLE 21–25: Rameau, *Nouvelle Suite No. 2: No. 5, The Hen*

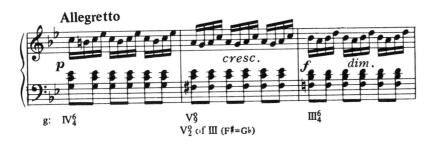

Irregularity of voice leading is common in the treatment of the diminished seventh chord. Voices are allowed to move freely by arpeggiation among the chord tones, over such "unmelodic" intervals as the augmented second and fourth, and diminished fifth and seventh. It should be remembered, however, that in examples like the following these are really instrumental voices.

EXAMPLE 21–26: Schubert, *Symphony No. 5*, III

Consecutive Diminished Sevenths

Successions of more than two diminished sevenths are often employed, the vagueness of the chord causing a temporary uncertainty of tonality.

EXAMPLE 21–27: Beethoven, *Sonata*, Op. 10, No. 3, II

In rapid harmonic movement, successive diminished sevenths progressing by half step in similar motion give the effect of a chord moving as layers of chromatic passing tones. Theoretically speaking, the chords are related harmonically, each chord being considered as the dominant of the next, with some enharmonic revision, but in actual practice the perception of real harmonic motion is suspended until a stable chord is reached. In the following example the parallel movement is disguised by the changes of position in the right-hand part.

EXAMPLE 21–28: Chopin, *Etude*, Op. 10, No. 3

Modulation Using the Diminished Seventh Chord

In modulation, the tonal ambiguity of the diminished seventh chord becomes a versatility unmatched by any other chord. A single diminished seventh chord, without enharmonic change, is capable, like any dominant chord, of the following analyses:

V
V of II
V of III (in minor)
V of III (in major)
V of IV
V of V
V of VI (in minor)
V of VI (in major)
V of VII (in minor).

Add to these the two nondominant forms raised II^7 and VI^7, and the dominant of the lowered second degree (V^0_9 of N^6), and we have twelve interpretations of one chord. Moreover, since the chord may be enharmonically written in four different ways without changing the sound, we may multiply the above by four, making a total of forty-eight possible interpretations.

There are, however, certain limitations upon the usefulness of the diminished seventh as an effective pivot chord in modulation. To begin with, it is not advisable to employ the dominant of the new key as the pivot chord, since the chord before it provides a better common ground between the two keys. Further, if a secondary dominant is selected, it may happen that its chord of resolution is also a basic chord in the first key and would be a more logical pivot chord than the diminished seventh.

EXAMPLE 21–29

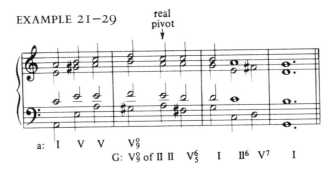

In the example above, the modulation may be effected in theory by the diminished seventh chord, but actually its chord of resolution is the real pivot chord, as it is both I in A and II in G, and introduces the dominant of the new key. If we wish to use V_9^0 of A as pivot chord in a modulation to G it is better to assume an enharmonic change (G♯ = A♭), making the dominant of IV in G. By resolving to the minor form of IV the key of A is excluded from the harmony following the diminished seventh chord.

EXAMPLE 21–30

The following are two examples of modulations that employ the diminished seventh as a pivot chord through enharmonic reinterpretation, involving remotely related keys.

EXAMPLE 21–31: Bach, *Mass in B minor*, Credo: *Confiteor*

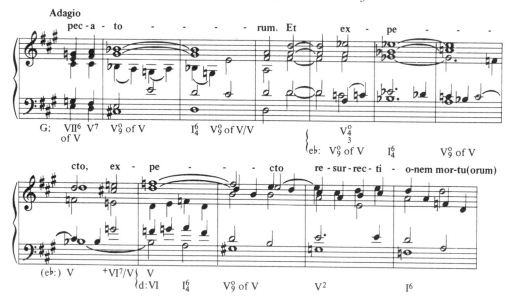

EXAMPLE 21–32: Mozart, *String Quintet*, K. 593, II

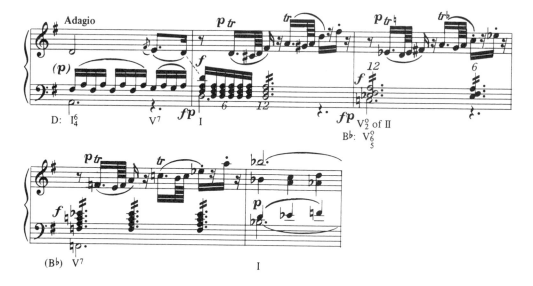

Formulae, to be played in all keys:

EXAMPLE 21-33

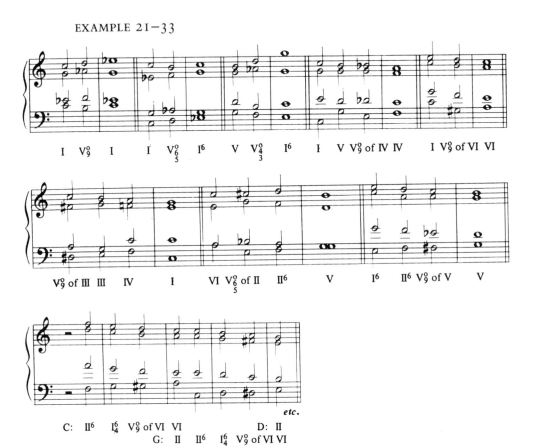

EXERCISES

1. Correct the notation of the following diminished seventh chords, to agree with the resolutions given.

2. Work out in four parts the following figured basses:

3. Write an analysis of the following chord as a dominant or secondary dominant in the keys named, using enharmonic change when necessary, and showing the resolution of the chord in each key.

Keys: G, A♭, B♭, C, E.

4. Construct a phrase using four diminished seventh chords in succession.

5. Harmonize the following melodies, employing at least two diminished seventh chords in each harmonization:

6. Harmonize the following unfigured basses, introducing diminished seventh chords:

22

The Incomplete Major Ninth

The Half-Diminished Seventh Chord

As we saw in the previous chapter, the seventh chord constructed on the leading tone and using the major mode bears a striking contrast to that from the minor mode, the diminished seventh. Both of these chords are dominant ninths without root, and both resolve regularly to the tonic triad, but they are different in several respects.

In the diminished seventh chord the interval (minor third) between successive factors is always the same, and its complementary interval, the diminished seventh, does not change when the chord is inverted. The diminished seventh chord is thus a perfectly symmetrical chord. The leading-tone seventh chord with major sixth degree, on the other hand, produces a major third between the two upper factors. This chord has a minor seventh between the outer parts, but also includes the diminished fifth, and thus is now widely referred to as the *half-diminished seventh chord*. Because this chord is made up of unequal intervals, there is a marked difference in the character of the inversions.

EXAMPLE 22−1

E.g. Ex. 23–22

The designation VII[7] has been used by some writers to distinguish the major V_9^0 from the diminished seventh chord. We will use VII[7] only to indicate such chords where the dominant feeling has been weakened, as before III.

The last inversion, with the ninth in the bass, is rarely found except as a dominant seventh chord in which the sixth degree appears as a suspension in the bass, resolving to the root. Indeed, there is a noticeable tendency throughout the common-practice period to treat the upper tone of the major ninth interval, with or without root, as a melodic tone, resolving it to the tone below before the resolution of the chord takes place (nonharmonic resolution). The very characteristic sonority of the major ninth, however, makes a harmonic effect, especially when the leading tone is present and the chord is in root position.

E.g. Exx.
8–43, 20–10

EXAMPLE 22–2: Schubert, *Sonata*, Op. 120, II

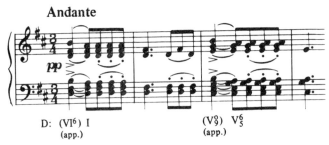

In the resolution, the presence of the perfect fifth between second and sixth degrees may lead to parallel perfect fifths in the voice leading. This is usually avoided by moving the second degree up to the third or by skip of a fifth down to the dominant. In neither case will the root be doubled in the tonic triad. (See Examples 22–3 and 4.)

EXAMPLE 22–3

EXAMPLE 22–4: Bach, Chorale No. 11, *Jesu, nun sei gepreiset*

If the upper voices are so arranged that the interval of a fifth is inverted to a fourth, all three may descend in parallel motion. However, this contrapuntal advantage is not more desirable than the typical sound of a major ninth heard in the top voice. Compare the sonority of the following with the disposition shown above.

EXAMPLE 22–5

Inversions

The six-five-three inversion must resolve to the first inversion of the tonic chord to avoid parallel fifths between the bass and the resolution of the ninth.

EXAMPLE 22–6

But see Exx.
8–40, 10–5

EXAMPLE 22–7: Mendelssohn, Overture to *A Midsummer Night's Dream*

The six-four-three inversion is more useful, as there are more alternative arrangements. It may resolve either to root position or first inversion. The arrangement in *d* below, with the ninth below the leading tone, is used less often than the others.

EXAMPLE 22–8

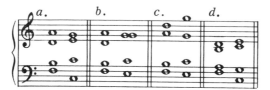

EXAMPLE 22–9: Grieg, *Lyric Pieces*, Op. 43: No. 1, *Butterfly*

Irregular Resolution

The regular resolution, to the major tonic, of the incomplete major ninth is really the only strong resolution this chord possesses. Unlike the diminished seventh chord, the incomplete major ninth is appropriate for use only in the major mode. The major sixth degree as a dissonance tends to descend, which it could not normally do in the minor scale without undue prominence of the false relation of the tri-

EXAMPLE 22–10

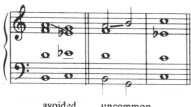

avoided   uncommon

tone between sixth and third degrees. If the sixth degree were purely melodic, it could ascend as a step of the melodic minor scale but would lose its harmonic significance as a ninth. (See Example 22–10.)

The progression to supertonic harmony is weak because all the tones of II are common to both chords. In the resolution to III the chord loses its identity as a dominant ninth without root and becomes a seventh chord on the leading tone (VII^7). This progression is most often seen in harmonic sequences.

EXAMPLE 22–11: Brahms, *Ballade*, Op. 118, No. 3

Secondary Dominants

The incomplete dominant major ninth is far less useful as a secondary dominant than the dominant minor ninth. This is because it cannot serve as the dominant of a minor tonic (Example 22–10). The degrees that may be preceded by a major ninth are I, IV, and V in the major mode, and III, V, and VI in the minor mode. In the case of III, its dominant in this form woud be identical with the seventh chord on the second degree.

EXAMPLE 22–12

See also Ex. 17–17

The dominant of the subdominant with major ninth resolves to the major form of IV.

EXAMPLE 22–13: Mozart, *String Quartet*, K. 458, II

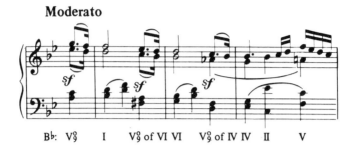

Most common secondary dominant in this form is the V_9^0 of V.

EXAMPLE 22–14: Franck, *Symphony*, I

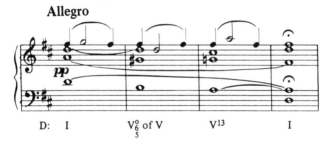

Modulation

From the foregoing it will be evident that the incomplete dominant major ninth offers somewhat limited opportunities as a pivot chord in modulation. There are no possibilities of enharmonic change as with the diminished seventh chord. The interpretations of the V_9^0 chord of the key of C are these:

V of IV in G major
V of V in F major
V of VI in E major
II^7 in A major

Formulae, to be played in all keys:

EXAMPLE 22–15

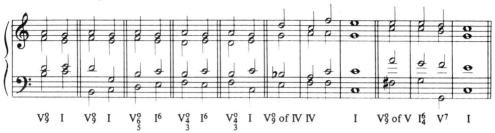

$$\text{V}^9_8 \quad \text{I} \quad \text{V}^9_8 \quad \text{I} \quad \text{V}^0_6 \quad \text{I}^6 \quad \text{V}^0_4 \quad \text{I}^6 \quad \text{V}^0_4 \quad \text{I} \quad \text{V}^0_8 \text{ of IV} \quad \text{IV} \quad \text{I} \quad \text{V}^0_8 \text{ of V} \quad \text{I}^6_4 \quad \text{V}^7 \quad \text{I}$$

EXERCISES

1. Construct three separate original phrases, illustrating three different modulations in which the pivot chord is the incomplete major ninth of the first key.

2. Work out the following figured basses:

3. Harmonize the following melodies, using the incomplete major ninth and its inversions where appropriate:

a.

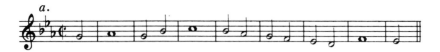

b.

c.

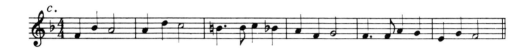

d.

4. Harmonize the following basses:

a.

b.

c.

23

Nondominant Harmony— Seventh Chords

Function of Dissonant
Nondominant Chords

It was stated earlier that most of the chord types in the common-practice period are either triads or various kinds of dissonant chords of dominant effect. Chromatically altered chords, to be discussed later in this book, account for some of the remaining types. In this chapter we will begin to examine the various kinds of nondominant harmony.

Dissonant chords of nondominant character are comparatively unusual in the common-practice period. When they do appear, it is usually as the result of contrapuntal writing, especially as suspensions or appoggiature and in sequences. Not until the nineteenth century are they exploited independently, that is, with their dissonant factors introduced without preparation. That kind of independence is a harbinger of the much more important role achieved by nondominant harmony after the common-practice period, when nondominant seventh chords, as well as more complex types, become fully independent sonorities, their dissonant factors neither prepared nor resolved.

Dominant harmony occupied such an important place in common practice that its characteristics became sharply defined through over two centuries of usage and convention. The presence of the leading tone a major third above the root, with its tendency toward the tonic, is the strongest characteristic of the dominant effect, and the root succession of V to I, whether up a fourth or down a fifth, is hardly less strong. A further reinforcement of the dominant function is provided by the addition of a seventh to the chord, a diminished fifth above the leading tone, and the combination of the leading tone and the seventh often suffices to establish the dominant quality even when the dominant root is absent, as in the two types of V_9^0.

It follows that harmonic formations that do not show these characteristics are by definition nondominant. The seventh chords, which will concern us first, are many and various, and in some ways their structure and function may be compared with dominant harmony. The nondominant seventh chords are distinguished from the dominant seventh above all by sound; beyond that, they are distinguished from each other by structural type.

Comparative Structure of Seventh Chords

The dominant seventh chord is the only seventh chord that can be constructed from the degrees of the major scale that has the structure of major third, perfect fifth, and minor seventh above the root, as the following comparison shows.

EXAMPLE 23–1

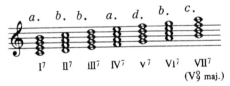

The nondominant seventh chords formed from the minor scales, including the mixed-mode types, are more numerous. All the possibilities are shown here.

EXAMPLE 23–2

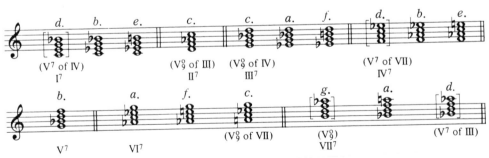

The chords in the two tables can be categorized in seven structural types, indicated by the letters.

a. Major third, perfect fifth, major seventh: these are called *major seventh chords.*

b. Minor third, perfect fifth, minor seventh: these are called *minor seventh chords.*

c. Minor third, diminished fifth, minor seventh: these are called *half-diminished seventh chords.*

d. Major third, perfect fifth, minor seventh: these are the familiar dominant seventh chords.

e. Minor third, perfect fifth, major seventh: some writers call this form the *major-minor seventh chord.*

f. Major third, augmented fifth, major seventh: this form has no specific name in common use.

g. Minor third, diminished fifth, diminished seventh: this is the familiar diminished seventh chord.

Chords enclosed in square brackets are already familiar; they include the various dominant sevenths (*d*) and the two forms of V_9^0 (*c, g*). Very infrequently, some of these may be found as nondominants (e.g., Example 5–31, third measure).

The other *c* forms in the table are equivalent to the incomplete major ninth used as a secondary dominant, but also have important values as nondominant sevenths as well. Their true identity becomes clear only on resolution.

The chords grouped under *a,* with major seventh, and those under *e* and *f,* with major seventh and various augmented fifths, have a certain pungency of sound. By contrast, the minor seventh chords, *b,* are of generally softer effect, with the minor seventh the only dissonant interval between any of the factors.

All seventh chords with strongly dissonant intervals have both typical and atypical resolutions, depending on the extent to which the dissonant factors are considered as harmonic or nonharmonic tones.

The Nonharmonic Element

The question of deciding whether a tone is a chord factor or a nonharmonic tone often comes to the fore in the study of harmony. What is more important is the appreciation of both sides of the issue. As we have often said, chords result from the coincidence of melodic parts, but certain coincidental chord types become established through usage and recur constantly under different melodic conditions, whereas others seem to depend on the assumption of an elementary harmonic form, such as a triad, as a basis.

Resolution

The seventh of a nondominant seventh chord customarily resolves by moving down one degree, as the seventh of the dominant seventh does. This rule applies to the major seventh as well as the minor, with the qualification that the major seventh also occurs fairly often as an upward-resolving appoggiatura, to the octave of the root. Harmonically, the regular resolution is to the chord whose root is a fourth higher, except in case of IV^7 and the minor VI^7, where the perfect fourth above would lie outside the scale. The resolutions are shown below.

Irregular resolutions are also employed, although not as often as the possibilities would lead one to expect.

The fifth, or the third, is sometimes omitted when the chord is in root position, especially when the resolution is to another seventh chord. In such a case the root is doubled.

The inversions resolve contrapuntally in much the same way as the root position, except that the root will usually remain stationary rather than moving up a fourth.

The Tonic Seventh

EXAMPLE 23–3

The regular resolution of the tonic seventh is to IV. In the minor mode the minor seventh degree is used in order to descend melodically to the minor sixth degree.

EXAMPLE 23–4: Brahms, *Intermezzo*, Op. 117, No. 2

The commonest irregular resolution is to II, the root remaining in position to become the seventh of the second chord.

In the following example, too, the root remains static, making a six-four chord of the subdominant triad. Note the apparent descending scale motion across the voices, from C down to G.

EXAMPLE 23–5: Grieg, *Sonata*, Op. 7, II

The Supertonic Seventh

The supertonic seventh regularly resolves to V. This chord is common in cadences, before the dominant or the tonic six-four chord. The minor form of II[7], obtained by adding A♭ to the following illustrations, is employed in both major and minor modes, but the major form is used only in major surroundings. Irregular resolutions are to I, III, VI, and the secondary dominants.

See also Ex.
7–20

EXAMPLE 23–6

| II⁷ | V | | II⁷ | V⁷ | | II⁶₅ | V | | II⁴₃ | V | | II² | V⁶₅ |

| II⁷ | I⁶ | | II(IV)⁶₅ | I⁶₄ | | II(IV)⁶₅ | I | | II⁷ | III | | II⁷ | VI |

More will be said about the minor form in the remarks on the half-diminished seventh chord later in this chapter.

EXAMPLE 23–7: Bach, *Three-Part Invention No. 11*

susp.

Bb: VI   II⁶₅   V⁷

EXAMPLE 23–8: Schumann, *Symphony No. 1*, II

Larghetto

p

c: VI⁶   II⁷   V   I

EXAMPLE 23–9: Berlioz, *Symphonie fantastique*, I: *Reveries, Passions*

Allegro agitato ed appassionato assai

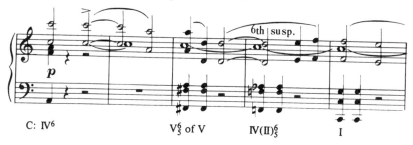

C: IV⁶   V⁶₅ of V   IV(II)⁶₅   I

The Mediant Seventh

The regular resolution of the mediant seventh is to VI. The two minor forms differ in the action of the fifth, which ascends when it is the leading tone and descends when it is the minor seventh degree. Irregular resolutions of III⁷ are to IV, II, and the secondary dominants.

EXAMPLE 23–10

III⁷ VI   III⁶₅ VI   III⁴₃ VI   III⁷ VI   III⁷ VI

EXAMPLE 23–11: Chopin, *Etude*, Op. 10, No. 1

Allegro

C: III⁷   VI⁷   II⁷   V⁷

EXAMPLE 23–12: Mattheson, *Gigue*

d: III⁷   VI⁷   II⁷   V⁷ of V   V   I

The Subdominant Seventh

EXAMPLE 23–13

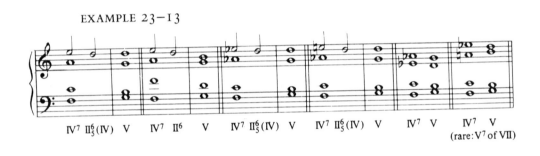

IV⁷ II⁶₅(IV) V   IV⁷ II⁶ V   IV⁷ II⁶₅(IV) V   IV⁷ II⁶₅(IV) V   IV⁷ V   IV⁷ V
                                                                   (rare: V⁷ of VII)

See also Exx.
8–44, 21–32

     The regular resolution of IV⁷ is not to the root a fourth above, which would be VII. In the majority of cases the seventh moves down before the progression of the other tones of the chord, making a form of II⁷, which then proceeds to V. The seventh is therefore usually considered an appoggiatura.

EXAMPLE 23–14: Bach, Chorale No. 59, *Herzliebster Jesu*

g: I   IV⁷   II⁴₃ V   V²   I⁶   VII⁶ I   V⁰₉ I   V
           (IV⁶)

EXAMPLE 23–15: Schubert, *Moments musicaux*, Op. 94, No. 6

The alternative analyses in these examples, where II is given parenthetically with IV, will be explained in the section on neighbor-note harmony later in this chapter.

When the fifth is omitted the root is doubled, and the supertonic chord which usually follows is a triad in first inversion.

EXAMPLE 23–16: Haydn, *String Quartet*, Op. 20, No. 4, I

Irregular resolutions to I and to several of the secondary dominants are practicable. The example below shows an unusual progression by parallel motion to III⁷.

EXAMPLE 23–17: Bach, *Sonata No. 1 for Unaccompanied Violin*, IV

The Submediant Seventh

EXAMPLE 23–18

VI⁷ II   VI⁷ II⁷   VI⁷ II₃⁴   VI⁷ V₅⁶   VI⁷ II₃⁴   VI⁷ IV₅⁶ II₃⁴

The regular resolution of VI⁷ is to II. When the third is present it is prolonged into the seventh of the II.

EXAMPLE 23–19: Handel, *Suite No. 8*: III, Allemande

f: VI⁷   II   V   I

As in the last of the progressions shown in Example 23–18, the voices may pass over a form of IV⁷ before reaching the II chord, or the resolution may sound like both IV and II. The harmonic rhythm may be either weak-to-strong or strong-to-weak. In the latter case the seventh will sound as appoggiatura to its note of resolution.

EXAMPLE 23–20: Mendelssohn, *Symphony No. 3* ("Scottish"), I

Andante con moto

a: III   VI⁷   II₅⁶(IV⁹)   I₄⁶   V⁷   I

Although the form of VI⁷ that combines the major sixth degree with the minor third degree ordinarily occurs when the sixth degree is part of an ascending melodic minor scale, it may also be found resulting from a descending chromatic motion.

EXAMPLE 23–21: Rameau, *Five Concert Pieces*: No. 1, *La Livri*

The Leading-Tone Seventh

This chord, usually an incomplete dominant ninth, partakes of non-dominant characteristics when it proceeds to III.

EXAMPLE 23–22: Bach, *French Suite No. 5*: VII, Gigue

Nondominant Sevenths in Sequence

The continuous series of seventh chords is a favorite device in nonmodulating sequences. The sevenths usually enter as suspensions, and when

See also Exx. 22–11, 23–11, 24–24

EXAMPLE 23–23

the chords are in root position every other chord will be incomplete, with its root doubled. (See Example 23–23.)

All inversions may be employed in these sequences, as well as ornamental resolutions of the suspensions and other melodic devices.

EXAMPLE 23–24: Krebs, *Partita No. 6*, Allemande

B♭: VI⁷ II⁷ V⁷ I⁷ IV⁷ VII⁷ III⁷ V of V V

Modulation

The nondominant seventh chords are useful as pivot chords in modulation. Since they are not of dominant effect they do not strongly suggest a key, and for each of these chords there is at least one other of identical sound. For instance, the II⁷ of C major may be interpreted also as I⁷ of D minor, III⁷ of B♭ major, IV⁷ of A minor, or VI⁷ of F major.

Irregular resolutions are sometimes useful in confirming the interpretation of the second key. For example, in a modulation from F to B♭, if the pivot chord is VI⁷ in F becoming III⁷ in B♭, the regular resolution will be heard as a chord still in F.

EXAMPLE 23–25

F: VI⁷   II
B♭: III⁷   VI

If, on the other hand, the irregular resolution III⁷ to IV is employed in B♭, it will be evident to the ear that a modulation has taken place, since the chord of resolution is not a usual chord in the key of F.

EXAMPLE 23–26

Bb: III⁷   IV
F: VI⁷

Neighbor-Note Harmony: The Triad with Added Sixth

An important category of nondominant chords originates in the harmonic relationship of the consonant neighbor note. Mention has already been made (Chapter 5, Example 5–9, and Chapter 11, Examples 11–18 and 11–19) of the first inversion of the supertonic triad, especially with the seventh present, used as a substitute for the subdominant triad. In such cases, one tends to hear the root-position triadic component of the chord as the most stable part of it, and the fourth degree, not the second degree, as the actual root.

EXAMPLE 23–27

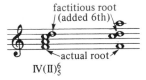

factitious root
(added 6th)
actual root
IV(II)⁶₅

This chord is an excellent illustration of the imbalance between practice and theory. According to theory, the root of this sonority should be D, the tones being rearranged to form a stack of thirds with D at the bottom. But the usage of this chord ever since the eighteenth century, especially in certain spacings, has shown that composers have usually considered it as a subdominant with root F, the D originating as a neighbor note or passing tone, or even as a purely harmonic dissonance analogous to the seventh in the dominant seventh chord. (It will be observed that in the major mode, this triad with added sixth contains only a single dissonance, the major second, the harmonic inversion of the minor seventh. The triad with added sixth could thus be said to possess an even milder dissonance value than the dominant seventh chord, which also contains the diminished fifth.)

EXAMPLE 23–28: Schumann, *Phantasiestücke*, Op. 12: No. 6,
                        Fabel

See also Exx.
5–31, 5–32,
8–27, 10–5,
15–2, 19–21,
26–9

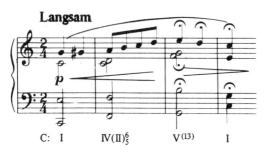

C: I   IV(II)⁶₅   V⁽¹³⁾   I

EXAMPLE 23–29: Brahms, *In stiller Nacht*

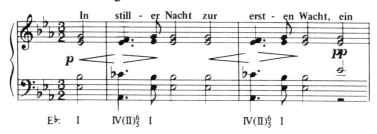

Eᵇ: I   IV(II)⁶₅ I   IV(II)⁶₅ I

The chord regularly proceeds to the dominant, as in the Schumann
example above, or to the tonic, as in the Brahms example. These are
normal progressions for II when in the first inversion, or for IV in any
position.

Whether one hears the chord as II or IV will depend on which tone
is stressed as a root. IV has the advantage as a root because it is in the
bass, but this may be offset by other conditions. Two examples from
earlier in the chapter may be compared for their relative harmonic effect.
In Example 23–7, the root C of the II⁶₅, the sixth above the bass, is
repeated three times in the measure, while the fifth (Bᵇ) above the bass
is suspended at the beginning; moreover the sequential pattern tends to
reinforce C as the true root. On the other hand, in Example 23–9, the
root D of the II⁶₅ is suspended while the F is sounded much more prominently, and one would more likely hear the harmony as a subdominant
with added sixth.

If the triad with added sixth thus represents a chord with two roots,
one real in the sense of actually perceived, and the other factitious, there

remains the problem of what to call the chord. In this book we will use the designation IV(II)$_5^6$, whenever it seems that the chord actually appears to have a function that is more strongly subdominant than supertonic.

The subdominant function of this chord is rather stronger in minor. This is because the supertonic component in the minor mode is a diminished triad, which, being dissonant, is relatively less stable than the minor triad.

A complete series of triads with added sixth can be constructed upon the notes of the major scale, thus:

EXAMPLE 23–30

I(VI)$_5^6$ VII$_5^6$ I$_5^6$ IV(II)$_5^6$ III$_5^6$ IV$_5^6$ V$_5^6$

Added-sixth chords constructed on the second and seventh degrees are identical with VII$_5^6$ and V$_5^6$ respectively, the well-known dominant forms. As for the others, the chords constructed on the third, fifth, and sixth degrees are not perceived with dual root, and are employed only as first-inversion seventh chords of I, III, and IV. That leaves the added

EXAMPLE 23–31: Chopin, *Sonata*, Op. 35, II

Gb: I (VI)$_5^6$ V$^{7(11)}$

EXAMPLE 23–32: Chopin, *Prelude*, Op. 28, No. 23

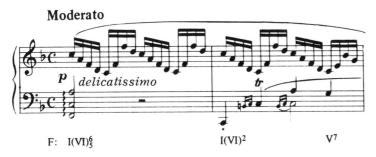

F: I(VI)$_5^6$ I(VI)^2 V^7

EXAMPLE 23–33: Wagner, *Five Poems of Mathilde Wesendonk*: No. 5, *Träume*

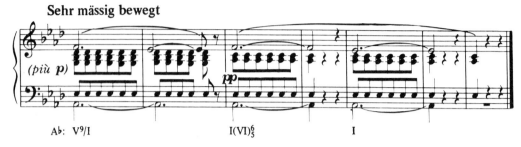

sixth chord constructed on the tonic, equivalent to the first inversion of VI[7]. This chord is frequently employed as a chord of tonic function in the common-practice period. (See Examples 23–31, 32, and 33.)

The origin of the added sixth as a rhythmically weak neighbor note is plain enough in the Chopin examples. In the Wagner example, the added sixth is rhythmically strong, the appoggiatura effect lasting a long time and interrupted by a rest before finally resolving. The final stage of evolution of this sonority can be seen in the last measures of Mahler's *Das Lied von der Erde*, where it is left unresolved (Example 30–30).

The minor form of this tonic chord, employing the major sixth degree, is less frequent in common practice. One is most likely to encounter it as a triad with nonharmonic sixth degree, from the ascending minor scale.

EXAMPLE 23–34: Beethoven, *Symphony No. 7*, II

In the works of several nineteenth-century Russian composers, the tonic sonority with added sixth appears as virtually a nationalist mannerism, even to the point of omission of the fifth, with VI[6] substituting for the tonic triad.

EXAMPLE 23–35: Borodin, *Polovetsian Dances* from *Prince Igor*, I

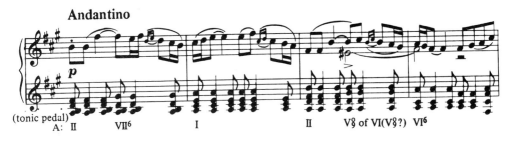

EXAMPLE 23–36: Rimsky-Korsakov, *Scheherazade*, III

Such usages reflect the interest of the Russian nationalists in harmony involving the natural minor scale, which appears, as does modal harmony generally, more strongly in their works than in the western European music of the time.

The major tonic with added sixth also shares a kinship with the pentatonic scale; it forms a basic sonority in pentatonic writing of the period following common practice.

The Half-Diminished Seventh Chord

EXAMPLE 23–37

Of the four half-diminished seventh chords that can be formed out of the notes of the major or minor scales, VII^7 is already familiar, and the second chord in the example above is given the somewhat awkward designation of VII^7 of IV. This leaves II^7 and VI^7, of which only the former occurs frequently. As we have just seen, VI^7 in the first inversion is relatively uncommon, while II^7 in the first inversion, as IV(II)$^6_5$, is very usual. In root position, II^7 with diminished fifth is freely used in strongly tonal contexts like any other seventh chord.

In the nineteenth century, composers began to take advantage of the tonal ambiguity of the half-diminished II^7. The principle suggested earlier, that in the first inversion this chord may appear to have two different roots in different contexts, seems to apply even when the triad is in root position; the diminished-triad component is harmonically weaker than the minor-triad component. This ambiguity makes the half-diminished seventh chord a useful nondominant adjunct in passages that modulate rapidly and repeatedly, where the composer wishes to avoid a stabilization of the tonality temporarily.

A characteristic use of the half-diminished II^7 occurs in the following example, showing the famous "Tristan chord." At first the II^7 resolves to a dominant with major ninth, the modal mixture adding a chromatic relationship to the progression; at the climax, the II^7 is reinterpreted enharmonically as an augmented sixth chord with appoggiatura, the pivot chord in a modulation to a remote key. (Compare Example 27–18.)

EXAMPLE 23–38: Wagner, Prelude to *Tristan und Isolde*

Langsam und schmachtend

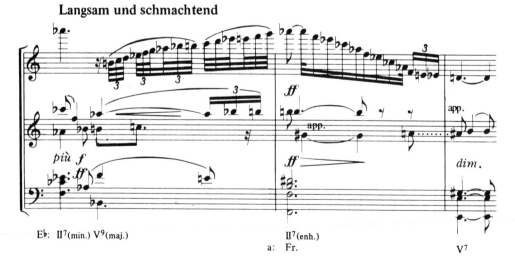

E♭: II^7(min.) V^9(maj.)   II^7(enh.)

                                        a: Fr.   V^7

In the following example the half-diminished seventh moves upward by parallel chromatic motion, much as the diminished seventh might do, with a comparable temporary suspension of the tonality. At the cadence, the stable harmony seems to be the F♯-minor triadic component of the chord, even though the D♯ is firmly established in the bass.

EXAMPLE 23–39: Dvořák, *Symphony No. 9* ("From the New World"), I

In the later nineteenth century the particular sonority of the half-diminished seventh chord was often exploited for its atmospheric quality.

EXAMPLE 23–40: Wagner, *Das Rheingold,* Interlude before Scene 2

EXERCISES

1. Work out the following figured basses:

2. Construct a phrase containing a sequence whose initial pattern is II^2–III^4_3.

3. *Road map.* Construct a musical sentence of three phrases, with the following specifications:

    a. The first phrase modulates from D major to F♯ minor by means of a nondominant seventh chord as pivot chord.

    b. The second phrase contains a modulating sequence ending in some key other than D.

    c. The third phrase returns to D major by a modulation using a nondominant seventh as pivot chord.

4. Harmonize the following unfigured basses, introducing nondominant seventh chords:

5. Harmonize the following melodies, introducing nondominant seventh chords:

a.

b.

c.

d.

24

Ninth, Eleventh, and Thirteenth Chords

The Complete Dominant Ninth

The complete dominant ninth chord, in both major and minor forms, is far less frequently found than the incomplete forms.

EXAMPLE 24–1

Reduction of this five-factor sonority to four-part writing necessitates omission of one factor. This is usually the fifth, which is unimportant contrapuntally compared to the other chord members, as it has no strong tendency, and the characteristic sound of the dominant ninth seems unaffected by its omission. In practice, however, it often happens that the voices move melodically so as to touch upon all the factors of the chord.

The regular resolution of the chord takes place as follows:

EXAMPLE 24–2

Treatment of the complete dominant ninth chord by composers of the eighteenth and nineteenth centuries has three important aspects:

1. The ninth may appear as a nonharmonic tone, resolving downward into the fifth degree, or sometimes, if it is the major ninth, up to the seventh degree, before the chord itself resolves. It is often an appoggiatura, in which case the harmonic color is very pronounced.

EXAMPLE 24–3: Schubert, *Symphony No. 8* ("Unfinished"), I

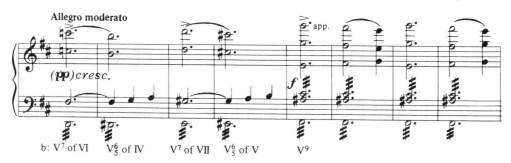

EXAMPLE 24–4: Bach, *Well-Tempered Clavier, II,* Fugue No. 5

See also Exx.
5–31, 5–32,
8–27, 10–5,
15–2, 19–21,
26–9

See also Ex.
8–46

2. The ninth may be used in a true harmonic sense as a chord tone but it may be absent from the chord at the moment of change. This is an important aspect of harmonic treatment of the ninth in common practice. It actually consists of the resolution by arpeggiation of a dissonant factor, a principle applied to no other dissonant chord (it is also called *dissolution* by some theorists). It is as though the ninth were regarded as an overtone in the dominant sonority, too high in the series to be involved in the reso-

lution effected by the seventh of the chord. Such treatment of the ninth implies a slowly moving root progression in comparison with the melodic activity.

EXAMPLE 24–5: Beethoven, *Piano Concerto No. 3*, III

EXAMPLE 24–6: Schubert, *Mass No. 6 in E♭*, Kyrie

Cf. Ex. 23–38

3. Finally, the ninth may act as a normal dissonant chord tone resolving to a tone of the following chord.

EXAMPLE 24–7: Wagner, *Das Rheingold*, Scene 2

EXAMPLE 24–8: Beethoven, *Symphony No. 3* ("Eroica"), II

In the Beethoven example above, the ninth in the upper voice is a dissolving ninth, doubled below by the A♭ resolving normally to G.

The minor ninth resolves to the minor tonic triad or, with modal mixture, to the major tonic. The major ninth, complete or incomplete, is used only before the major tonic.

The major dominant ninth has further limitations; it represents a harmonic color characteristic of the end of the common-practice period rather than the eighteenth century. Employed as in the third of the aspects just described, it is rarely encountered until the latter part of the nineteenth century. We will meet the dominant major ninth again in Part Two of this book in connection with impressionistic harmony, in which it is of great importance both as an independent, quasi-consonant sonority and as an adjunct to the triad in modal harmony.

Spacing

When the root of the dominant ninth chord is present, and the chord is used in the usual harmonic sense (see No. 3, above), care is taken to place the ninth at least a ninth above the root. It is practically never found below the root and the arrangement of the chord in which the leading tone is below the ninth rather than above it is preferred.

It is, of course, possible to place the factors close together, all within the range of an octave (*a* below). The effect of this is not of a ninth chord, however, but rather of a chord built with intervals of a second, or what is known in the twentieth century as a *tone-cluster*.

EXAMPLE 24–9

Considering the dispositions above: *a* is not heard as a ninth chord; *b* is usually avoided since the root is higher than the ninth; *c* has more of the characteristic sound of the dominant ninth chord, with the ninth below the leading tone; *d* shows the importance of the leading tone, by its omission, in the typical ninth-chord sound; *e* is the most usual arrangement.

The strident sound of the following minor ninth chord is largely due to the spacing, as well as to the position of the root D close to the ninth E♭.

EXAMPLE 24–10: Beethoven, *Symphony No. 9*, IV

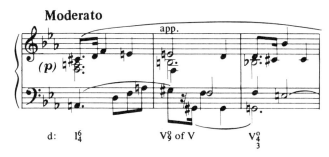

The root may appear above the minor ninth in a nonharmonic function, as appoggiatura to the seventh. This effect is not uncommon

EXAMPLE 24–11: Chopin, *Mazurka*, Op. 56, No. 3

and should be regarded as a diminished seventh chord, the root non-harmonic. (See Example 24–11.)

Inversions

The complete dominant ninth chord in inversion is not often found in the common-practice period, but occasional examples do exist. To assure the characteristic sonority of the chord, the spacing in the inversions should follow the restrictions regarding the relative positions of ninth, root, and leading tone, with the higher-numbered factors generally placed in upper positions in the chord.

In figuring basses for the inversions the spacing is not taken into account, the arabic numerals simply identifying the notes to be used in arranging the chord.

EXAMPLE 24–12

The fourth inversion is not used, as that would place the ninth below the root. The second inversion, with the fifth in the bass, is less used than the other two.

EXAMPLE 24–13: Lalo, *Symphonie espagnole*, Op. 21, IV

EXAMPLE 24–14: Haydn, *Sonata No. 7*, II

Largo e sostenuto

F: IV(II)$_5^6$ V$_2^4_3$ I^6 II^6 I$_4^6$ V^7 I

Secondary Dominants

The complete ninth chord may serve as a secondary dominant, with the reservation that the major ninth cannot introduce a minor tonic. Irregular resolutions of the secondary dominant ninths are occasionally employed, as shown in the first of the following examples.

EXAMPLE 24–15: Wagner, *Die Meistersinger*, Act III, Finale

Mässig

C: V^7 I^6 V$_3^4$ V^9 of VI IV V$_9^0$ of V
                        (VI of VI)

EXAMPLE 24–16: Chopin, *Nocturne*, Op. 72, No. 1

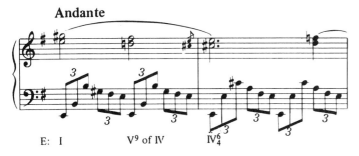

Andante

E: I V^9 of IV IV$_4^6$

EXAMPLE 24–17: Mussorgsky, *Songs and Dances of Death*: No. 3, *Death's Serenade*

Modulation

The ninth chord shares the disadvantage of all dominant chords as pivot chords in modulation, namely that the pivot chord is preferably not the dominant of the new key. It is, therefore, more effectively used as a secondary dominant in the second key, or even in both. Irregular resolution of the pivot chord is an added resource. The presence of the root takes away the possibilities of enharmonic change, which were so numerous in the incomplete minor ninth chord.

The following example shows a shift, or modulation without pivot chord, with three common tones at the junction point.

EXAMPLE 24–18: Grieg, *Piano Concerto*, I

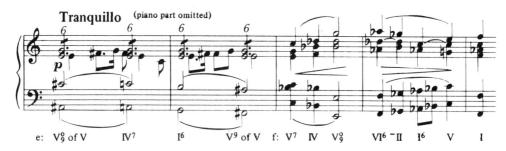

In the following example, the ninth chord appears as the chord of resolution in the deceptive cadence in D. Hence it is taken as the pivot chord in the sudden modulation to B♭, in order that the formula of the deceptive cadence may be preserved in the analysis.

EXAMPLE 24–19: Franck, *Symphony*, I

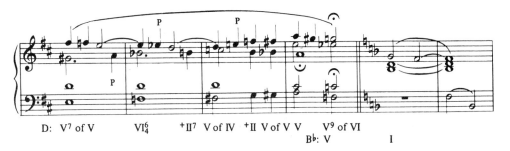

D: V⁷ of V   VII⁶₄   ⁺II⁷ V of IV ⁺II V of V V   V⁹ of VI
                                                B♭: V   I

Nondominant Ninth Chords

The nondominant ninths most often used by composers are generally found on the roots I, II, and IV, less often on III or VI. They are brought about in nearly all cases by the presence of one or more appoggiature or suspensions. The appoggiatura to the octave above the bass, if sufficiently prominent harmonically, will create the effect of a ninth chord. If the seventh is not present the true chord is a triad in root position.

EXAMPLE 24–20

(I⁹) I   (II⁹) II   (IV⁹) IV

When the seventh is included and both seventh and ninth resolve, as a double appoggiatura, the fundamental harmony is a triad in first inversion.

EXAMPLE 24–21

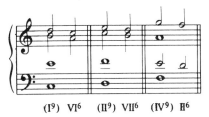

(I⁹) VI⁶   (II⁹) VII⁶   (IV⁹) II⁶

Cf. Ex. 23–20

Both fifth and seventh may be included with the ninth, representing a seventh chord in first inversion.

EXAMPLE 24–22

(I^9) VII^6_5 (II^9) VII^6_5 (IV^9) II^6_5

All of the appoggiature shown may occur in the form of suspensions, in which case they would enter as tied-over notes from the preceding chord and would, of course, be weak instead of strong rhythmically. These effects are also used in the minor mode, the lowered seventh degree being employed when it descends to the sixth.

The ninths representing harmony of II or IV are the commonest of the nondominant ninths.

EXAMPLE 24–23: Beethoven, *Violin Sonata*, Op. 30, No. 2, II

A^b: I $(IV^9)II^6$ II   V

In the following sequence, the ninths arise by suspension from the fifth of the preceding chord, the sevenths from the preceding third.

EXAMPLE 24–24: Verdi, *Messa da Requiem*: No. 1, *Requiem aeternam*

a: II^7 of III V^9 of III $(V^7$ of III)III^7 $VI^9$$(IV^9$ of III)(VI^7) II^7 V^9 (V^7) I II^7 of V V of V V

Appoggiature with Delayed Resolution

Sometimes the appoggiatura or suspension is delayed in its resolution so that a change of harmony takes place before the melodic tone is resolved. The nondominant ninth seems under these circumstances to possess more independence as a chord, although its contrapuntal origin is still apparent.

EXAMPLE 24–25: Beethoven, *Symphony No. 2*, I

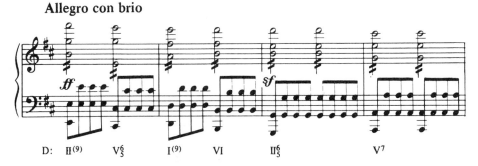

The following example is unusual in that all factors of the supertonic ninth chord are sounded.

EXAMPLE 24–26: Grieg, *Sonata*, Op. 7, II

The Unresolved Appoggiatura

As a final stage in the evolution of a chord the contrapuntal tone is left unresolved. It is nevertheless essential in the nondominant ninth chord, as well as in the chords of the eleventh and thirteenth, that the character of these higher factors, as contrapuntal tones whose resolution is only implied, be recognized. The effect is somewhat different from that of the dominant ninth similarly treated, in which case the sense of the vertical structure in thirds is strongly felt.

In the following example, the ninth is resolved in the accompaniment, but this resolution is barely audible by comparison with the melody as orchestrated. The syncopated chords are given to divided violas, while all the violins, both first and second, play the upper melody. A clearer sense of resolution is to be had by hearing the upper line as a compound melody, the G in the first measure resolving to the F in the second.

EXAMPLE 24–27: Schumann, *Symphony No. 2*, III

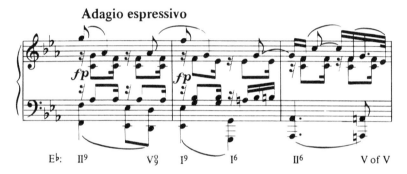

The ninth in the example below cannot in any sense be said to resolve. Note also that the chord is in the first inversion. Inversions of these chords are not common, the interval of the ninth being ordinarily formed with the bass.

EXAMPLE 24–28: Franck, *Piano Quintet*, I

Part of the charm of the cadence in the following example derives from the uncertainty as to the contrapuntal significance of the double appoggiatura, E and C♯. It is as though the seventh and ninth of the subdominant were held over from the tonic chord and the group of sixteenth notes were decorated neighbor notes.

EXAMPLE 24–29: Mozart, *Piano Concerto*, K. 488, I

Eleventh and Thirteenth

As we have seen, in both dominant and nondominant harmony the ninth is often both a melodic and a harmonic tone, depending upon its prominence as a harmonic ingredient. This ambiguity becomes even more marked in the chords of the eleventh and thirteenth. The omission of factors weakens the sense of structure in thirds and allows the ear to accept the higher factors as melodic tones dependent on a simpler harmonic construct, usually a triad or a dominant seventh chord. On the other hand, when most of the lower factors are present, and the higher-numbered factors are prominently sounded in the uppermost voices, then there will be a greater likelihood of hearing these factors as actual elements of the harmony.

   In the following example, a thirteenth chord is shown (*a*) with all its factors, a sonority quite foreign to the common-practice period. It is also shown (*b*) as it usually occurs. Playing this second version will demonstrate the high improbability of the missing thirds, especially A and C, and will also show the strong implication that the note E represents D, whether or not it actually resolves to it.

EXAMPLE 24–30

Eleventh and thirteenth chords arise from melodic tones such as the appoggiatura and the suspension, and also through the tonic or dominant pedal. The commonest of these is the tonic eleventh effect created by a dominant seventh chord above a tonic bass, first described in Chapter 8 as "five over one." It may happen that the tonic part of this sonority is represented by an actual chord or arpeggio below the dominant chord. We then have all the factors of a tonic eleventh chord, but there can be no doubt that the upper factors are heard as contrapuntal tones over a simple triad, rather than as chord members.

*See also Exx.
5–27, 8–8,
11–13*

EXAMPLE 24–31: Beethoven, *Sonata*, Op. 2, No. 2, IV

The dominant eleventh is ordinarily the subdominant triad sounding over a dominant pedal.

EXAMPLE 24–32: Brahms, *Sonata*, Op. 5, II

*See also Ex.
25–13*

Or the dominant eleventh may include the fifth, in which case the chord may be considered to contain a supertonic-seventh element.

EXAMPLE 24–33: Grieg, *Piano Concerto*, I

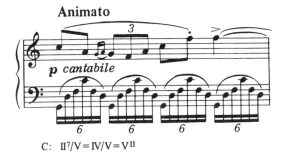

Animato

C: II⁷/V = IV/V = V¹¹

The eleventh may appear as a nonharmonic tone over the dominant ninth.

EXAMPLE 24–34: Beethoven, *Symphony No. 9*, I

Allegro ma non troppo, un poco maestoso

d: V   V of V   II$^4_3$ V¹¹   V⁹

Eleventh chords may be found on II and IV, resulting from appoggiature.

EXAMPLE 24–35: Liszt, *Sonata*

Andante sostenuto

F♯: I   VI⁷   II^(11)   V⁹

The thirteenth is as high as it is possible to go in the series of thirds, since the fifteenth would coincide with the double octave. The dominant thirteenth of contrapuntal origin is a fairly common chord effect. It has been pointed out that the third degree, that degree being the thirteenth above the dominant, tends to be absorbed into the dominant *See Ex. 23–28* harmony when it stands above a dominant bass, as in III⁶ and I⁶₄. It is this third degree which gives rise to the expression "dominant thirteenth," especially when it occurs as an appoggiatura in combination with the dominant seventh chord (Example 24–30*b*).

In the following example the thirteenth appears as an appoggiatura, prepared as a neighbor note, to the fifth of the chord. In the third *Cf. Ex. 19–19* measure, the minor thirteenth, prepared in the previous measure, appears and is not resolved, but is unobtrusively prolonged into the secondary tonic that follows.

EXAMPLE 24–36: Chopin, *Prelude*, Op. 28, No. 13

If the following example contained a leading tone in the first three measures the chord would sound like a real thirteenth. Without that factor the separation of subdominant harmony from the dominant bass is quite marked, so that a pedal effect is clearly present, continued from the preceding measures.

EXAMPLE 24–37: Dvořák, *Symphony No. 9* ("From the New World"), I

Cf. Ex. 22–14

The following example is a clearer instance of a true dominant thirteenth, with only the eleventh missing. The thirteenth resolves by dissolution, arpeggiating downward to the major ninth, which in turn resolves upward. The spacing makes the chord warm and sonorous, comparable to the distribution of natural overtones.

EXAMPLE 24–38: Wagner, *Die Meistersinger*, Act III, Finale

A tonic thirteenth results from placing a dominant ninth over the tonic bass as a pedal, or with the dominant as an appoggiatura chord. The dominant ninth thus used may be either major or minor and may occur without root.

EXAMPLE 24–39: Bach, *Well-Tempered Clavier*, *II*, Prelude No. 9

Cf. Ex. 21–15

EXAMPLE 24–40: Mendelssohn, *Song without Words*, Op. 85: No. 5, *The Return*

In the following example the complete tonic thirteenth is formed by a combination of the dominant ninth and the tonic triad. The dominant is represented by four suspensions, which resolve into the tonic harmony.

EXAMPLE 24–41: Brahms, *Intermezzo*, Op. 119, No. 1

Formulae, to be played in all keys:

EXAMPLE 24–42

EXERCISES

1. Work out the following figured basses:

2. Construct original examples of the following harmonic effects, showing their introduction and resolution:

a. II^9 in G major, without seventh

b. IV^9 in E♭ minor, with fifth and seventh

c. I^9 in A major, resulting from an appoggiatura with delayed resolution

d. IV^9 in F minor, the ninth an unresolved appoggiatura

e. an inner dominant pedal

f. a tonic eleventh chord

g. a subdominant eleventh chord made by a double appoggiatura

h. a dominant thirteenth chord in which the thirteenth is an unresolved appoggiatura

3. Harmonize the following unfigured basses, using some chords of the ninth, eleventh, and thirteenth:

4. Harmonize the following melodies, using some chords of the ninth, eleventh, and thirteenth:

25

Chromatically Altered Chords: The Raised Supertonic and Submediant

In a literal sense an altered chord is any chord affected by an accidental, signifying that one of its tones is changed from its original form as established by the key signature. There are three possible reasons for these chromatic alterations, but only one of these will apply to the term *chromatically altered chord* as we wish to define it more narrowly in this chapter.

The first reason for the use of an accidental may be said to arise from the deficiency of our system of key signatures, inasmuch as these do not permit the interchangeability or mixture of the modes. Hence we will not speak of a chord as being a chromatically altered chord when a sharp, flat, or natural is used to indicate a normal scale degree, as for example in the following:

EXAMPLE 25–1

c: III   VI⁷   VI⁷   V⁰₉

The second category of chords affected by accidental signs includes all the secondary dominants. These chords are not really altered chords. The process of deriving a secondary dominant involves the consideration of a temporary tonality in which the chord exists as the normal, unaltered dominant. (Some theorists use the expression *borrowed chords* for the secondary dominants, implying, for instance, that the D-major triad in the key of C is a dominant "borrowed" from G.) This category probably accounts for the majority of the accidentals seen in music, except perhaps in instances of actual modulations when the key signature has not been changed.

That leaves a third category of chords in the common-practice period having chromatic signs, and these we shall consider as true chromatically altered chords. The important members of this group are the raised supertonic and the raised submediant, the Neapolitan sixth, the chords of the augmented sixth, and those with altered fifth.

II⁷ and VI⁷ with Raised Root and Third

The seventh chords on supertonic and submediant, derived from the major mode, and having root and third chromatically raised, are non-dominant diminished seventh chords. It was pointed out in Chapter 21 that the identity of a diminished seventh chord is determined by its resolution. These two chords resolve to I and V⁷ respectively.

EXAMPLE 25–2

In root analysis, we use plus and minus signs to indicate chord factors which have been chromatically raised or lowered. A plus sign at the upper left of the roman numeral indicates that the root is raised. Thus ⁺II⁷ and ⁺VI⁷ will designate the chords discussed in this chapter, the third being understood as also raised.

Note that ⁺VI⁷ has the same relationship to V as ⁺II⁷ does to I, the voice leading being different in only one factor. In resolving to V⁷ the raised submediant strengthens the tonality by making the dominant harmony stronger.

The resolutions show that a chromatically altered tone tends to resolve in the direction of its alteration. Both chords contain raised tones whose tendency is upward, like leading tones or appoggiature. The root being thus altered does not seem like a harmonic root, but more like a melodic tendency tone. Thus the names $^+$II^7 and $^+$VI^7 are really more a matter of convenience than an accurate description of independent supertonic or submediant harmony. These chords are comparable to V$^0_9$, or II^7 and VI^7 (ascending) in the minor mode, in that the lowest factor of a diminished-triad component is not heard as a true root.

Notation

Composers have generally been indifferent to the grammatical notation of these diminished seventh chords. The raised second degree is often written as minor third degree and the raised sixth as minor seventh degree.

EXAMPLE 25-3

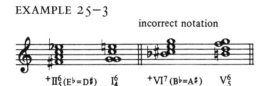

The note E$\flat$ functions as D$\sharp$, resolving to E$\natural$; similarly the note written as B$\flat$ behaves like an A$\sharp$. The first chord, therefore, is not V$^0_9$ of V, but rather $^+$II^7; the second chord is not V$^{\circ4}_2$ of II, but $^+$VI^7. Each chord is properly identified by its resolution.

EXAMPLE 25-4: Bach, *Well-Tempered Clavier*, I, Prelude No. 3

EXAMPLE 25-5: Beethoven, *Symphony No. 2*, II

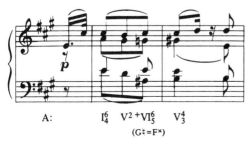

Music is fortunately a matter of sound rather than symbols, and there is no doubt that the second violins in the Beethoven example instinctively give the G♮ its proper meaning, that is of an F×.

The problem is more difficult in the example below.

EXAMPLE 25–6: Schubert, *String Quintet*, Op. 163, I

Here the E♭ in viola part obviously should be D♯. But the melodic outline of the first violin part would be very strange if D♯ were substituted for E♭. A compromise must be effected in performance between the harmonic and the contrapuntal, a compromise that is continually necessary in music of chromatic style, especially where enharmonic notation is used.

Rhythm

The harmonic rhythm of the ⁺II⁷ and ⁺VI⁷ chords and their resolutions may be either strong-to-weak or weak-to-strong. The following two examples are identical in their kind of melodic preparation, but different in harmonic rhythm. The first example shows an appoggiatura chord, the second an auxiliary chord.

EXAMPLE 25–7: Tchaikovsky, *The Nutcracker: Waltz of the Flowers*

EXAMPLE 25–8: Rossini, Overture to *William Tell*

See also Ex.
8–12

G: I   +II² I

When the altered tones enter as chromatic passing tones the chord is a passing chord.

EXAMPLE 25–9: Schumann, *Dichterliebe*, Op. 48: No. 7, *Ich grolle nicht*

C: V   VI⁷   +VI⁷   V⁶₅   I

EXAMPLE 25–10: Chopin, *Valse brillante*, Op. 34, No. 1

A♭:   V⁹   +VI⁶₅ V⁴₃

These chords may also serve as independent chords of equal rhythmic value with the surrounding harmony. ⁺VI⁷ is a useful chord for introducing the dominant half cadence to emphasize the key (Example 25–

9, above), and $^+$II^7 often appears prominently before the cadential six-four chord.

EXAMPLE 25–11: Mozart, *Concerto for Two Pianos*, K. 365, III

Eb: IV $^+$II$^{o}_{5}$ (Gb=F♯)   I$^{6}_{4}$

Cross-Relation

The two altered tones of either chord are sometimes found in a melodic group of double thirds or sixths forming two reaching tones. In this case the resulting cross-relations are not avoided. The altered tones may be first or second in the group.

EXAMPLE 25–12

These progressions contain not only the cross-relation, but also the unusual interval of the diminished third, F to D♯ and C to A♯. In the example below there are two cross-relations, Ab to A♮ and F♮ to F♯. The melodic diminished third, Ab to F♯, is accompanied in the top voice by the interval of a diminished fourth, Db to A♮.

EXAMPLE 25–13: Wagner, *Die Meistersinger*, Act II, Scene 4

(voices omitted)

(dominant pedal)
Ab: I   IV $^+$VI^7 V^7 I

Mode

The raised supertonic and submediant chords are more at home in the major mode than the minor. $^+VI^7$ contains the major third degree and $^+II^7$ implies it by the raised second degree. Both chords may, however, be used in the minor mode. If the resolution of $^+II^7$ is treated not as tonic, but as V of IV, there is no difficulty in continuing in minor. The following example shows $^+VI^7$ used in predominantly minor surroundings.

EXAMPLE 25–14: Haydn, *String Quartet*, Op. 76, No. 4, I

Irregular Resolution

Irregular resolution of a diminished seventh chord in the sense of progression to an irregular root is rare. Variations in the form of the chord of resolution can be employed, however, without destroying the identity of the diminished seventh.

$^+II^7$ may resolve to V of IV, either as a dominant seventh chord or as in incomplete ninth, usually minor. In the second case, diminished seventh chords move parallel. (See Examples 25–15 and 16.)

EXAMPLE 25–15

EXAMPLE 25–16: Beethoven, *Symphony No. 3* ("Eroica"), III

The submediant chord may also resolve to an incomplete ninth.

EXAMPLE 25–17: Bach, *Well-Tempered Clavier*, I, Prelude No. 8

eb: IV   (app. E♮)   ⁺VI⁶₅ (D♭=C♯)   V⁰⁴₃
                                    (F♭=E♮)

Modulation

As we have seen, the diminished seventh chord functioning as an ordinary dominant, V⁰₉, serves in many ways as a pivot chord in modulation, and the nondominant functions, ⁺II⁷ and ⁺VI⁷, make the diminished seventh even more flexible for this purpose. The modulation in which a dominant becomes a nondominant is especially effective and somewhat unexpected. For instance, if the incomplete dominant minor ninth of C is left as II⁷ raised, the new key will be A♭ major. If it is left as VI⁷ raised, the distant key of D♭ will be introduced.

EXAMPLE 25–18

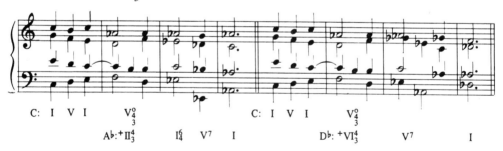

C: I V I   V⁰⁴₃   C: I V I   V⁰⁴₃
        A♭:⁺II⁴₃   I⁶₄ V⁷ I   D♭:⁺VI⁴₃   V⁷   I

If the pivot chord is to be ⁺VI⁷ or ⁺II⁷ in the first key, there are two problems. Since the identity of these chords depends upon their resolution, their function in the first key must be made clear before the point of modulation. The best method of doing this is to present the chord with its resolution in the first key, using it as a pivot chord only after its identity has already been established. The second problem is to avoid weakening the modulation by allowing the pivot chord to be the dominant of the second key. This can be arranged by using a secondary dominant.

Both of these procedures are seen in the following example. The $^+$VI in second inversion (root F$^\times$, notated as G$\natural$) proceeds to V and back again, only to be reinterpreted enharmonically as a dominant (ninth D$\flat$, notated as C$\sharp$), which resolves nonharmonically (compare Example 21–22). (The enharmonic notations in this example make it easier for the performers to read, but more difficult for the analyst.)

EXAMPLE 25–19: Beethoven, *Symphony No. 7*, II

The following example shows both the $^+$II^7 and $^+$VI^7 in a pattern which is the basis of a modulating sequence. It is given here in reduced form because the tempo is very fast and each harmony stretches over four measures; the entire sequence, with some slight deviations from the pattern, lasts for eighty measures, or twenty measures per unit, in a big crescendo modulating from D minor to C major.

EXAMPLE 25–20: Schubert, *Symphony No. 9*, IV (harmonic outline)

Formulae, to be played in all keys:

EXAMPLE 25-21

$^+II_3^4$ I_4^6 V^7 I $^+II_5^6$ I_4^6 V^7 I I $^+II^2$ I I $^+II^2$ I

II^6 I_4^6 V $^+II_5^6$ $^+VI^2$ V^7 $^+VI^7$ V_5^6 $^+VI^7$ V_9^o I V^7 $^+VI^2$ V^7

EXERCISES

1. Work out the following figured basses:

a.

6   7   6   6   6   6
    #   5   4   4   7
                   2

b.

6#   6   6×   6   2   6   7   6   7
4×   4   5   4   #
3   3

c.

6   7   7   7   7♭   6   6   6♮   6   7♭
4   ♮   5   4   5♭
2

d.

6   3   6   7   6   7♮   4   6   7♮
4   #   2
2

e.

7   6#   4   7♭   6   6   6   4#   7
   5   3   5♮   5   4   2#
         3♮

2. *Road map.* Construct a musical sentence of three phrases according to the following specifications:

   a. The first phrase shows a diminished seventh chord used first as V of V, then as $^+$II^7 (with enharmonic change).

   b. The second phrase modulates by means of a pivot chord which becomes $^+$VI^7 in the second key.

   c. The third phrase returns to the original key by a pivot chord which is $^+$II^7 in the final key.

3. Construct a modulating sequence, the pattern of which contains the chord $^+$VI^7.

4. Harmonize the following unfigured basses, introducing chords of the raised supertonic and submediant:

a.

b.

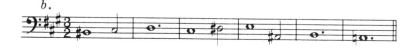

c.

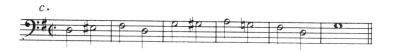

5. Harmonize the following melodies, introducing chords of the raised supertonic and submediant:

a.

b.

c.

d.

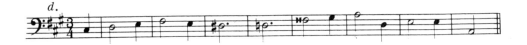

26

The Neapolitan Sixth

Definition, Resolution, Preparation, and Doubling

The major triad whose root is the chromatically lowered second degree of the scale is known as the *Neapolitan sixth*. It is difficult to say what is "Neapolitan" about this chord, but the name is universally accepted. In the eighteenth century it was used primarily in the first inversion, hence the *sixth*. Later in the nineteenth century the triad was called a Neapolitan sixth even when it was used in root position.

Far from wishing to discard a designation so securely established, we shall welcome the convenience of the identifying label attached to this chord. In this way we may be permitted the unscientific but quite understandable expression, "the Neapolitan sixth in root position," and the use of the commonly accepted symbol N in lieu of the roman numeral II. When the roman numeral is used instead of N for the Neapolitan, as in the examples in this book, it should be preceded by a small minus sign at the upper left, indicating chromatic lowering of the root.

The Neapolitan sixth is a major triad, and is therefore not a dissonant chord. However, the chromatic alteration of the second degree gives that tone a downward tendency, so that it makes for a downward resolution as though it were a dissonant tone.

Although derived from the minor scale, and most often used in the minor mode, the Neapolitan sixth is freely used in the major mode as well. It is a chord of strongly subdominant character, progressing most frequently to some form of the dominant chord. Note that the bass is the best tone to double, as it is a tonal degree. (See Example 26–1.)

In any resolution to V, the preferred voice leading of the altered second degree is downward by a skip of a diminished third. Examples such as *d* and *e* above, where the altered tone moves upward, contrary to the direction of alteration, are unusual (Example 26–4).

EXAMPLE 26–1

The progressions shown in the example contain the cross-relation between D♭ and D♮. This cross-relation has not been avoided by composers, although many arrangements of the progression to V without it are possible. When the dominant chord contains a seventh, for example, its fifth may be omitted so that no cross-relation will occur.

EXAMPLE 26–2: Beethoven, *Sonata quasi una fantasia*, Op. 27, No. 2, I

Adagio sostenuto

The bass may remain in place as the harmony changes, resulting in the third inversion of the dominant seventh.

EXAMPLE 26–3: Bach, *Orchestral Suite No. 2*: VII, *Badinerie*

Allegro

See also Ex. 26–16

If the sixth degree, the fifth of the chord, is continued into the next harmony, a ninth chord will result.

EXAMPLE 26–4: Beethoven, *Sonata*, Op. 90, I

e: I   IV   ‾II⁶   V⁹

Very often the dominant chord will first be represented by the cadential tonic six-four, the sixth and fourth as double appoggiature. This allows a smooth stepwise progression in all voices, the three upper parts moving in contrary motion to the bass. The root progression is, of course, still II to V. There is no sense of cross-relation because of the intervening harmonic effect of I.

EXAMPLE 26–5: Mozart, *Piano Concerto*, K. 488, II

f♯: I   VI   ‾II⁶♮   I⁶₄   V⁷   I

Other chords are sometimes interpolated between the Neapolitan sixth and the dominant. These are for the most part substitutes for supertonic harmony. The problems of voice leading vary; if the chord is dominant of the dominant, there will be several chromatic progressions in the voices. Note, in the example below, that the cross-relation between the altered and unaltered second degree (G♮, G♯) makes it possible for the lowered tone in the soprano to descend according to its tendency. The other two chromatic progressions occur each within a single voice.

See also Ex.
28–29

EXAMPLE 26–6: Schumann, *String Quartet*, Op. 41, No. 3, II

Un poco adagio

f♯: ⁻II⁶   V⁶₅ of V   V⁷   I

In the following, the interpolated harmony is the incomplete dominant ninth chord. The fifth of the Neapolitan is doubled, and the root moves upward, contrary to its tendency. In the first measure the melodic figuration over the Neapolitan harmony is the scale of the temporary tonality, the lowered second degree, here D major.

EXAMPLE 26–7: Beethoven, *Sonata quasi una fantasia*, Op. 27, No. 2, III

Presto

(cresc.)

c♯: ⁻II⁶   V⁰₉ of V   I⁶₄

The altered tone may appear as appoggiatura to the tone below. The fundamental harmony will then be subdominant, although the color of the Neapolitan sixth is recognizable. It is also reasonable to consider the tonic as a passing tone, as in the following example:

EXAMPLE 26–8: Mozart, *String Quintet*, K. 515, I

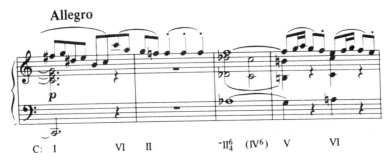

Allegro

C: I   VI   II   ⁻II⁶₄ (IV⁶)   V   VI

The example above shows the adaptability and coloristic effect of this chord employed in a major-mode context.

The harmonic rhythm of the following cadential passage gives unusual prominence to the Neapolitan six-four.

EXAMPLE 26–9: Weber, Overture to *Der Freischütz*

The Neapolitan sixth is not used only in cadential formulae. It may be found in any part of the phrase, and may even begin the piece.

EXAMPLE 26–10: Chopin, *Ballade*, Op. 23

In its subdominant capacity it progresses occasionally to I or V of IV.

EXAMPLE 26–11: Handel, *Concerto Grosso*, Op. 6, No. 5, IV

See also Ex.
11–30

The Neapolitan sixth may be used as subdominant harmony in a plagal cadence, followed by either major or minor tonic harmony.

EXAMPLE 26–12: Brahms, *String Quartet*, Op. 51, No. 1, I

In the nineteenth century the Neapolitan sixth chord was employed with increasing frequency in root position. This gave it much more independence and stability, the lowered second degree being treated in this case not as a melodic tendency tone, but as a true harmonic root, which would thus be doubled. The doubled root and the augmented fourth relationship to the dominant help to emphasize the remoteness of this harmony from the main tonal center.

EXAMPLE 26–13: Brahms, *Violin Sonata*, Op. 108, IV

Secondary Relationships

In the example below, the root-position D♭-major triad in the second measure is clearly IV of VI, the two measures being sequentially related. At the end of the piece, however, the identical triad is in Neapolitan relationship to C minor.

EXAMPLE 26–14: Chopin, *Prelude*, Op. 28, No. 20

c: I   IV⁷   V⁷   I   VI IV of VI V⁷ of VI VI   VI ⁻II V⁷   I

The secondary-subdominant relationship above accounts for the rare appearance of what could be called a "Neapolitan minor," but of course this chord does not function as a true Neapolitan. The following progression incorporating the minor IV of VI was used several times by Schubert.

EXAMPLE 26–15: Schubert, Overture to *Fierrabras*

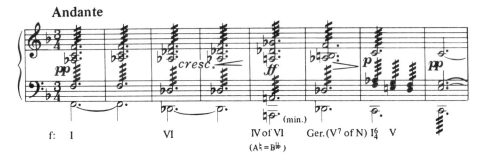

f: I   VI   IV of VI   Ger.(V⁷ of N) I⁶₄ V
                                (A♮ = B♭♭)

V of the Neapolitan

The Neapolitan sixth may be preceded by its dominant, thus adding another to the list of secondary dominants available in one tonality. The independence of the root-position Neapolitan is greatly strengthened by the presence of the secondary dominant, V of ⁻II⁶. It is plain, however, that the two chords constitute an extension of the main tonality rather than a weakening of it.

EXAMPLE 26–16: Schubert, *Symphony No. 9*, II

Intermediate Modulation

The Neapolitan sixth chord is often felt to be of sufficient strength to cause a momentary shift to its root as a tonal center. This may be due simply to the length of time it occupies.

EXAMPLE 26–17: Chopin, *Prelude*, Op. 28, No. 6

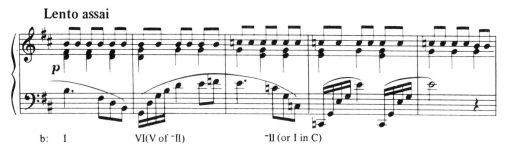

Or it may be because of the attendant harmonies. In Example 26–

EXAMPLE 26–18: Beethoven, *Sonata*, Op. 106 ("Hammerklavier"), III

18 the last chord in the first measure is the raised supertonic in the key of G, followed by the tonic six-four. The use of the subdominant of G confirms this impression, but we know that the G triad is only the Neapolitan sixth chord of the key of F♯.

Cf. Ex. 26–5

The intermediate modulation may of course be analyzed without invoking the symbols of a modulation, the chords foreign to the tonality being referred to the secondary tonic. Enharmonic equivalents are employed here so as to avoid notating such triads as B♭♭ major.

EXAMPLE 26–19: Chopin, *Etude*, Op. 10, No. 6

Modulation with the Neapolitan

The Neapolitan sixth is a useful pivot chord in modulation. As a simple major triad it is capable of many interpretations. It is common ground between distantly related keys, as in the following modulation from F to E:

EXAMPLE 26–20: Beethoven, *Sonata*, Op. 14, No. 1, III

Such modulations to keys a semitone distant are often brought about with the aid of the augmented sixth chord, the enharmonic equivalent of the dominant of the Neapolitan; augmented sixth chords are discussed in the next chapter.

See also Ex. 20–16

The Neapolitan six-five-three appears as a pivot chord in the dramatic and dissonant climax of the following well-known passage:

EXAMPLE 26–21: Beethoven, *Symphony No. 3* ("Eroica"), I

Formulae, to be played in all keys:

EXAMPLE 26–22

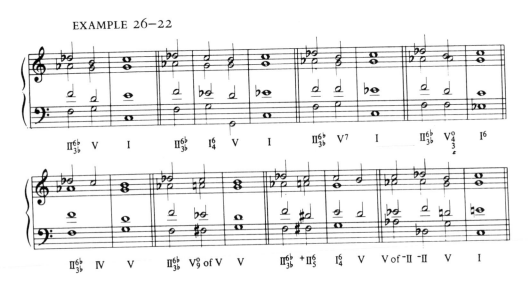

EXERCISES

1. Work out the following figured basses:

2. Construct a modulating sequence in which the pivot chord is the Neapolitan sixth in the second key.

3. Harmonize the following unfigured basses, introducing Neapolitan sixth chords:

4. Harmonize the following melodies, introducing Neapolitan sixth chords:

a.

b.

c.

d. **Mazurka**

27

Augmented Sixth Chords

The four chords comprising the group known as *augmented sixth chords* have in common the interval of the augmented sixth created by the minor sixth degree and the chromatically raised fourth degree. The name derives from the usual arrangement of the chords, in which this characteristic interval is found between the bass and an upper voice.

Origin as Secondary Dominants

The raised fourth degree, as leading tone to the dominant, is the clue to the secondary dominant function of three of the four augmented sixth chords. The augmented sixth interval expands in its normal resolution to the octave on the dominant.

EXAMPLE 27–1

V

The augmented sixth interval does not come from a subdominant with raised root, but from V of V with lowered fifth. The following example shows its contrapuntal origin.

EXAMPLE 27–2

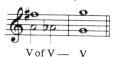

V of V — V

Definitions

Normally all four augmented sixth chords will have the minor sixth degree in the bass and the raised fourth degree in any upper voice. The tonic is always in some other voice, making three factors common to all four chords. Each member of the group will then be distinguished by the fourth voice. The four augmented sixth chords are shown below with their regular resolutions.

EXAMPLE 27–3

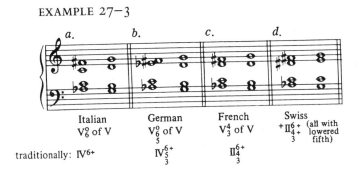

a is called the *augmented sixth*;
b is called the *augmented six-five-three*;
c is called the *augmented six-four-three*;
d is called the *doubly augmented fourth*.

The names *Italian sixth* (a), *German sixth* (b), and *French sixth* (c), have won wide, if not universal, acceptance over the years. As with the Neapolitan sixth, there seems to be no good explanation for the origin of these names. We might propose the adoption of the name *Swiss sixth* for the d chord above, because it does include characteristics of both the German and French sixths.

Many harmony texts, including the earliest editions of this book, have described a and b above as chords having the raised fourth degree as root, and c as an altered supertonic seventh. The difficulty with the traditional labeling of a and b as IV is that the presumptive underlying triad is diminished and therefore not easily heard as a true subdominant. It is probably more accurate, then, to think of a above as a type of VII⁶ (V⁰₆) of V, that is, an incomplete V⁷ of V with lowered fifth. The actual root of the chord would then be D, as in the complete form, c in the example above. As for b, it may be considered an altered diminished seventh chord, V_9^0 of V with lowered fifth. If *c*, traditionally called II_4^{6+}, is interpreted in a similar manner, it becomes a V^7 of V with lowered fifth. Thus all three chords *a*, *b*, and *c* have a family resemblance, being various types of V of V, as their usual resolutions imply. The *d* chord is readily explained as the result of lowering the fifth of the raised supertonic seventh.

Because the exact labelings "V_6^0 of V with lowered fifth," "V_6^0 of V with lowered fifth," "V_3^4 of V with lowered fifth," and "$^+II_4^{6+}$ with lowered fifth" are somewhat cumbersome, it is more practical to use "It.," "Ger.," "Fr.," and "Sw." respectively, regardless of inversion; the national abbreviations are readily understood as referring to augmented sixth chords, and there is no danger of confusing the roman-numeral labels with those of unaltered forms of V of V or II.

Note that *b* is like *a* with minor seventh added; *d* sounds like *b*, but the difference between E♭ and D♯ becomes clear on the resolution of the chord; *c* is distinguished from *b* by the presence of the second degree in place of the minor third degree; *a*, *b*, and *d* sound like dominant sevenths of the Neapolitan, which makes them useful as pivot chords in modulation.

Resolution

The regular resolution of the augmented sixth chords is to V or, in the case of the doubly augmented fourth, to major I_4^6. The raised fourth degree moves up a half step, the minor sixth degree moves down a half step, and the tonic either moves down directly to the leading tone or remains in place as a suspension or appoggiatura before descending.

The fourth voice will vary in movement according to its identity. Since there are but three factors in *a*, the plain augmented sixth chord, the tonic will be doubled. It is not customary to double either of the tones making the interval of the augmented sixth. The fourth voice usually moves up by step.

EXAMPLE 27–4

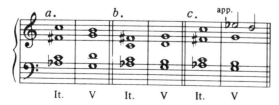

See also Exx.
16–18, 20–9

The fourth voice can move up by the interval of a fifth to the dominant, often a desirable melodic skip in the upper voice.

EXAMPLE 27–5: Beethoven, *Symphony No. 5*, I

In the augmented six-five-three or German sixth (*b* in Example 27–3), the fourth voice forms an interval of a perfect fifth with the bass. The parallel fifths arising from the natural progression to the dominant are always considered acceptable, except when occurring between soprano and bass. They are most often seen between tenor and bass. The third degree is, however, frequently tied over as a suspension, or repeated as an appoggiatura, before continuing down to the second degree.

The augmented six-five-three strongly suggests the minor mode, since it contains both minor third and minor sixth degrees.

EXAMPLE 27–6

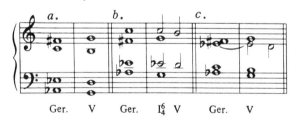

EXAMPLE 27–7: Mozart, *Sonata*, K. 332, I

The parallel fifths are more noticeable in the following example:

EXAMPLE 27–8: Franck, *Symphony*, I

d: V⁷ of V   Ger.   V⁷

Because the augmented sixth chords have two factors in common with IV, and a third factor which is the raised fourth degree itself, it follows that IV is a good preparation for the augmented sixth chords, the raised fourth degree arising contrapuntally (Example 27–2). The augmented sixth chords often appear as connectors between IV⁶ and V, especially in cadences. Here is an example of the augmented six-five-three preceding a cadential six-four chord.

EXAMPLE 27–9: Mozart, Overture to *Don Giovanni*, K. 527

d: IV⁶   Ger.   I⁶₄   V

The French sixth, or augmented six-four-three, has a more obvious secondary dominant function than do the other augmented sixths. The presence of the actual root, the second degree, affords a common factor with the dominant chord, and this will usually be repeated or tied over in the chord of resolution; or it may progress to an appoggiatura of the second degree, as in a cadential six-four chord (*c* in the following example).

EXAMPLE 27–10

See also Ex.
12–10

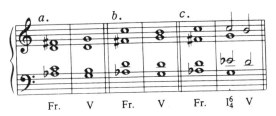

EXAMPLE 27–11: Schubert, *String Quartet*, Op. 125, No. 1, IV

The augmented six-four-three is employed with chords of both major and minor modes, contributing thereby to the impression of modal interchangeability.

EXAMPLE 27–12: Chopin, *Nocturne*, Op. 48, No. 2

In the chord of the doubly augmented fourth, or Swiss sixth, the distinguishing factor is the raised second degree, implying a resolution to the major third degree. This interval of the doubly augmented fourth, formed between the minor-sixth-degree bass and the raised second degree, is enharmonically identical with the perfect fifth. The chord can be distinguished from the augmented six-five-three only upon its resolution.

EXAMPLE 27–13

EXAMPLE 27–14: Chopin, *Ballade*, Op. 47

Composers often write the Swiss sixth incorrectly as an augmented six-five-three. The same indifference to the notation of the raised second degree was observed in the supertonic seventh chord with raised root and third. The two chords are closely related, differing only in the form of the sixth degree.

EXAMPLE 27–15: Mozart, *Sonata for Piano Four Hands*, K. 521, III

When the augmented sixth is followed by a dominant seventh chord, the raised fourth degree descends chromatically, somewhat in the manner of the irregular resolution of a leading tone. If the augmented six-five-three is used, the progression sounds like a succession of dominant

seventh chords and is often incorrectly written as such. The steps in the
evolution of this progression might be outlined as follows:

EXAMPLE 27–16

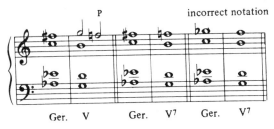

In the following example, the parallel motion is interrupted by the
appoggiatura in the upper voice.

EXAMPLE 27–17: Beethoven, *Sonata*, Op. 57 ("Appassionata"), II

Coloristic possibilities of the augmented sixth combined with
chromatic nonharmonic tones are suggested in the following well-known
excerpt:

EXAMPLE 27–18: Wagner, Prelude to *Tristan und Isolde*

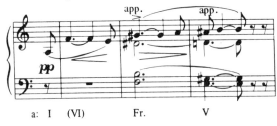

The appoggiatura forming the interval of a diminished octave with
the raised fourth degree is of fairly frequent occurrence.

EXAMPLE 27–19: Mozart, *Sonata*, K. 576, II

f#:   I   VI⁷   Ger.   V

Inversions

When the augmented sixth chords are inverted, the characteristic interval will no longer be found between the most prominent voices. The augmented sixth interval itself may be inverted to produce a diminished third. This accounts for such analyses as "the German sixth in the six-four-three position," meaning an inversion in which the augmented six-five-three appears with the tonic in the bass. Such inverted chords nevertheless do not seem to lose their identity as augmented sixth chords, nor their characteristic harmonic color.

When the raised fourth degree is in the bass the resultant interval of a diminished third resolves with no less emphasis to the octave of the dominant. The diminished third is usually found as its compound interval, the diminished tenth; it less often appears as a simple diminished third in contiguous voices, with resolution to a unison.

EXAMPLE 27–20: Bach, *Mass in B minor*, Credo: *Crucifixus*

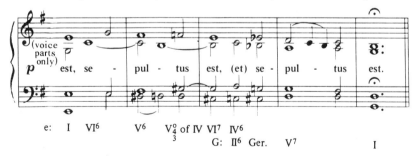

e: I   VI⁶   V⁶   V⁰₄ of IV VI⁷ IV⁶
                   3   G: II⁶ Ger.   V⁷   I

In the example above, the position of the chord is a natural consequence of the melodic progression of the two outside voices in chromatic contrary motion. The melodic movement of the bass is usually the reason for a choice of any factor other than the sixth degree as the lowest note.

As a dissonant chord over a dominant pedal the augmented sixth is strikingly effective.

EXAMPLE 27–21: Chopin, *Scherzo*, Op. 20

b: Ger./V

Like the Neapolitan sixth, the augmented sixths may be found anywhere in the phrase, even at the beginning of the piece.

EXAMPLE 27–22: Schumann, *Dichterliebe*, Op. 48: No. 12, *Am leuchtenden Sommermorgen*

$$Bb: \quad II_{4\ 3}^{6+} \qquad\qquad I_4^6 \qquad V^7$$

Irregular Resolutions

The augmented sixth chords have few irregular resolutions. Most of those we do encounter result from voice leading, as in the smooth suspension of the tonic note into the I_4^6 preceding V. Others involve the contrapuntal possibilities of nonharmonic tones (Example 27–18).

Modulation

As a pivot chord in modulation the augmented sixth is most often employed for its enharmonic similarity to a dominant seventh chord.

The raised fourth degree then becomes the seventh of the chord, a tone of downward tendency. Since the minor sixth degree is interpreted as a dominant the two tonalities will be a half step apart.

EXAMPLE 27–23: Chopin, *Polonaise*, Op. 40, No. 2

In the example above the modulation is enharmonically notated. Modulations to semitonally higher keys using the augmented sixth are common in the nineteenth century. Because the pivot chord is the dominant of the new key, the modulation seems abrupt, with the new dominant more strongly perceived than the augmented sixth relationship to the old key. The following is analyzed with a pivot chord, but is more likely to be heard as a shift, without a pivot chord.

EXAMPLE 27–24: Schubert, *Symphony No. 9*, III

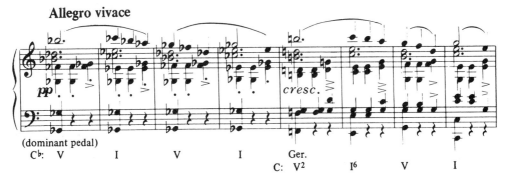

Of somewhat different character is the reverse arrangement, that is, modulation to the key a semitone lower, where the pivot chord is the augmented sixth chord in the second key. Both modulations may be described as sudden, in the sense that the changes are to distantly related tonalities.

EXAMPLE 27–25: Schubert, *Symphony No. 8* ("Unfinished"), II

Exceptional Forms

A few cases may be found of chords having the same interval structure as those of the augmented sixth group but derived from other scale degrees. One of these will be discussed in the next chapter—the chord formed by the lowered second degree in a dominant seventh chord. It is mentioned here as an instance of the comparatively rare treatment of the augmented sixth as a primary dominant.

See Ex. 28–14ff.

EXAMPLE 27–26: Schubert, *String Quintet*, Op. 163, IV

The supertonic seventh chord with major sixth degree and raised root is sometimes used in progression to I. It is equivalent to the augmented six-five-three in the relative minor with irregular resolution.

EXAMPLE 27–27: Schubert, *Symphony No. 9*, IV

In addition to the four-part formulae given in Examples 27–4, 27–6, 27–10, and 27–13, the following sequences are recommended for keyboard practice. They should not be written out, but played from the patterns given.

EXAMPLE 27–28

EXERCISES

1. Work out the following figured basses:

2. Write a modulating sequence in which the pivot chord is V⁷ of IV becoming the doubly augmented fourth chord (Swiss sixth) in the second key.

3. *Road map*. Construct a musical sentence of two phrases according to the following specifications:

a. The first phrase modulates from B to B♭ by means of a pivot chord which is an augmented sixth chord in the second key.
b. The second phrase returns to B by means of a passing modulation through a third key.

4. Harmonize the following unfigured basses, introducing augmented sixth chords:

b.

c.

d.

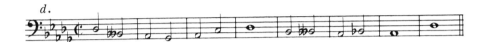

5. Harmonize the following melodies, introducing augmented sixth chords:

28

Other Chromatic Chords

Enharmonic Restrictions of
Altered Scale Degrees

Thus far, we have studied chromatic tones in the following harmonic groups: secondary dominants; raised II^7 and VI^7, Neapolitan sixth, and augmented sixths. A few altered chords in the vocabulary of common-practice composers remain to be discussed. While it is physically possible to use chromatic alteration to create many new chords, just as one can invent new words with the letters of a language, our purpose in this study is to define the harmonic vocabulary as composers have actually used it.

You can learn much about chromatic harmony in common practice by experimenting with the possible alterations of existing chords with a view to discovering reasons why some forms were used in preference to others. You should do this by examining each chord and systematically altering each of its factors in turn, appraising the results for intervallic content and the relation of the chord to the original tonality.

You will observe immediately that a large proportion of the chords made by this method are really familiar chords spelled enharmonically, so that the apparent new form exists only on paper. A few such results are given here:

EXAMPLE 28–1

$$\text{C:} \quad I_{3\flat}^{5\#} = VI^6 \qquad I^{6\flat} = III \qquad III^{5\#} = I^6 \qquad V_{4\#}^{6\#} = V \text{ of } V_{5\flat}^7$$
$$\qquad\qquad\qquad\qquad\qquad\qquad\qquad\qquad\qquad\qquad {}_{3\#}$$

434

The harmonic interpretation of these chords depends upon the ear's acceptance of the tones as particular scale degrees of a particular key and mode. In the example above, the key of C is arbitrarily chosen but, as we know, a key can be established only through association of several harmonic elements; in other words, a tonal context must be defined within which the chromatic tones are to be interpreted.

The following example contains a chromatic passing tone, G♯, which forms the augmented triad on C. If, however, the third of the chord is minor, the passing tone will be heard as the minor sixth degree instead of the raised fifth, and the bracketed progression is diatonic rather than chromatic.

EXAMPLE 28–2

C: I___ VI   c: I VI___

The following observations are made as to chromatic alteration of the scale degrees:

The tonic may be raised, but if lowered it is heard as the leading tone.

The supertonic may be either raised or lowered. When raised it is sometimes heard as the minor third degree.

The minor mediant if raised becomes the major mediant; if lowered it is heard as supertonic.

The major mediant if raised is heard as subdominant; if lowered it becomes the minor third degree.

The dominant may be raised, sometimes being heard thus as the minor sixth degree. When lowered it will usually be heard as leading tone of the dominant.

The minor submediant when raised becomes the major submediant; if lowered it is heard as the dominant.

The major submediant may be raised, sometimes being heard thus as the minor seventh degree. When lowered it becomes the minor sixth degree.

The leading tone if raised is heard as tonic. It may be lowered.

A general principle may be derived from these observations: if a scale degree, upon alteration, results in the enharmonic equivalent of another scale degree, major or minor, in the same tonality, the enharmonic and not the altered function will probably be the function more strongly perceived.

The Augmented Fifth

Chords with fifth raised to make the interval of the augmented fifth above the root are found in I, IV, and V.

The tonic chord so altered is practically always major. The altered tone is of course not doubled and the chord resolves regularly to the subdominant.

EXAMPLE 28–3

It also leads smoothly into the supertonic seventh chord, especially when the third degree is doubled.

EXAMPLE 28–4: Bizet, *l'Arlésienne*, Suite No. 1: No. 3, *Adagietto*

The presence of the tendency tone brings out the inherent quality of the major tonic as dominant of the subdominant. There are many examples of V[7] of IV with augmented fifth.

EXAMPLE 28–5: Beethoven, *String Quartet*, Op. 18, No. 4, II

Andante scherzoso quasi allegretto

C: V$^6_5$ V^2 of IV IV^6 V$^6_5$ of IV IV II I$^6_4$ V^7 I

In dominant harmony the raised degree is the supertonic, suggesting the major mode by its implied resolution to the major third degree.

EXAMPLE 28–6

V$^{5\sharp}$ I V$^{5\sharp}_7$ I

Note enharmony with III (aug.) in minor mode (Chap. 4)

EXAMPLE 28–7: Brahms, *Piano Concerto No. 2*, IV

Allegretto grazioso

B♭: I V$^{6\sharp}$ I V$^{6\sharp}$ I

The raised second degree is a tendency tone added to those already present in the dominant seventh chord. Resolution of these tendency tones results in doubling the third of the tonic triad. The augmented sixth interval between two of the factors, as in V^7 of IV in Example 28–5, does not mean that these chords should be regarded as augmented sixth chords. The characteristic interval here is the augmented fifth, not the sixth.

EXAMPLE 28–8: Schubert, Overture to *The Devil's Pleasure Palace*

The additional tendency tone reduces the number of practicable irregular resolutions. The following shows an effective resolution of the augmented triad on V to the incomplete major ninth V of V.

EXAMPLE 28–9: Wagner, *Siegfried*, Act III, Scene 3

Sehr ruhig und mässig bewegt

The subdominant chord with raised fifth differs rhythmically from the two chords described in that it is nearly always an appoggiatura chord. The raised tonic is an appoggiatura to the second degree, and if seventh and ninth are present they act as appoggiature to the third and octave of a II⁶.

EXAMPLE 28–10

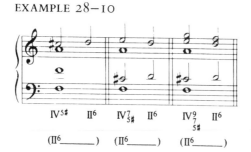

EXAMPLE 28–11: Liszt, *Sonata*

Allegro energico

B: IV$^7_{5\sharp}$ II

The augmented triad has a certain vagueness due to the fact that all of its positions sound alike. Much as the diminished seventh chord divides the octave into four equal parts, the two major thirds of the augmented triad divide the octave into three equal parts, with the upper interval, the diminished fourth, being the enharmonic equivalent of the major third. This symmetry suggests the origin of the whole-tone scale.

EXAMPLE 28–12

A chromatic succession of augmented triads loses the sense of definite tonality. The following passage continues for twenty-two measures before augmented-triad harmony yields to a minor triad; this justly famous beginning sets the tone for the entire work.

EXAMPLE 28–13: Liszt, *A Faust Symphony*, I

Lento assai

The Diminished Fifth

Chromatic lowering of the fifth is found in dominant harmony. In the second inversion of the dominant seventh this produces a chord similar to the augmented six-four-three, but of dominant function.

See also Ex. 27–26

EXAMPLE 28–14

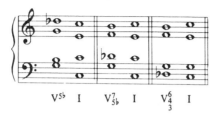

$$V^{5\flat} \quad I \quad V^{7}_{5\flat} \quad I \quad V^{6}_{4\,3} \quad I$$

EXAMPLE 28–15: Brahms, *Symphony No. 4*, IV

Allegro energico e passionato

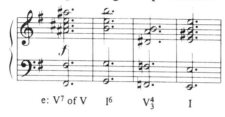

$$e: V^7 \text{ of } V \quad I^6 \quad V^{4}_{3} \quad I$$

The chord may resolve to a minor tonic as well.

EXAMPLE 28–16: Chopin, *Nocturne*, Op. 27, No. 1

Larghetto

$$c\sharp: I \quad {}^{-}II^6 \quad V^{7}_{5\natural} \quad I$$

If this alteration (lowered second degree) is applied to the dominant minor ninth without root, the chord sounds like the augmented six-five-three used as a primary dominant. (See Example 28–17.)

Example 28–18 shows the same kind of chord, but in the four-three position, which, like the ordinary $V^{\circ}_{4\,3}$, has a subdominant effect when it resolves to root-position I (compare Example 20–15). Here the chord sounds rather like a Neapolitan. In combination with the tonic pedal it gives the unusual result of A, B♭, and C♭, all sounding simultaneously (compare Example 27–21).

EXAMPLE 28–17: Schubert, *Schwanengesang*: No. 13,
            Der Doppelgänger

EXAMPLE 28–18: Beethoven, *Fidelio*, Act I, Finale (Prisoners'
            Chorus)

The Raised and Lowered Fifth

It may happen that the altered chord contains a factor which has been
both raised and lowered. Often this will be the fifth of a dominant triad
or dominant substitute, combining the effects of V with lowered fifth
and V with raised fifth.

EXAMPLE 28–19

V_4^6 I

In the example below, the altered chord is the pivot chord in an unexpected modulation from B♭ major to G major, in which the B♭ is reinterpreted as A♯. The expected resolution would be to IV⁶ in B♭ major.

EXAMPLE 28–20: Schumann, *Dichterliebe*, Op. 48: No. 12, *Am leuchtenden Sommermorgen*

Ziemlich langsam

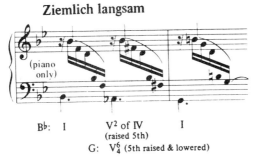

B♭:   I   V² of IV   I
                (raised 5th)
        G: V⁶₄ (5th raised & lowered)

The minor triad with raised and lowered fifth is enharmonically equivalent to a dominant seventh chord or to an augmented sixth chord, either of which would resolve irregularly. Its commonest use is as an altered tonic in a progression between I and II⁷ or V⁷ of V, a harmonic gesture that became popular in the nineteenth century.

EXAMPLE 28–21: Liszt, *Piano Concerto No. 2*

Adagio sostenuto assai

A: I   (5♯)   V⁷ of V   V⁹
               (F=E♯)

EXAMPLE 28–22: Brahms, *Piano Trio*, Op. 87, I

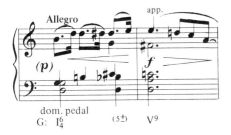

EXAMPLE 28–23: Nevin, *The Rosary*

The raised and lowered fifth may also occur in other functions, such as the supertonic. The notation in the following example indicates that the altered II might also be thought of as V[7] of III in minor, with irregular resolution.

EXAMPLE 28–24: Schubert, *Rosamunde*: Entr'acte No. 1

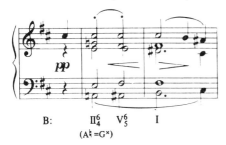

This description of an altered II offers a possible harmonic explanation for a favorite chromatic progression of the common-practice period called the *omnibus*. The succession *a* below is the commonest

EXAMPLE 28–25

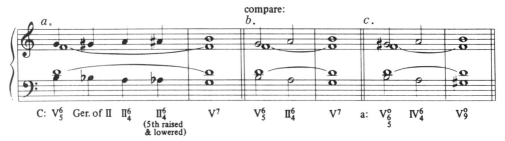

compare:

C: V⁶₅ Ger. of II II⁶₄   II⁶₄   V⁷   V⁶₅   II⁶₄   V⁷   a: V°₆   IV⁶₄   V°₉
                            (5th raised   ₅
                            & lowered)

form of the omnibus; it is also found with the soprano and bass lines inverted.

It is easy to see how the addition of chromatic passing tones to the contrary-motion voice exchange in progression *b* brings about the omnibus. Composers have traditionally avoided the doubly augmented octave (the A♯ and A♭ together in the first example above) in their notation of the omnibus, as the example below shows.

EXAMPLE 28–26: Schubert, *Sonata,* Op. 42, I

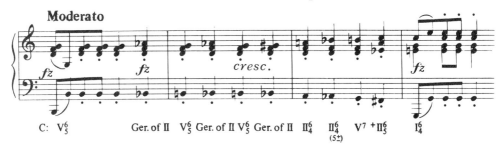

Moderato

fz   *fz*   *cresc.*   *fz*

C: V⁶₅   Ger. of II V⁶₅ Ger. of II V⁶₅ Ger. of II II⁶₄   II⁶₄   V⁷ ⁺II⁶₅   I⁶₄
                                                                  (5±)

The simplicity in the voice leading of the omnibus is in stark contrast to its cumbersome harmonic analysis. One can easily understand the second step of the progression as an augmented six-five-three of II, but the fourth step is more problematic. With the voice leading given, it is a supertonic six-four chord with raised and lowered fifth; considered enharmonically, with B♭ in the soprano and G♯ in the bass, it is an inversion of the augmented sixth chord, but resolving irregularly, the diminished tenth expanding to a major tenth. However it is notated, the progression is very unorthodox, perhaps not even comprehensible, when considered merely as a succession of roots and altered factors. But as the product of linear chromatic motion over sustained tones it is entirely transparent to the ear. The omnibus offers an excellent illustration of the power of clear and simple chromatic motion to generate harmonic relationships that are only tenuously associated within one diatonic scale, a phenomenon that is increasingly characteristic of the chromatic harmony of the later nineteenth century.

The five-step omnibus begins and ends with the same dominant seventh chord but in different positions, and can thus be called a prolongation of dominant harmony. The three-step sequential omnibus, on the other hand, is used as a modulating device. In this sequence, the successive dominant sevenths are enharmonically reinterpreted as the augmented sixth chords of the next key. The model below is given in strict (that is, not enharmonic) notation, a process which cannot be carried very far without encountering triple sharps.

EXAMPLE 28–27

Example 28–28, from a work on the borderline of common practice, carries the three-step omnibus through two cycles and into a third before breaking off; this is the farthest that a pedal can be sustained in the progression.

EXAMPLE 28–28: Mussorgsky, *Boris Godunov*, Act III, Scene I

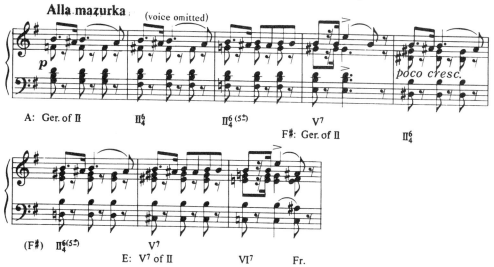

Many variants of the omnibus can be found which preserve the general pattern but depart from the strict chromatic motion.

EXAMPLE 28–29: Schubert, *Winterreise*, Op. 89: No. 20, *Der Wegweiser*

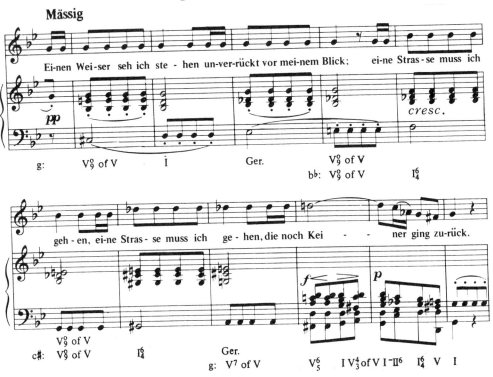

Appoggiatura Chords

It is customary to speak of a combination of appoggiature as an *appoggiatura chord*, and in Chapter 8 we learned about such diatonic appoggiatura chords as "five over one," in which an entire harmony is superposed over the root of another, in a position of rhythmic strength. Nevertheless, in chromatic harmony, appoggiatura chords typically include chords forming the weak part of a weak-to-strong progression, in which case the chord members could hardly be called appoggiature.

   The method of forming these chords consists of preceding some or all of the factors of a given chord, such as a triad or seventh chord, by tones a half step above or below, so that they resolve upward into the chord factors as leading tones or downward as chromatic appoggiature. There are many different possibilities that may result from this melodic process; a few characteristic examples are given here.

In the following example the first chord is an unusual form of IV⁷, with root and third raised and fifth omitted. Its function is readily understood when it is compared with the effect of the raised submediant seventh as an introductory chord to the dominant.

EXAMPLE 28–30: Brahms, *Intermezzo*, Op. 116, No. 6

When the subdominant triad appears with all its factors raised, leading to the dominant, it becomes a chord whose root is separated from the tonic by an augmented fourth, the farthest distance possible.

EXAMPLE 28–31: Liszt, *Sonata*

In the following example, the unaltered supertonic seventh chord of A major appears as a pivot in the key of A♭ major, where it is like the familiar raised supertonic seventh, but with the fifth and seventh also raised; in other words, it is a II⁷ with all of its factors raised. The unorthodox resolution of the two additional raised factors contributes to the tonal surprise of the progression.

EXAMPLE 28–32: Liszt, *A Faust Symphony*, II

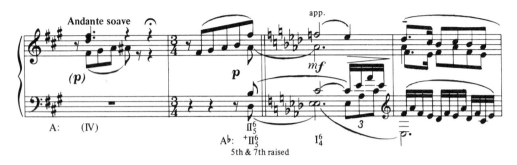

The following chord resembles VI[7] except for the presence of the subdominant E.

EXAMPLE 28–33: Franck, *Prelude, Chorale, and Fugue*

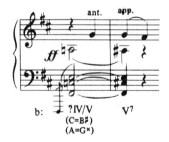

The next example is similar. The G♭ is incorrectly written for F♯, the raised submediant, while the F♭ is an appoggiatura to the seventh, not a lowered root.

EXAMPLE 28–34: Wagner, *Die Götterdämmerung*, Act I, Scene 2

Sehr gemässigt und etwas zögernd

In the next example we have a chord that might properly be called an appoggiatura chord because of its rhythm. It is questionable whether a weak-to-strong progression can be heard here, as the position of the barline suggests. The leading tone in both chords creates a dominant feeling throughout.

EXAMPLE 28–35: Brahms, *Capriccio*, Op. 76, No. 8

True appoggiatura chords are shown by asterisks in the following example. These chords have a perceptible harmonic effect, but a root analysis seems less appropriate than a melodic description. Melodically, the chords are made up of four half-step appoggiature to the factors of the dominant seventh chord; harmonically, the chords are augmented triads on the minor sixth degree, the third of the triad appearing simultaneously in both raised and unaltered form.

EXAMPLE 28–36: Mozart, *Symphony No. 40*, K. 550, I

The lowered tonic, C♮, in the submediant triad in the example below, imparts a dominant quality to the chord, since it sounds like a leading tone back to the C♯ in the succeeding harmony.

EXAMPLE 28–37: Franck, *Piano Quintet*, I

The examples just given by no means represent an exhaustive list of chromatic appoggiatura chords, but they will serve to indicate the circumstances in which such chords appear. The student should note down examples of similar chords discovered in music of the eighteenth and nineteenth centuries, taking special notice of those combinations that are used several times.

Characteristic Chromaticism

New chords are the result of harmonic and melodic, vertical and horizontal, influences. Harmonically, they arise from the desire for harmonic interest and variety by the creation of a sonority hitherto unheard, or by the use of an established form in an unaccustomed position in the tonality. Melodically, the altered tones forming the new chord are introduced as tendency tones imparting melodic direction and continuity.

These two aspects are not entirely separate. Some of the altered chords appear most often as the result of chromatic passing tones, appoggiature, or other nonharmonic tones. The altered factors in the raised supertonic, for example, usually arise in this way. Those vertical combinations that seem to have been brought about deliberately should be recognized as chords, their nonharmonic components notwithstanding. It will be recalled that this point of view was taken with respect to purely diatonic chords, beginning with the six-four chord and some seventh chords, as well as the more complex chromatic chords.

The development of a vocabulary of chromatic harmony is of course part of the history of the common-practice period; all the same, one becomes aware that, in the expanded chromatic harmony of the later nineteenth century, the formation of new chords becomes increasingly a matter of the individual composer's practice, or even of the idiosyncrasies of an individual work. The student should try to single out such individualities and relate them to common practice, insofar as this is possible. It will be apparent that harmonic analysis of such music becomes inseparable from questions of contrapuntal relationships, and indeed becomes involved in the relationships of tonality and form in different ways in different works. Some of this analysis will be discussed in Part Two of this book.

We will conclude this part of our study with three examples illustrating the community of a chromatic harmonic language over a century and a half of common practice. The characteristic differences between the three examples are more matters of texture and style than of harmony, and it is fair to say that in their harmony they are rather more like each other than they are different. All three examples show the use of more or less the same kinds of chords, the same kinds of nonharmonic tones, the same kinds of distant triadic relationships and tonicizations, and above all an elegance and economy of smooth connection from chord to chord, by means of common tones and stepwise relationships.

EXAMPLE 28–38: Bach, Chorale Partita, *O Gott, du frommer Gott*

EXAMPLE 28–39: Chopin, *Prelude*, Op. 28, No. 9

EXAMPLE 28–40: Wagner, *Tristan und Isolde*, Prelude

EXERCISES

1. Work out the following figured basses:

a.

b.

c.

d.

e. **Leicht bewegt**

2. *Road map.* Construct a musical sentence of three phrases according to the following specifications:

a. The first phrase modulates by means of a pivot chord which is a chromatically altered chord in both keys.

b. The second phrase contains a modulating sequence whose pattern includes a dominant seventh chord with lowered fifth. The phrase ends in a key not found in the first phrase.

c. The third phrase returns to the initial key by a pivot chord which is an augmented triad.

3. Harmonize the following unfigured basses, introducing chromatically altered chords:

a.

b.

c.

4. Harmonize the following melodies, introducing chromatically altered chords:

a.

b.

c.

II

After Common Practice

29

Harmonic Practice
Historically Considered

In the first part of this book we sought to define the common practice of composers over a period of about one and a half centuries, assuming arbitrarily that Bach, Mozart, Chopin, and Dvořák were contemporaries and that harmonic practice did not change, let alone evolve. While conceding these assumptions for their value in the study of harmonic practice, let us also concede that this book is not the place for a thorough historical consideration of harmony. A few general observations, nevertheless, will be useful before we take up the extremely varied developments of the last century.

At the time of J. S. Bach's first compositions (about 1703), twelve-tone equal temperament (see Appendix I) had not yet achieved wide acceptance. In the tuning systems then popular, music was ordinarily restricted to the simpler keys, that is, those having at most two or three flats or sharps in the key signature. Keys and chromatic tones further around the circle of fifths were too out of tune to be used effectively. Equal temperament did away with these limitations. By distributing the collective intonational defects of the circle of fifths evenly over the chromatic scale, equal temperament made every interval (except the octave) out of tune by an equal but tolerable amount. This meant that, for instance, the C♯-major triad or the C♭-major triad sounded no more out of tune than the C-major triad, and therefore composers were free to write in any key they wished. Bach himself promoted the general adoption of equal temperament by composing the two books of the

Well-Tempered Clavier (1722, 1744), each book containing a prelude and a fugue in each of the twelve major and the twelve minor keys.

*Review Chap. 14
(first section)*

Most of the composers of Bach's time and for some years thereafter nevertheless kept not only to the simpler keys but also to the simpler relationships among the keys. Tonal unity of their individual works would be best ensured by avoiding modulations remote from the main tonality and favoring the nearest keys instead—particularly dominant, subdominant, and relative major and minor. Part of this tonal limitation can be attributed to the relative brevity of individual pieces and movements; of equal importance was the preference of late Baroque composers for sectional musical forms (such as the concerto forms and dance forms) rather than narrative ones, and for contrapuntal forms (such as the fugue) rather than harmonic. With the subsequent emergence in the Classical period of the more homophonic forms, the close association of tonic–dominant and relative-minor–relative-major key relationships became part of the very basis of the sonata–allegro form, thus confirming the long-established preference for closely related keys.

Throughout this time there existed some notable exceptions to one or another of these tendencies. For example, the episodic form of the keyboard fantasia, where continuity of themes was not a concern, permitted a freer succession of keys. Thus Bach's *Fantasia in G minor for Organ* modulates as far afield as D♭ minor. (One may wonder how well this sounded on the nontempered organs of the time.) This work, as well as the opening section of Mozart's *Fantasia for Piano in C minor*, K. 475, which has a similarly wandering tonality, is comparable to the operatic recitative in not being formally tied to a closed phrase structure and in its essential freedom to move from chord to chord. Mozart's *G minor Symphony*, K. 550, is a good example of the extent to which one of the most innovative composers of the time was willing to explore the resources of chromatic modulation. The key relationships between the first and second themes of the sonata-form movements are according to the usual patterns, but the development sections show a tendency toward rapid and far-reaching modulation.

*See also Ex.
31–62*

We have already seen how the era of tonal counterpoint was able to justify on contrapuntal grounds the momentary vertical concurrence of practically any diatonic combination of four or five tones. The same could be said for a large number of possible chromatic combinations of tones that would hardly be conceivable as self-standing harmonies. The vocabulary of independent harmonies we have studied was basically

complete even in Bach's time, although, for instance, complete dominant ninths are uncommon and augmented sixth chords are quite rare.
The incidence of such usages at different times in the period of common
practice is just one of the complex questions that must be considered in
a historical study of harmony.

See Ex. 27–20

Another such question would be the differences between common
practice and individual practice. This question, let us repeat, is never
fully answered by the attempt to define common practice. Some generalizations are easy enough to make, but require a good deal of effort
to test analytically. For instance, one tends to think of Beethoven as
somewhat less interested in the expressive possibilities of chromatic
harmony than his predecessors, if only because one finds a number of
examples in Bach and Mozart that seldom have a counterpart in Beethoven. At the same time it is demonstrable that Beethoven habitually
used a wider range of keys in his developmental structures than any
composer before him; this is less a question of harmony than of tonality. Similarly, Schubert, who achieved few innovations in musical form
comparable to Beethoven's, nevertheless shows a remarkable degree of
harmonic originality, including a personal chromaticism that often goes
beyond Beethoven's. Some of Schubert's harmonic practices are, for
their time, so individualized that they are a distinguishing feature of his
music; not until Chopin do we have a composer so identifiable by his
harmonic language.

*E.g., Ex.
14–21*

Like Beethoven before him, but on a much larger scale, Wagner
achieved a revolution in musical form, and part of this revolution included
an extension of the very comprehensiveness of tonality as a structural
principle. Before Wagner, the tonal unity of even a multiple-movement
composition could be sensed as a background for the entire work, such
as C minor–C major in Beethoven's *Fifth Symphony*. Even in an opera
like Mozart's *Magic Flute*, which begins and ends in E♭ major, the individual numbers in a variety of keys represent stable tonal units, per-
ceivable as related, to one extent or another, to each other and to the
"main" tonality. But in Wagner's music-dramas the dimensions are so
large and the changes of key so numerous that the idea of a "main
tonality" becomes virtually meaningless. While it may be possible to
speak of *Die Meistersinger* as being "in C major" just because that is the
key in which the opera begins and ends and has some important epi-
sodes, the C-major tonality is more symbolic than actual. In the same
way D♭ major comes to symbolize Valhalla in Wagner's *Ring*, if only

*E.g., Ex.
26–15*

See Exx.
23–38, 27–18,
30–17

because of the association of the key with certain leitmotives and scenes and, at the end of *Die Götterdämmerung*, with the destruction of Valhalla.

From the harmonic standpoint Wagner's *Tristan und Isolde* is in every way the most remarkably innovative achievement of the last part of the common-practice period. Though when considered on a chord-to-chord basis the harmony of *Tristan* is no more radical than the chromatic explorations of Chopin, or even of Bach for that matter, the dimensions and continuity of the work carry the conceptions of tonality far beyond anything that had been realized before in closed, tonally self-limited symphonic forms. What was pointed to in *Tristan* at the time as "unending melody" might better be called "unending progression," in which the listener is led on a journey from one key to another for over four hours. Many points of tonal stability exist, but always only relatively; deceptive cadences, abrupt modulations, motivic chord progressions, and chromatic alterations are so ubiquitous that the listener is forced to accept them as the harmonic norm, abandoning any expectation that a particular key, defined by simple root progressions, will be established for more than a relatively short time. This radical approach to tonality, which in its day was considered destructive of the very idea of tonality, was at the heart of the psychological necessities of the drama, exactly as Wagner intended. What was not immediately understood was that Wagner accomplished it entirely within the resources of classical voice leading; other than the chromatic context, there is no essential difference between the counterpoint of *Tristan* and that of the C-major Prelude of Book I of Bach's *Well-Tempered Clavier*. The essentials of this counterpoint are contiguity, common tones, controlled motion, and restricted harmonic relationships.

The mature music of Debussy offers the severest contrast to Wagner's chromaticism, although that was one of its aesthetic influences. While it was influenced also to some extent by his somewhat older countrymen, such as Franck, Lalo, Fauré, and Chabrier, Debussy's style is essentially original, the originality residing in its anticlassical approach to harmony, counterpoint, and form. Parallel motion of perfect fifths, triads, seventh chords, and ninth chords, in any succession, in any position, and to any degree of the chromatic scale, is a fundamental characteristic. So is the use of all manner of scales, including major, minor, chromatic, modal, pentatonic, and artificial, as well as the whole-tone scale (whose use in Debussy's music, though abundant, has been overemphasized by many writers). In his later works Debussy added quartal, quintal, and polychordal sonorities to his vocabulary. Debussy's distinctive harmonic language was a conscious attempt to do away with what he perceived as the restrictively systematic relationships of classical tonality, and as such was as genuinely revolutionary as anything in the history of music. At the same time it succeeded, in ways that are difficult to define, in creating an idiosyncratic tonal logic that depends not on counterpoint or ordinary root relationships (the V–I relationship, for instance, appears only infrequently) but on maintenance of tone-centers, nonclassical "tonics," and an essentially diatonic, triadic background.

At about the same time that Debussy was using his carefully controlled nonsystematic tonal language to create a new and essentially French musical aesthetic, Wagner's successors in Austria and Germany were continuing to explore the world that *Tristan und Isolde* had opened up for them. The more adventurous of these probed into chromatic counterpoint of ever-increasing complexity, in which the harmonic element, at least in the classical sense, was progressively attenuated until, in the works of Schoenberg, Berg, and Webern, beginning about 1907–08, tonality disappeared altogether. Remaining in its place was a dense, nontriadic chromaticism regulated by various abstract means, which were usually intrinsically bound up with the autonomous structures of the individual works. Eventually a principle called serialism emerged, which was based on the composer's precompositional definition of certain different pitches to be projected in a stated intervallic succession. Schoenberg's invention, in the early 1920s, of what came to be called the twelve-tone system, was an application of the serial principle to the twelve different pitch-classes of the chromatic scale, which would be ordered by the composer in a certain way, the entire composition then being referable to the initial ordering, subject to certain conditions and defined states. The twelve-tone system, as its best practitioners demonstrated, allowed for a remarkable degree of compositional freedom and clearly was a convincing way of regulating atonality; it has been immensely influential in the music of the last half-century.

While the revolution in chromatic harmony initiated by *Tristan und Isolde* represented one pole of the development of Austro-German music after Wagner, another pole was destined to serve as an international restorative force in twentieth-century tonality. This was the aesthetic movement that came to be called neoclassicism, which drew its inspiration from the masters of the eighteenth century. As early as the middle of the nineteenth century we find composers like Brahms and Saint-

Saëns reacting against what they regarded as the excessive tendencies
of Wagner in general and the Wagnerian music-drama in particular, in
favor of "absolute" music, classical forms and contrapuntal devices,
and restrained chromaticism. Wagner himself contributed to the movement with *Die Meistersinger*, which in keeping with its historical subject
is much more diatonic and classically contrapuntal than his other mature
operas. Nevertheless, as a genuinely forceful trend in music, neoclassicism did not begin to flourish until the third decade of the twentieth
century, when an entire generation of composers, led by Ravel, Stravinsky, Hindemith, and Prokofiev, wrote an impressive body of works
that projected a new kind of diatonic tonality. (Oddly enough there
was also at this time an atonal neoclassicism, led by Schoenberg; this is
just one aspect that makes neoclassicism a complex historical phenomenon.)

Even if it is roughly true, it is an oversimplification to say that
diatonicism and chromaticism, or tonality and atonality for that matter,
represent the broad categories of twentieth-century harmony. Neither
in theory nor in practice does such a division account for the abundance
of harmony wherein the two domains merge, and we have already seen
numerous instances in eighteenth- and nineteenth-century music where
diatonic harmony is colored or elaborated by chromaticism. Nor does
the categorization give much idea of the tremendous variety, both possible and actual, of diatonic and chromatic harmony.

For it becomes obvious at once that the evolution of harmony after
Wagner is unparalleled in its richness, in its wealth of new discoveries,
and in the variety of individual practices. The period ending about 1914
was particularly fruitful in these respects. At the same time, all this
harvest of originality has posed a problem for theorists and historians
of music because of the increased complexity of tonality and formal
structure that it embodies. The decline of nineteenth-century common
practice was not followed by a twentieth-century one, nor even by
several, but by more like dozens of practices which could be said to
have some kind of acceptance at one time or another, and which in
many cases overlapped.

In the remainder of this book we shall concern ourselves with aspects
of post–common-practice harmony that can in some ways be accounted
for, analyzed, or described. What follows this chapter should not be
thought of as more than a relatively small part of the harmonic cosmos
after common practice. Rather, it should serve as an introduction to
just a few of the many ways by which the student may begin to be

familiar with the many modes of compositional thought that have marked the past century. As has been noted before, theory does not precede practice but follows it, and is never complete; if it were, presumably we would have a consistent theory of twentieth-century music as well as of earlier music. You will find ample opportunity, in examining the examples that follow, to find alternative explanations and interpretations, with the reassurance that, on many of the questions posed here, no substantial agreement has been achieved today even by the most accomplished analysts.

Exercises are not given for these chapters. The standard exercises in harmonization and figured bass, of use in common-practice training, do not lend themselves to complex diatonic or chromatic harmony. Most of your work on these chapters will consist of analysis of the examples and comparison with such other relevant excerpts as you can find in the literature. Nevertheless, you will find it instructive to compose phrases or short pieces incorporating some of the harmonic types described, and to test the range of possibilities inherent in some of the systematic procedures shown.

30

Extensions of Common Practice

No simple dividing line separates common-practice harmony from what came after it. The individualities of the common-practice composers reveal numerous instances of uncommon practice, in some cases fore-runners of much later kinds of harmony; these exceptions, seen in increasing numbers in the later part of the period, are found to be extensions or extremes of established procedures more often than direct contradictions. Some composers, like Mussorgsky, Fauré, and Mahler, can be said to have begun in common practice and gradually developed away from it; others, like Debussy and Schoenberg, gained this libera-tion more quickly and completely, in both cases achieving a new kind of harmonic language whose ties to the past are nevertheless apparent. And indeed, many features of common practice persist in some way even in much of the music of the present day.

One of the striking features of the period extending approximately from 1880 to 1920 is the way common practice gave way to individual practice, at first gradually and later more rapidly. Even composers who were close contemporaries came increasingly to develop styles that were characterized in large part by individualities of harmony. Fauré's har-mony, for example, often does not resemble Chabrier's; Mahler's har-mony is significantly different from Richard Strauss's. On examination, the works of even two such popularly associated composers as Debussy and Ravel are seen to be clearly distinct in their harmonic languages, despite many aspects common to both.

In some ways it is possible to argue convincingly that the forty-year period that supplies most of the examples in this and the following chapters represents the climax of the "harmonic period," for it certainly includes the most music wherein composers seem to have been interested in the expressive qualities of individual harmonies chosen for their own characteristic sound, that is, kept relatively free from contrapuntal considerations. With the revitalization of counterpoint in neoclassical tonality after the First World War, that tendency markedly declined. This does not mean that the new counterpoint was in itself any less harmonic, but it does mean that the era of new discoveries in harmony had by then essentially passed. This fact of history will necessitate one more limitation on our study. Much of the music of this century—as indeed of previous centuries—is less meaningfully analyzed as harmony than as counterpoint, and in laying a groundwork for twentieth-century harmonic analysis we do not wish to go beyond the announced scope of this book.

The purpose of this chapter will be to describe the early manifestations of the new tendencies and to relate them in various ways to each other and to the common background from which they arose. For when all is said and done, even the most radical of the harmonic discoveries after common practice appear to be an evolutionary result of the past.

Modal Scales and Modal Harmony

The use of modal scales is a convenient subject with which to begin our departure, because it represents a tendency, even though only an occasional one, that persisted through the common-practice period. The church modes, a legacy from pretonal music, can be viewed in common practice as variants of the major–minor system, having different harmonic effects in their application. Thus the Dorian and Phrygian modes, with minor third degree, yield a minor tonic triad, and so should be regarded as essentially minor in sound, whereas the Lydian and Mixolydian, with major third degree, are essentially major for the same reason. The Dorian and Mixolydian modes form a minor dominant triad, whereas the Phrygian mode, with lowered second degree, produces a diminished triad on the dominant. From the standpoint of the major–minor system the effect of all these modal scales is to weaken the perception of the classical tonic.

The deliberate use in the common-practice period of modal scales, or at least of some of their distinguishing features, seems to have reflected

Review beginning of Chap. 5

composers' desires to increase harmonic possibilities on the one hand, and, on the other, to provide a certain feeling of archaic style, especially in religious music. The Bach fughetta furnishing the example below, based on a sixteenth-century Mixolydian chorale melody, could be said to be in G major with a Mixolydian flavor. The F♯ leading tone, absent from the key signature, is worked into the harmony at some points and replaced by F♮ at others. The final measures emphasize G by repetition of the tonic note; at the same time, subdominant harmony is stressed by the presence of F♮ as the seventh of V[7] of IV. The final cadence

Cf. Ex. 21–15   ingeniously partakes of both tonal regions; the leading tone rises to G as in V–I, while the C and E♭ in the bass proceed as in IV–I.

EXAMPLE 30–1: Bach, Fughetta on *Dies sind die heil'gen zehn Gebot'*

G: I   IV V[7] I   V[7]   I (V of IV)   IV   II   I (V of IV)   IV   V°[3 / 4] I
(tonic pedal)   (V/IV)

The "Dankgesang" movement of Beethoven's *String Quartet*, Op. 132, pointedly labeled "in the Lydian mode," is perhaps the most famous example in the common-practice period of a systematic attempt to employ a modal scale. In that piece, as well as in the example below by Chopin, tonal functions are often obscure; it is hard to say where the tonic is. Strong dominant-to-tonic relationships occur seldom, and when present are interfered with by the increased emphasis on root-position modal-degree triads, the latter occurring without preceding secondary dominants. The modal feeling is increased by the avoidance of the leading tone relationship in the dominant of A minor, which would introduce an accidental. The Chopin example is drawn from the first section of the work, where fifty-six measures appear consecutively without a single accidental.

EXAMPLE 30–2: Chopin, *Mazurka*, Op. 24, No. 2

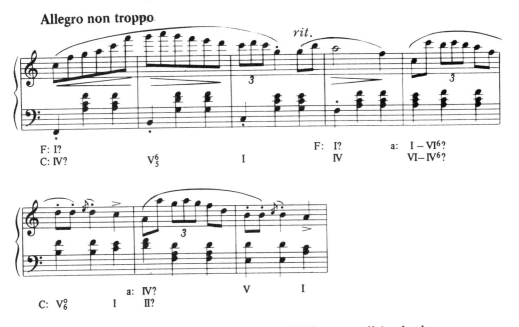

The increasing prevalence of such "modal harmony" in the later nineteenth century can be traced to the use of modal scales in folk music, which had a wide influence on the so-called nationalist composers. The tendency was perhaps greatest in eastern Europe, most notably among the Russian composers, whose often starkly chordal homophonic styles reflect the influence of the a cappella choirs of the Orthodox Church. In the example below, a pentatonic melody is accompanied by chords that first stress VI, V, and III, and only then turn toward the tonic; the V of V abruptly following suggests a touch of Lydian mode.

Review Chap. 23: Neighbor-Note Harmony

EXAMPLE 30–3: Mussorgsky, *Pictures at an Exhibition*, Promenade

The familiar March from Tchaikovsky's *Nutcracker* begins and ends on the G-major triad, but contains numerous references to E minor throughout. Several phrases end on either the E-minor triad or the E-minor half cadence; the entire middle section is based on an E pedal. Like Chopin's *Scherzo*, Op. 31, and a number of other works in the nineteenth century, this March seems to merge relative major and minor into a tonality that is simultaneously single and dual.

EXAMPLE 30–4: Tchaikovsky, *The Nutcracker*, March

The following example illustrates a typical use of the Aeolian mode, that is, the natural minor, without the leading tone:

EXAMPLE 30–5: Borodin, *Symphony No. 3*, I

In the example below, the use of differently inflected modal degrees is entirely harmonic and coloristic; because of the changing third degree, the passage projects an alternating quasi-minor and quasi-major, with no single modality prevailing.

EXAMPLE 30–6: Balakirev, *Symphony No. 1*, II

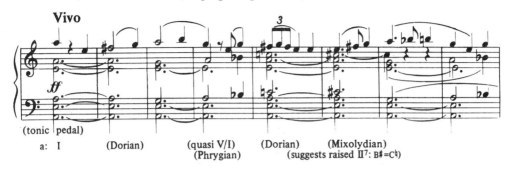

The following example of Lydian mode sounds like an alternation between I and V of V, irregularly resolving:

EXAMPLE 30–7: Mussorgsky, *Boris Godunov*, Act III, Polonaise

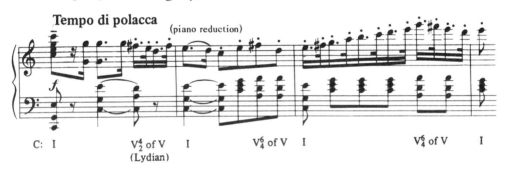

The following examples incorporating the minor seventh degree show different ways of circumventing dominant harmony:

EXAMPLE 30–8: Berlioz, *Requiem*: No. 2, *Dies irae*

EXAMPLE 30–9: Dvořák, *Symphony No. 9* ("From the New
World"), IV

Cf. Ex. 30–4

The Phrygian mode, as used in the opening measures of Debussy's
String Quartet, projects a feeling of E♭ major that is offset only by the
repetition of the G-minor triad and by the use of the leading tone at the
end of the second measure. Later in the movement Debussy changes
the harmonization of the melody so as to emphasize an actual E♭ major.

EXAMPLE 30–10: Debussy, *String Quartet*, I

As the examples given here demonstrate in various ways, the most
important determinant of modal perception is the extent to which a
strong tonic is felt, for if the tonic is made clear by reiteration, all the
modal functions will relate to it even if they weaken it in the classical
sense. More comprehensive examples can be found, of course, particularly in twentieth-century popular music, where systematic use of a
single mode within a simple repetitive harmonic scheme is a common
procedure.

The Decline of Dominant Harmony

It was stated earlier (Chapter 16) that the common-practice era was marked by a definite preference for dominant harmony over nondominant harmony, and we have already seen many examples of how this preference was projected. Tonicizing chords, such as secondary dominants progressing to their respective tonics, and including diminished seventh chords and the various chromatically altered chords that are either secondary dominants themselves or point to dominants, form the most significant general category of chord functions in common practice. *Review also Chap. 23*

Though the period after common practice did not dispense with dominant harmony, even introducing more complex forms not previously employed, it must be acknowledged that a number of composers sought and achieved ways of weakening the dominant effect, even to the point of extinction. In part this can be accounted for by the resurgence of interest in modal harmony, in which triads on modal degrees were used more frequently and prominently. A natural concomitant of this was the appearance of the cadential minor dominant resolving to either a major or a minor tonic. (See Examples 30–11, 12, and 13.)

EXAMPLE 30–11: Grieg, *Piano Concerto*, III

Poco più tranquillo (Allegro marcato)

F: I   V⁷(min.)   (V⁹)   I

EXAMPLE 30–12: Chabrier, Overture to *Gwendoline*

Allegro con fuoco

c: V⁷ of V   I⁶   IV(II)⁶₅ V(min.)   I

EXAMPLE 30–13: Ravel, *Menuet antique*

These examples differ from common practice only by their substitution of the minor seventh degree for the leading tone.

The anticlassicism of Debussy included, as forcefully as anything else, an avoidance of dominant-to-tonic progressions everywhere in the phrase. His works furnish the most consistent and abundant examples of evasion of the dominant in its most traditionally dependable usage, the final cadence.

EXAMPLE 30–14: Debussy, *Suite bergamasque*: No. 3, *Clair de lune*

Debussy's final cadences range over a variety of types during the course of his development. In the early works dominant chords in other than root position or with nonharmonic tones may precede the final tonic; in the later works even the final tonic sonority may contain unresolved dissonances. It is not that V–I relationships cannot be found in Debussy, but they are rarely found unmixed with extra factors, and in any event they are relatively infrequent.

The following example, from the final measures of the movement, shows a dominant seventh with unresolved chromatic appoggiatura (the C in the third measure) reinterpreted enharmonically as the dominant seventh of a tritone-related key. The root of V^7 in $C^\flat$ major is the lowered fifth of V^7 in F major, and the raised fourth above the root of the V^7 in $C^\flat$ is the root of the V^7 in F. This progression illustrates a harmonic substitution often used in jazz.

Cf. Ex. 31–69

EXAMPLE 30–15: Debussy, *Sonata for Flute, Viola, and Harp*, II

Remote Tonal Relationships

Music of the eighteenth and early nineteenth centuries is rich in examples of harmonic successions between distantly related triads and modulations between distantly related keys. These are accomplished by a variety of well-established and coherent means, such as pivot tones, enharmonic relationships, chromatically altered chords, and modal mixture or mode change, as well as by unorthodox types of dissonance preparation and resolution. The use of such means does not ordinarily result in more than a momentary weakening of tonality—which may indeed be the effect desired by the composer—because the context of the remote tonal relationship is ordinarily a well-established key both before and after. It was only when these means were applied continuously, frequently, and in combination, with the result of straining the sense of tonal predictability, that common practice was exceeded.

EXAMPLE 30–16: Fauré, *Nocturne No. 6, Op. 63*

A: I   IV⁷   IV/V(V¹¹)   I(V⁷ of IV)   V⁷ of IV
                                Db: Ger.(V of V)   V⁴₃ of V   V⁷ ⁽¹³⁾

(Db:) V⁷/I   I

The example above contains few, if any, instances of harmonic progression or dissonance treatment that considered separately could not be found widely in common practice, but the phrase when considered as a whole constitutes a chain of events that would hardly be likely to occur before Fauré. The irregular voice leading in the resolution of the dominant eleventh, the ambiguity of I and V⁷ of IV, the enharmonic reinterpretation of the V⁷ of IV as an augmented sixth chord, the interpolation of an unaltered V of V between the augmented sixth and its resolution, and the presence of an unresolved thirteenth in the resolution itself—these all add up to a distinctive succession, an example of the individuality of Fauré's style. It is worth noting that the passage contains only a single chromatic alteration (the augmented sixth chord) and a single chromatic motion (the resolution of V of V to V).

The following excerpt from Wagner's *Tristan und Isolde* illustrates the continuous chromatic modulation for which the opera is famous. It shows how the principle of contiguity operates to bring about the association of remote keys by contrapuntal means. Nearly every harmony in the passage has at least one tone in common with the preceding or following harmony; most of the tones that move in succession move stepwise. The reduction shows this more clearly than does the example itself. An S-shaped curve is used to show the connection where an octave change is involved. The harmonically stronger triadic formations are indicated by white notes; except for the G-major triad, the only triad in the excerpt that is preceded by a strong dominant, they are related by the interval of a minor third (triads beamed together). The motivic sequential progression, I–V–III, involves a mode change between V and III.

EXAMPLE 30–17: Wagner, *Tristan und Isolde*, Act II, Scene 2

REDUCTION, omitting doublings and some nonharmonic tones.

   The example shows that even the most remote harmonic relationships, in an advanced chromatic idiom, can result from the smooth connection of melodic lines, even under the elementary contrapuntal restrictions of suspension and stepwise motion, and can be fully comprehended as harmonic progressions. The chromaticism of the post-Wagnerian composers is often seen to proceed just as smoothly, though the root motions may be only tenuously related from chord to chord or from cadence to cadence.

Examine the complete score and find the Db-major passage earlier in the movement

The passage by Berlioz given below, composed in 1830, may be cited as an example of freakishly uncommon practice, deliberately written for its grotesque effect. From the standpoint of common practice, the root relationships are so remote as to have no apparent connection. The noncontiguous harmony may indeed be unique for its time, but before the end of the nineteenth century such progressions came to be heard frequently, and within a few years (see the Satie example following) were commonplace.

EXAMPLE 30–18: Berlioz, *Symphonie fantastique*: IV, *March to the Scaffold*

EXAMPLE 30–19: Satie, *Three Pieces in the Shape of a Pear*, No. 7

The Reevaluation of Counterpoint

Contrapuntal technique in the nineteenth century can be described as embodying the following general principles:

a. smooth connection of harmonies;
b. regulation of parts, even in the most complex figurations and textures, by elementary voice leading, and by the characteristics of nonharmonic tones;
c. avoidance of prohibited motions.

The explanation and elaboration of these principles have already been a major concern of this book. We will now examine the ways in which music after common practice set new values on these principles and departed from them.

The traditionally prohibited parallel motions were the first to be set free, to be employed as a resource in new kinds of harmony. We have already seen some examples of parallel perfect fifths in common practice that can be explained in various ways, such as those resulting from the combination of nonharmonic tones, from the resolution of the German sixth chord, or even sometimes from inadvertence or extramusical reasons. *Review Chap. 19*

An example like the following probably cannot be attributed to any such causes. The fifths in the first measure are part of a smooth motion from a tonic triad with doubled third. Certainly the fifths are not overlooked as fifths by the discerning ear, but the listener should think of them as a manifestation of a self-consistent style, not as a flaw in common-practice harmony. *Cf. Ex. 19–19*

EXAMPLE 30–20: Fauré, *Pelléas et Mélisande, Prelude*

G: I (VI⁶)(IV⁶)V   II(VII⁶₃)VI

The following is an example of what may be considered as doubling fifths. The texture of the piano accompaniment is really that of an upper melody with collateral part in thirds, and a bass with collateral part in fifths, the two elements combining to form four-part harmony. Parallel fifths of this kind become increasingly common in the works of the post-Wagnerian composers.

See also Ex.
10–19

EXAMPLE 30–21: Wolf, *Spanish Song Book*: No. 3, *Nun wandre, Maria*

Doubling an upper melody in fifths is a coloristic device of impressionist harmony. Instances like the following abound in the works of Debussy, Ravel, and later composers.

EXAMPLE 30–22: Debussy, *La Mer*, I

The systematic application of parallel fifths will also be considered later in the discussions of independent sonorities, parallel harmony, and quintal harmony.

The following is an extreme instance of parallel dissonant intervals, resulting from the addition of a countermelody to a minor-mode version of the well-known round *Frère Jacques*. The passage occurs in a funeral march, which contains a number of such deliberately grotesque gestures.

EXAMPLE 30–23: Mahler, *Symphony No. 1*, III

The counterpoint of the following example is anything but smoothly connected.

EXAMPLE 30–24: Mahler, *Symphony No. 4*, I

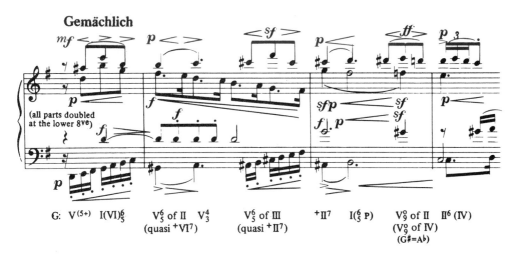

The two upper melodies and the bass line are all variants of themes that have already been extensively developed earlier in the movement in many versions; thus in part it is the hearer's recognition of themes

that supports the counterpoint. Nevertheless, the note-to-note connections in the melodic lines, with so many wide leaps, multiple appoggiature and reaching tones, and irregular resolutions, make it difficult for
the ear to form a harmonic connection between them. Only on repeated
hearing does it become clear that the passage is a complex elaboration
of the following melodic progression, in which all the chromatic tones
are passing tones.

EXAMPLE 30–25

The harmony, and the underlying melodic motion, are certainly
typical of common practice, but this is hardly true of the counterpoint.

The Independent Vertical Sonority

A piece of tonal music presupposes a context of selected keys, and a
beginning and ending with continuity in between. The continuity is
maintained by melodic and harmonic progression, which is always
present, whether the progression is smooth or abrupt. Thus in one sense
there can be no vertical arrangement of tones completely independent
of a context. We will nevertheless use the term *independent vertical sonority* to indicate a harmony whose origin and resolution are mostly,
even if not completely, independent from voice-leading considerations.

We have already seen a hierarchy of chordal types, beginning with
the dominant seventh, whose dissonant factors may arise without preparation. Some of these chords, such as ninth chords, may have their
dissonant factors resolved internally by arpeggiation, and a few examples may be found in common practice in which such dissonances have
no apparent resolution. There are also many instances of chords
"resolving" by parallel chromatic motion over a distance, as in the case
of the sequential diminished seventh chord, where in most cases the
resolution is postponed until after the last chord of the succession. Other
complex sonorities have been treated similarly:

EXAMPLE 30–26: Wagner, *Die Götterdämmerung*, Act III, Scene 2

The passage above, occurring after an uncomplicated authentic cadence in C major, initiates a complex series of chromatic modulations that eventually returns to C. The pedal point provides a tonal anchor without which the tonality would be momentarily suspended. *Cf. Ex. 23–39*

Chromatic succession of root-position chords in parallel motion is a characteristic invention of the end of the common-practice period. *Cf. Ex. 27–16*

EXAMPLE 30–27: Fauré, *Impromptu No. 2*, Op. 31

This example could be explained as a modulating sequence of augmented sixth chords, but it is not really heard that way. It is rather a dominant seventh moving as one line up the chromatic scale, not only against the tendency of the natural resolution of the seventh but with parallel motion of root and fifth; the figuration helps to conceal the parallel motion. The chromatic scale serves as a regulating influence on parallel motion of this sort, even permitting, as we saw in Chapter 27, the chromatic resolution of parallel fifths in the augmented sixth chord. *For a horrible example, see Ex. 19–17*

The next departure was to allow dissonant chords to move diatonically in parallel motion.

EXAMPLE 30–28: Debussy, *Nocturnes*: I, *Nuages*

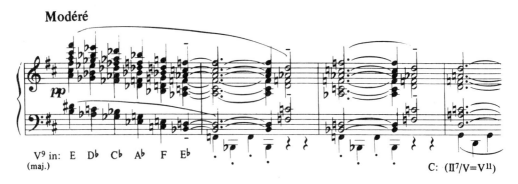

This is a typical example of parallel writing in block chords, a type that will be discussed more thoroughly in the next chapter. What is notable about it in the context of the present discussion is that all the chords are independent dominant major ninths. The sevenths and ninths move along with their supporting triads, but do not resolve. The chords have the dominant-ninth structure, but they are not dominants that refer to actual tonics in the music. They are purely chordal, their dissonant factors being treated as though they were consonant.

EXAMPLE 30–29: Debussy, *Fantasy for Piano and Orchestra*, I

EXAMPLE 30–30: Mahler, *Das Lied von der Erde*, VI

Another quasi-consonant sonority is the triad with added sixth, which had already achieved some degree of independence in common practice but was later much more widely and freely used. Examples 30–29 and 30 on the facing page show the tonic triad with added sixth used at the beginning of one work and at the end of another.

Students of jazz techniques will recognize that an entire harmonic vocabulary based on the complete set of added–sixth chords and non-dominant sevenths and ninths exists in that art, indeed defining the normative chordal states in a harmony where pure triads are rare. Examples such as those shown here illustrate the ancestry of such harmony.

The chordal types shown thus far have been cited as harmonies established in common practice which came to have an independent existence later. More complex independent sonorities include chords with various kinds of unresolved nonharmonic tones, to be discussed in the next chapter.

New Definitions of Tonality

Tonality without effective dominant relationships is difficult to envision in common-practice terms. Strongly modal harmonic relationships, in contexts that avoid the V–I relationship, tend to weaken the tonic and to bring about a fluctuating sense of relative-major–relative-minor mixture, as we have seen even in common-practice instances. Whatever confusion this may cause for the harmonic analyst, it is clear that the unsettled tonality of such music was not looked on as a drawback by its practitioners. But even in the period after common practice, the evidence indicates that in many cases composers were intent on preserving the feeling of some kind of tonal center, a point of harmonic gravitation fully comparable to the classical tonic but defined by a non-classical array of harmonic conditions.

The most important means of defining a tonal center, in the absence of a preceding dominant, became and remained the solitary tonic element in itself, asserted vigorously or subtly but always definitely, whether as a triad or as a single pitch used somewhat like a pedal point, or even as a dissonant element in a chord.

The well-known passage quoted in Example 30–31 illustrates the establishment of the tonic C through nondominant means. The two harmonies are related enharmonically as V^7 of D♭ and V^7 of G, with C

EXAMPLE 30–31: Mussorgsky, *Boris Godunov*: Prologue, Scene 2

Cf. Ex. 28–31

and F♯ (G♭) as common tones, but the tonic triads of D♭ major and G major do not appear anywhere in the constant oscillation of the two dominants, which continues beyond the excerpt for thirty more measures without harmonic change. In the classical sense the two dominants are independent sonorities, but they nevertheless reinforce the common tone C as a nonclassical tonic. (F♯–G♭ is also a common tone but C is stressed as a pedal much more strongly.)

The following example shows the first sixteen measures of a remarkable pedal-point passage:

EXAMPLE 30–32: Debussy, *Nocturnes*: II, *Fêtes*

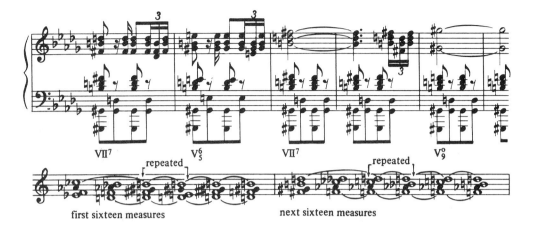

VII⁷   V⁶₅   VII⁷   V°₉

first sixteen measures   next sixteen measures

The A♭–G♯ pedal remains in the bass throughout. In the initial harmony it is the root of a triad with added major sixth; the avoidance of the leading tone in the first four measures gives the melodic parts a touch of Dorian harmony. The next four measures have the A♭ pedal as the seventh of an independent secondary dominant sonority. Then comes an alternation of what could be called a VII⁷–V relation in A major, or a II–V, over the G♯ pedal which is the quasi-root of a half-diminished seventh chord; this yields at the end of the phrase to a diminished seventh on G♯. The reduction of the entire thirty-two-measure succession, given below the excerpt, shows clearly the considerable amount of common-tone association and contiguity between the successive chords; next to the A♭–G♯ pedal itself, the strongest contributor to the tonal centricity of the A♭ minor triad is the C♭–B. Not a single functional dominant is present. The entire passage is characteristic of Debussy's quite original approach to tonal organization of larger contexts.

The first of Debussy's *Nocturnes*, *Nuages*, shows if anything a more radical tonal outlook, and the student would find it a profitable exercise to analyze the entire piece. Part of the tonal organization depends on Debussy's use of a special scale, discussed in the next chapter, which has a diminished tonic triad on B and no functional dominant. Through subtle reiteration of the B and its companion F♮, Debussy defines and accumulates special harmonic regions related through one or the other of these tones, ultimately leaving only the single note B to define a tone center at the end (see Example 31–12). The following example shows the beginning of the piece:

EXAMPLE 30–33: Debussy, *Nocturnes*: I, *Nuages*

Another means of defining a tone center is illustrated by the following example, which seems to project G (Mixolydian) major and A (natural) minor simultaneously, or at least interchangeably. The ostinato bass is more oriented towards G than A, the A seeming like a neighbor note to the G. On the other hand, the upper parts gravitate toward the pedal A, which is also the goal note of the first melodic phrase. The situation shown here may be compared with the uncertain tonal center

EXAMPLE 30–34: Stravinsky, *l'Histoire du soldat*, Music to Scene I

of the Chopin example shown earlier (Example 30–2); on the other hand it is also comparable to bitonality, which will be discussed in the next chapter.

More complicated questions of tonality in the twentieth century will be discussed in Chapter 32.

31

Scalar and Chordal Types

The Pentatonic Scale

The pentatonic scale, whose intervallic pattern corresponds to that of the black keys on the piano, is very ancient, having been used in the music of Oriental cultures perhaps longer even than the diatonic scale in the West.

EXAMPLE 31–1

It is also the scale used in many European folksongs, particularly those of the British Isles.

Cf. the major tonic triad with added sixth (Chap. 23)

Because the pentatonic scale corresponds to only five of the seven major-scale degrees, it is sometimes called a *gapped scale*. Only two triads are possible, corresponding to relative major and minor, and with no leading tone or indeed any semitone, the perception of any kind of dominant harmony is doubtful. Many pentatonic folk melodies, heard without accompaniment, seem to suggest an ambiguous tonal center, which may be relative major at one moment and relative minor the next.

See Ex. 10–18

Chopin's *Etude* for piano in G♭ major, Op. 10, No. 5, popularly called the "Black Key" Etude, uses only the black keys in the right hand. The left hand, however, uses a number of white keys to complete the diatonic harmony. Thus this piece does have a normal diatonic basis, even though at times it suggests harmony made up entirely of pentatonic degrees. Debussy's *Pagodes* is a good deal closer to an example of "pure" pentatonic writing, even though parts of the piece show many departures from the scale.

EXAMPLE 31–2: Debussy, *Estampes*: I, *Pagodes*

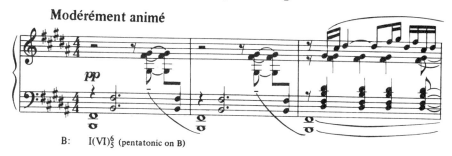

In the following example a pentatonic melody is harmonized with one triad at first, then with a fuller harmony using B♮ and E♯, the degrees which with the pentatonic scale would complete the natural minor scale on D♯. The B♯ on the cadencing chord adds a further change of modal color.

EXAMPLE 31–3: Debussy, *Nocturnes*: I, *Nuages*

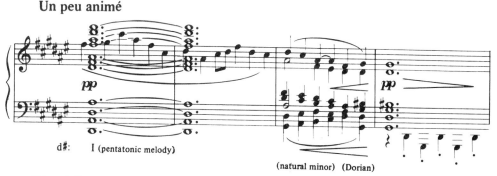

The following example is based exclusively on the E pentatonic scale, but it sounds characteristically diatonic. The second degree, F♯, appears as a passing tone between E and G♯; only the sixth degree dangles slightly, though it seems to be associated with the tonic triad like an added sixth. The passage, from one of Debussy's early works, is a good illustration of a subtle, rather than a radical, departure from common practice.

EXAMPLE 31–4: Debussy, *Arabesque No. 1*

Melodies using the pentatonic scale are found in many twentieth-century works in all types of harmonic contexts, from purely pentatonic to densely chromatic. Often the use has a programmatic significance, such as a connection with Oriental subjects (Ravel, *Mother Goose Suite*, No. 3; Stravinsky, *The Nightingale*; Bartók, *The Miraculous Mandarin*; Mahler, *Das Lied von der Erde*, No. 3).

The Whole-Tone Scale

As was mentioned before (Chapter 28), the six-note whole-tone scale is a symmetrical partitioning of the chromatic scale.

EXAMPLE 31–5

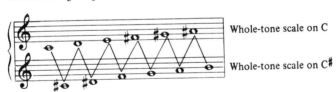

In this scale all triads are augmented and no intervals except the octave are perfect. All thirds are major or diminished, sixths are minor or augmented, seconds are major, sevenths are minor, fourths and fifths are augmented or diminished, all of these irrespective of enharmonic notation.

The whole-tone scale is occasionally seen in the common-practice period, though never as an independent generator of harmony. Mozart used it for deliberately disruptive purposes in his *Musical Joke*, K. 522. At other times it appears as a companion to the chromatic scale, as in the bass line of the following example.

EXAMPLE 31–6: Chopin, *Prelude*, Op. 28, No. 19

The harmony in the passage above, like most instances of consecutive diminished sevenths, suspends the tonality between the triads surrounding it, and can be regarded as a harmonic, though not triadic, thickening of the chromatic scale. A similar situation is found in the example below. All four parts move chromatically in two opposing layers, each vertical cross-section coinciding with the whole-tone scale.

EXAMPLE 31–7: Schoenberg, *String Quartet*, Op. 7

The pairing of chromatic and whole-tone scales here should be compared with the opening of Liszt's *Faust Symphony* (Example 28–13).

Debussy's use of the whole-tone scale is just one of many distinctive aspects of his style. In the earlier works it appears in augmented triads harmonizing the chromatic scale, as in the Schoenberg example above, or sometimes as an incidental detail in prevailing diatonic harmony, growing out of the dominant seventh with raised fifth, or the augmented six-four-three, as in Example 31–8.

The use of the suspended third degree and the irregular resolution to the tonic would be unlikely to be found in common practice; the sonority contains five of the six possible whole-tone degrees.

EXAMPLE 31–8: Debussy, *Prélude à l'Après-midi d'un Faune*

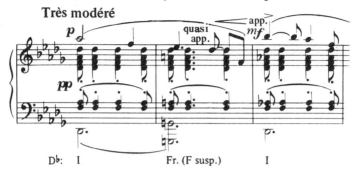

Db: I   Fr. (F susp.)   I

In Debussy's more typical use of the whole-tone scale, tonality can hardly be defined in terms of classical triads and progressions. Only two triads are possible, both of them augmented, and, as has already been noted, all inversions sound alike. All "progressions" tend to have the same tonal character. What one hears are tone centers rather than tonics, and only when these are stressed, as by repetition or duration.

EXAMPLE 31–9: Debussy, *l'Isle joyeuse*

It cannot be denied that the small number of possible different intervals and nonequivalent chords available in the whole-tone scale results in a soft-edged, neutral kind of sound lacking in tonal contrast. For certain types of atmospheric effects, however, whole-tone harmony suited Debussy's purposes admirably. Though he used it often, he seldom used it for more than a few measures at a time, always contrasting it with more conventionally diatonic harmony.

Whole-tone harmony only rarely appears in the works of Ravel, and with some frequency in the earliest works of Stravinsky and Bartók. It is found occasionally in Schoenberg's and Berg's early works, within a context of advanced tonal chromaticism. Since the 1930s, whole-tone harmony, like much else that Debussy discovered, has become one of the platitudes of the "Hollywood style."

Artificial Scales

It is apparent that the major and minor scales and the modal scales do not exhaust the possibilities of diatonic scales, that is, seven-note scales composed of successive half steps and whole steps in various distributions. An *artificial scale* is defined to be a scale that is neither major, minor, chromatic, nor one of the church modes. We will concern ourselves in this section with artificial scales that are subsets of the twelve-tone tempered scale, leaving aside the whole-tone and pentatonic scales just discussed, as well as nontempered scales, such as those found in Oriental music, and microtonal scales, such as the quarter-tone scale (twenty-four tones to the octave) and others that even today are considered experimental.

Already in the common-practice period we have encountered the use of the harmonic minor scale, with one augmented second, as a basis of melody, even though in such cases it is usually possible to think of this as the result of alternating between different melodic minor forms. The so-called Hungarian scale (Chapter 5, Example 5–1), with two augmented seconds, turns up now and then in the melodic writing of the Hungarian nationalists, beginning with Liszt, but not as a basis for harmony. Other comparable patterns may be occasionally found in nineteenth-century melodic writing, in isolated instances where the appearance of one or more nonclassical interval successions is likely to be brought about by momentary chromatic alteration in the major or minor scale, and we have seen how the use of the chromatically lowered second degree in the Neapolitan sixth does not of itself proclaim the use of the Phrygian mode.

A more compelling instance of an artificial scale is afforded by Debussy's *Nuages*, the first of his three *Nocturnes* for orchestra, in which the following scale appears as the basis of both melody and harmony during a large part of the piece:

EXAMPLE 31–10

At a glance this is no more than the natural minor scale of B with lowered fifth degree, but that one difference has a considerable effect on the tonality. The tonic triad is diminished, being absorbed into the sound of the submediant seventh chord, which itself sounds like the dominant of C, a tone not present in the scale.

EXAMPLE 31–11: Debussy, *Nocturnes*: I, *Nuages*

Debussy never considered the exclusive use of a particular scale in a composition to be an imperative, and *Nuages* is no exception; the extensive passages in which the artifical scale appears are contrasted with various kinds of ordinary B minor, with F♯ as the fifth degree. But it is precisely that condition that makes *Nuages* such an important departure from common practice. The distinction between B–D–F♯ as

EXAMPLE 31–12: Debussy, *Nocturnes*: I, *Nuages* (final measures)

the tonality-organizing triad and G–B–D–F as the companion chord of the tone B becomes blurred, and eventually any classical association with B minor vanishes, leaving at the end only the single pitch B as a tone center. (See Example 31–12.)

One of the "Six Inventions" that constitute the final act of Berg's opera *Wozzeck* is a scene described by him as an "Invention on a six-note chord," that chord being the D♭ pentatonic scale with an additional note, the minor third degree.

EXAMPLE 31–13

From this collection of pitch-classes (that is, including their enharmonic and octave equivalents) most of the pitches of the scene are drawn. (Some parts of the scene use the transposed collection, others add chromatic passing tones; one climactic point uses the collection as one chordal layer, adding below it, in a cluster, the other six tones of the chromatic scale, forming a twelve-tone chord.) Thus the six-note "chord" is also to be considered a scale in the same sense that only its pitch-classes are used, in a variety of combinations with each other, triadic and otherwise, and in both scalar and nonscalar order. The convergence of this scale with the pentatonic scale lends a loose quasi-tonality to the scene, one of the relatively few places where such a thing occurs in this mostly atonal opera.

EXAMPLE 31–14: Berg, *Wozzeck*, Act III, Scene 4

Parallel and Antiparallel Harmony

We have already seen how chords with classical values of dissonance, such as the dominant seventh and ninth, came to be used as independent vertical sonorities, dissociated from their classical voice-leading tendencies and free to move even in strict parallel motion. A tendency of several composers in the late nineteenth century was to emphasize particular kinds of chords for their own sonorous qualities, often in a homophonic texture with parallel connections of the chords. Debussy's style, particularly in his piano works, came to make extensive use of parallel chords of all types, often in block chords without any textural differentiation. The following shows parallel chords made up of unequal intervals, the structure of the chord being one that might occur in common practice only as the result of coincidence of nonharmonic tones with chord tones.

EXAMPLE 31–15: Debussy, *Danse sacrée* for harp and strings

The parallel motion may employ only triads in root position.

EXAMPLE 31–16: Bartók, *Bluebeard's Castle*

The following example shows successive root-position triads applied to a melodic line, much like a classical harmonization in block chords. Some of the successive chords show parallel perfect intervals, while others do not. This is a good example of a nonsystematic antiparallel harmony.

EXAMPLE 31–17: Debussy, *String Quartet*, I

In cases where the parallel motion is continuous, it is possible to regard the block chords as a harmonic expansion, or thickening, of a single line. An analogous procedure was widespread in common practice with parallel triads in the first inversion, as will be remembered from Example 6–12. The parallel chromatic motion of diminished sevenths in common practice is a somewhat different matter, because such motion is ordinarily connective rather than inherently melodic; it is as though the entire succession were a prolonged passing chord from the initial to the final harmony. Only after common practice did parallel chordal motion come to include the intervals of perfect fifth or octave between the outer voices, subordinating everything to the progress of the line. With these considerations in mind, one can imagine the possibility of lines in combination, each thickened by parallel chords.

EXAMPLE 31–18: Stravinsky, *Petrushka*, Tableau I

Such combined lines or layers naturally give rise to complex chords whose vertical relationship cannot be accounted for other than by such "contrachordal" interpretations, just as certain complex sonorities in common practice result from the contrapuntal combination of nonharmonic tones. In an example like the one above, the use of only diatonic degrees results in what has been called *pandiatonic* harmony, discussed later in this chapter. With a chromatic element, the structure of the harmony may be much more complex, even when the contrapuntal origin is relatively straightforward. The harmony of the upper parts in the following example progresses systematically from an initial sonority by means of chromatic contrary motion of the voices, a favorite procedure of Berg in both his tonal and atonal works.

EXAMPLE 31–19: Berg, *String Quartet*, Op. 3, II

The same kind of mirror counterpoint is often found in the music of Bartók, whose fondness for parallel intervals is evident in other examples in this chapter. The chromatic parallel thirds of the following example should be compared with those of Example 31–7, showing whole-tone sonorities.

EXAMPLE 31–20: Bartók, *Suite*, Op. 14, No. 4

Tertial Harmony

The term *tertial harmony* means harmony based on chords constructed by superposing intervals of a third. In the larger sense this would include all of common-practice harmony, but we shall discuss here only harmony in which the superposition of thirds and the treatment of the resulting chords go beyond common practice.

Beginning with Debussy, composers came to realize the possibilities of nondominant seventh and ninth chords treated independently, without consideration of how these might be fitted into a context by classical voice leading. The following passage from Ravel's *Menuet antique*, for example, shows how Ravel imagined the voices to move, but this movement is hardly what one would expect to find in common practice. It seems likely that Ravel was as fully interested in the sonorous peculiarities of the chord as in any contrapuntal considerations.

EXAMPLE 31–21: Ravel, *Menuet antique*

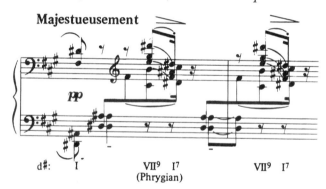

In the following example, the accumulation of thirds certainly does not arise from the counterpoint, but neither does it obscure the under-

EXAMPLE 31–22: Ravel, *Le Tombeau de Couperin*: No. 4, *Rigaudon*

lying classical root progression, probably because the passage is entirely diatonic in C major.

Stacks of thirds can also result from the intersection of melodic layers.

EXAMPLE 31–23: Holst, *The Planets*: II, *Venus*

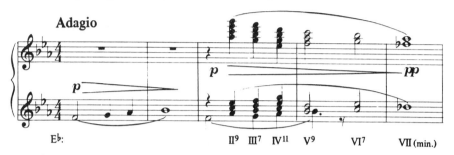

The example above can be analyzed strictly in the manner shown, but one does not really hear this as a succession of true roots any more than one hears a succession of parallel first-inversion triads as moving roots, independently of other features of the music. It is more realistic to think of it as the convergence of two lines thickened by layers of superposed thirds, with the possibility that some functional values, such as the dominant ninth, can be discerned.

Nor would one be likely to perceive the following admittedly extreme example as an independent supertonic twenty-seventh chord, where the bass is just one more factor that happens to be the "root."

EXAMPLE 31–24: Stravinsky, *Petrushka*, Tableau II

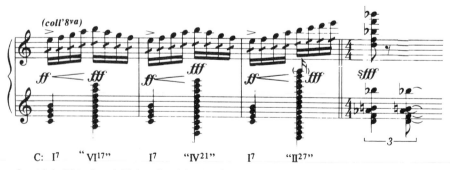

Quartal Harmony

In triadic music the interval of the perfect fourth is a consonant component only of triads in the first inversion, or when the root is doubled in root position. As a dissonant interval it is marked by its tendency to shrink to a third. Perfect fourths heard in superposition seem to compound this tendency and thus are seldom heard in common practice. In the absence of a triadic basis, the ear finds it difficult to determine a root unless other harmonic elements are involved.

The structure of superposed fourths in the following example, ingeniously arranged to account for the open strings of Beckmesser's lute, is actually a II^7 over a dominant pedal, as the resolution shows.

EXAMPLE 31–25: Wagner, *Die Meistersinger*, Act II, Scene 5

D: $II^7/V(V^{11})$ V^7

The regular use of chords built of superposed fourths does not appear until the early twentieth century, with works like Schoenberg's *Chamber Symphony*, Op. 9, which remains an isolated phenomenon in Schoenberg's output, but which had a considerable influence elsewhere. In the following example, a chromatically descending series of

EXAMPLE 31–26: Berg, *Sonata*, Op. 1

fourth chords settles on a five-tone quartal sonority (circled), whose factors then creep chromatically into a whole-tone chord on E, having the structure of a dominant seventh with raised fifth (B♯). The notation of the example follows the practice of Schoenberg and his disciples of providing accidental signs on nearly every note, even when a key signature was used.

The following example shows separate lines doubled in fourths, becoming parallel, and finally moving as a single layer of fourths.

EXAMPLE 31–27: Bartók, *Sonata for Two Pianos and Percussion*, I

The harmonically neutral sound of superposed perfect fourths is not substantially affected by the addition or removal of factors in the chord. The alteration of one of the intervals within, however, revises the entire structure of the chord and introduces a definite coloristic change. The inclusion of one augmented fourth in the vertical structures of the following example gives the impression of a succession of independent dominant thirteenths.

EXAMPLE 31–28: Satie, *Le Fils des étoiles*, Prelude

En blanc et immobile

Quintal Harmony

The sonority of superposed perfect fifths is similar to but different from that of fourths. It seems to be qualitatively more stable, if only because the ear can imagine a root in the bass, and sometimes a third in between the root and fifth. Beyond two superposed fifths, however, it is difficult to carry this process of mental extrapolation; one does not hear three superposed fifths as a thirteenth chord with third, seventh, and eleventh missing.

The beginning of Liszt's *Mephisto Waltz* is like the Wagner example above in that it is a musical depiction of tuning up a stringed instrument. Note how the tones in the stack of fifths move so as to change the sonority to something more closely related to triadic harmony.

EXAMPLE 31–29: Liszt: *Mephisto Waltz No. 1*

Allegro vivace (quasi presto)

In the example below, Debussy uses oscillating chords of two perfect fifths in the left hand, together with a melody doubled in perfect
fifths and octaves, to give an archaic atmosphere to his impressionistic
"sunken cathedral," in which he seems to be recalling parallel organum
of the Middle Ages. A marking at the beginning of the piece says "in a
gently sonorous fog."

EXAMPLE 31–30: Debussy, *Preludes*, Book I: No. 10, *La
Cathédrale engloutie*

Profondément calme *(sans nuances)*

The following comparable example combines fourth chords with
a surrounding stack of six fifths.

EXAMPLE 31–31: Ravel, *Daphnis et Chloé*, beginning

The Casella excerpt is firmly rooted on C, with an implication of
alternating tonic and dominant.

EXAMPLE 31–32: Casella, *Sonata No. 2 in C major for Piano and Cello*

Largo molto e sostenuto

The harmony of the following example is in two quintal layers in contrary motion. Sometimes these intersect to form octave doublings or an unbroken stack of fifths, while at other times the variable interval separating the two layers introduces a new color.

EXAMPLE 31–33: Bartók, *Piano Concerto No. 2*

Adagio

Secundal Harmony

Chords built of seconds are of several types. When only major seconds are superposed, a whole-tone sonority results. Chords built of adjacent diatonic scale degrees have major and minor seconds; these and chords built only of semitones are described as tone-clusters.

A melodic line in parallel major seconds was a device particularly favored by the impressionist composers.

EXAMPLE 31–34: Debussy, *La Boîte à joujoux*, Tableau II

Parallel major seconds are found abundantly in the works of many later composers, including Bartók, who was also one of the first to use parallel minor seconds.

EXAMPLE 31–35: Bartók, *Suite*, Op. 14, IV

The following pair of clusters for the piano, an important leitmotive in Berg's *Lulu*, uses all twelve pitch-classes of the chromatic scale. The example is given in Berg's notation.

EXAMPLE 31–36: Berg, *Lulu*, Prologue

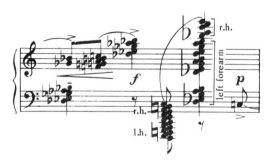

A similar passage is found in Ives's *"Concord" Sonata*, where the pianist uses a measured strip of wood to press the keys. Ives's use of clusters is an important aspect of his style, in ensemble music as well as his works for the piano. The following drastically expressive passage forms the climax to a short song.

EXAMPLE 31–37: Ives, *Charlie Rutlage*

Tone-clusters containing many different chromatic pitches closely packed will ordinarily have no tonal basis. They are usually employed for rhythmic, percussive accents, only occasionally for soft, atmospheric color.

EXAMPLE 31–38: Bartók, *Sonata*, III

Pandiatonicism

In the previous part of this chapter we examined harmony in which the superposition of equal intervals is employed systematically to produce characteristic sonorities. These special harmonic types were thoroughly explored by composers beginning in the first decade of the twentieth century, and in varying ways became incorporated into the diatonic vocabulary. However, these sonorities account for only part of the nontriadic harmony of the twentieth century. Composers were equally cognizant of harmony based on the diatonic scale but not having any specifically intervallic organization. The terms *pandiatonicism* and *white-note harmony* have been coined in recognition of the entire spectrum of diatonic harmony that is not limited to chords originating from triads.

The opening measures of Stravinsky's *Octet* demonstrate E♭ major clearly enough at the very beginning by means of tonic triad and dominant seventh; the chords that follow combine elements of both, then proceed to a half cadence on V of VI.

EXAMPLE 31–39: Stravinsky, *Octet for Wind Instruments*, I

E♭:   V⁷   I V⁷ (V, I) V/I V of VI (app.)   V of VI   V♭₉ of V V

The dissonances in some of these chords are not to be explained by the conventional determinations of preparation and resolution, but by the composer's choice of individual harmonic and melodic relationships. Another passage from later in the piece shows a more contrapuntal genesis of the pandiatonic harmony; it has no chromatic tones at all. In its lack of triadic basis, this passage may be compared to the Casella example earlier, in which there is a perception of roots and melodic lines but not of identifiable chordal structures per se. Such pandiatonic writing became a strong characteristic of tonal neoclassicism from the early 1920s on, especially among American composers.

Cf. Exx. 31–30, 31–32

EXAMPLE 31–40: Stravinsky, *Octet for Wind Instruments*, I

V, IV, I mixed   II, I/V   I

EXAMPLE 31–41: Copland, *Billy the Kid*

Polychords and Polytonality

Polychords result from the combination of two or more triads or other simple chords. Normally the term is used to designate only combinations of relatively remotely related triads. A chord resulting from superposition of a D-minor triad over a G-major triad, for example, would normally be a V^9 of C major, and not a polychord. Nevertheless the differentiation is not always an easy one to make, because the effect of some polychords is to have one of the components harmonically predominating, and the other members heard to a greater or lesser degree as nonharmonic tones.

Review Chap. 8: The Pedal

A wide variety of polychordal types can be found in the works of many composers, beginning in the first decade of the twentieth century. These types range from combinations of incomplete triads to combinations of seventh and ninth chords and altered chords. It is char-

acteristic of the period that the polychords used by composers are chosen for their individuality of sound and not for their systematicity of
structure. Thus it is not at all unusual to encounter harmonies in which
a particular member of a polychord may be explainable as a factor of
one particular triadic component, or as an altered factor of another, or
as an unresolved appoggiatura, or a combination of these.

The extraordinary chord that appears seemingly out of nowhere in
Mahler's *Tenth Symphony* is a good illustration of the insufficiency of
our descriptive language in its present state.

EXAMPLE 31–42: Mahler, *Symphony No. 10*, I

It is possible to analyze this sonority as a combination of three
groups, a diminished seventh (G♯–B–D–F), a half-diminished seventh
(B–D–F–A), and a minor triad (C–E♭–G), over a pedal C♯. With equal
validity it could be considered as a stack of thirds reaching as far as the
nineteenth (though the omission of the third between the low C♯ and
G♯ makes a big difference), but with several chromatic alterations; as a
complex dominant over a C♯ root the chord is directly related to the
main tonality of the movement, F♯ major. But neither of these analyses
seems to go very far toward explaining why such a chord should be
chosen at all; only a closer analysis of the context, perhaps including
the entire movement, would be likely to illuminate that question.

The relationship of a tritone between two major-triadic components is the basis of Stravinsky's so-called "Petrushka chord," although
other composers, such as Ravel in his *Jeux d'eau*, used it at least ten
years before *Petrushka*. (See Example 31–43.)

From the standpoint of the circle of fifths, the tritone relationship
is the remotest possible (cf. Example 28–31). One should compare the

EXAMPLE 31–43: Stravinsky, *Petrushka*

Petrushka sonority also with the "Boris chords" as shown in Example 30–31.

The following example is relatively simple to resolve into two layers, a sustained D-minor triad with most if its weight in the bass, and an oscillating pair of D♯- and C♯-minor triads in the upper parts.

EXAMPLE 31–44: Stravinsky, *The Rite of Spring*: Part II, Introduction

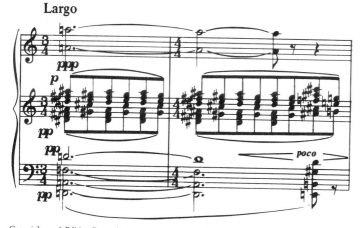

The melodic activity of the upper parts seems to define a Phrygian D♯-minor tone center, strong enough to overbalance the D-minor bass, which acts as a sort of "false tonic," even the sustained upper-register A sounding like a leading tone to the A♯. This interpretation is not the only possible one, however, nor even necessarily a preferred one. The outstanding characteristics of the harmony of this passage, as in so much music of the period, are its autonomous structure and individualized sound, and not the way in which it may or may not fit into some formal tonal scheme.

Polytonality is a situation somewhat different from the mere use of polychords. In polytonality, the intention is to create the impression of more than one key at the same time, a sort of counterpoint of keys.

EXAMPLE 31–45: Wagner, *Die Meistersinger*, end of Act I

In the example above, the listener has already heard the Apprentices' Song earlier, with the harmony shown. Here it is incorporated into a slower-moving passage over a dominant pedal in F major, a key that has been well established for some time. The different meter and different texture make it possible to hear the song as a simultaneous different music, anchored by the C in the bass, and the impression of two keys, though delicate and fleeting, is not hard to hear.

In twentieth-century bitonality the key relationships are likely to be more remote and contrasting. It is easier to distinguish the two keys mentally if one of them is established first and then the other is added.

EXAMPLE 31–46: Poulenc, *Mouvements perpétuels*, I

By permission of J & W CHESTER / Edition Wilhelm Hansen London Limited.

In the example above, the Gb-major scale shares most of its pitches with the Bb-minor scale, so the difference between the two keys (Bb and Gb) is not as great as the difference between the two modes (Bb major and Bb minor).

Another aid to aural separation of the two keys is to have one of them relatively inactive harmonically, like a pedal point.

EXAMPLE 31–47: Ravel, *l'Enfant et les sortilèges*, Dance of the Shepherds

Sometimes one of the keys may be defined by as little as an ostinato bass of tonic and dominant.

EXAMPLE 31–48: Ravel, *Daphnis et Chloé*

In another passage in *Daphnis et Chloé*, the upper layer of triads does not seem to define a single separate key because the triads are not all closely related to each other; rather there is the feeling of a series of polychords related by their melodic succession in the upper layer and by the sustained dominant seventh in the bass.

EXAMPLE 31–49: Ravel, *Daphnis et Chloé*

When there is much harmonic activity in both bitonal layers the separate keys may be difficult to distinguish. One hears instead a synthesis of the two into a complex harmony that sounds more chromatic than diatonic.

EXAMPLE 31–50: Ravel, *l'Enfant et les Sortilèges*, final scene

Examples like the foregoing make it apparent that the simultaneous perception of different keys is not necessarily easy, and that it depends on more than just the constitution of the chords involved. Rhythmic, melodic, and contrapuntal separation may have a good deal to do with how the different keys are heard, and spacing may be especially important.

Modal Mixture

The interchangeability of parallel major and minor modes, noted in Chapters 5 and 14 as a resource of common practice, continued into twentieth-century tonality. One perceives an actual change of mode when it is the tonic triad that changes, as in Example 5–28. Triads from the opposite mode, other than the tonic triad, do not usually create the impression of a shift in the main mode, but rather appear as chords lent temporarily from the other mode. IV from the minor followed by I in the major, for example, does not change the prevailing major mode; the progression is found everywhere in common practice. The prevalent use in the major mode of such chords as the various forms of dominant minor ninth, the Neapolitan sixth, and the augmented sixth chords, all of which contain the minor sixth degree, attests to the adaptability of the different modal degrees without disturbing the stability of the major mode. This property is comparable to the use of inflected triads with the ascending melodic minor scale, which do not in themselves weaken the hegemony of the surrounding minor mode. Rather less frequent than these is the use of VI from the minor progressing to I in the major, two major triads involving a change of the modal third degree. On the other hand, the inverse of this progression, VI from the major progressing to I in the minor (two minor triads), is definitely not common practice.

EXAMPLE 31–51: Mahler, *Symphony No. 3*, IV

Other such progressions entered the harmonic vocabulary as the use of modal scales increased. As we have seen, the Lydian and Mixolydian scales are essentially "major" because the tonic triad is major; similarly the Dorian and Phrygian are essentially "minor." (See Example 31–52.)

EXAMPLE 31–52: Janáček: *The Diary of One Who Vanished*, No. 9

Another aspect of modal mixture that has already been pointed out is the cross-relation of leading tone with minor seventh degree in dominant harmony, the leading tone ascending and the minor seventh descending as part of the melodic minor scale (Example 8–28). In common practice this is generally an appoggiatura relationship, but in the twentieth century it became an independent harmonic structure.

EXAMPLE 31–53: Bartók, *The Wooden Prince*

The addition of a minor third to dominant seventh and dominant ninth harmony is an example of what jazz musicians call a "blue note." The first composer to make systematic use of such harmony was Ravel, who made it a distinctive stylistic characteristic.

EXAMPLE 31–54: Ravel, *Miroirs*: No. 4, *Alborada del gracioso*

The following example shows a dominant with major and minor third, and another with major and minor seventh (the major seventh as chromatic neighbor note):

EXAMPLE 31–55: Ravel, *Rapsodie espagnole*: I, *Prélude à la nuit*

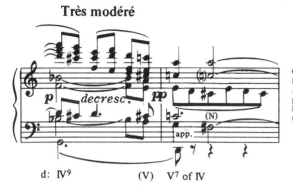

The following example is more complicated. To the third, fifth, and seventh of each dominant is added an appoggiatura a major seventh (or diminished octave) above. This may be an extension of the principle of major-minor mixture, but the effect is of a polychordal sonority, rather like the *Daphnis et Chloé* example earlier (Example 32–49). Despite the complex dissonance in the upper register, the classical sequence of dominant basses is clear and effective.

EXAMPLE 31–56: Ravel, *Piano Trio*: II, *Pantoum*

The Inverted Ninth Chord

Like its counterpart in common practice, the dominant minor ninth with major and minor third may appear as an incomplete chord without the root.

EXAMPLE 31–57

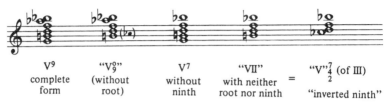

V^9	"V_9^o"	V^7	"VII"	"V"$^7_{4\ 2}$ (of III)
complete form	(without root)	without ninth	with neither root nor ninth	= "inverted ninth"

See also Ex.
31–24

In the spacing shown, the complete chord of six factors is not without some polychordal feeling, rather like V^7 in the lower four voices combined with V^7 of III in the upper four. When the root is left out, the chord no longer sounds like an incomplete dominant, but like a complete and different dominant, $V^7_{4\ 2}$ of III, with a different root (the upper voice, in the example). The chord called "VII" above, implying an incomplete V^7 with major and minor third, is often seen in the enharmonic notation shown. This enharmonic version is seen to have notationally the structure of a dominant minor ninth in the fourth inversion, with root but without seventh. In this inversion the ninth is

But see Ex.
24–11

below the root, a situation that does not occur in common practice (see Chapter 24), but that is characteristic for this sonority in the twentieth century.

EXAMPLE 31–58: Ravel, *Gaspard de la nuit*: No. 1, *Ondine*

Rapide et brillant

The following example contains three harmonic layers, the middle showing parallel inverted ninth chords. The upper layer (with a somewhat different chordal doubling) and the parallel-fifth ostinato bass have previously been heard together without a middle layer. The overall effect is generally one of dense major-minor polychords.

EXAMPLE 31–59: Stravinsky, *The Rite of Spring*: Part I, *Round Dance*

Sostenuto e pesante

The example below is of similar effect, made particularly pungent by the B♮–B♭ semitone in the middle of the cadencing sonority.

EXAMPLE 31–60: Berg, *Wozzeck*, end of Act I

Andante affetuoso

Appoggiatura Chords

Appoggiatura chords in common practice, defined in Chapter 28 as vertical combinations of appoggiature, are dependent for their meaning on expected resolution to consonant sonorities. By extension the term includes chords resulting from combinations of other types of nonharmonic tones. Many such chords are possible, and even the most mordantly dissonant combinations are well understood if the melodic motion and the surrounding harmonic context are clear.

EXAMPLE 31–61: Bach, *Brandenburg Concerto No. 1*, II

EXAMPLE 31–62: Mozart, *String Quintet*, K. 614, II

Common practice also included, as we have seen, a category of so-called harmonic dissonances—the seventh and ninth in dominant harmony, and the added sixth above a root-position triad—which in some circumstances were appoggiature or suspensions, but in others were less restricted in their preparation and resolution, that is, closer to being autonomous chords. In our discussion of independent sonorities we saw that after common practice it was chords embodying these harmonic dissonances that were the first to achieve a freedom of motion and connection comparable to that enjoyed by pure triads.

Appoggiatura chords in the twentieth century are extensions of common-practice forms of chordal dissonance. They include several basic types. One type is represented by common-practice appoggiatura ninth, eleventh, and thirteenth chords and chords over pedal points, the dissonant factors being left unresolved; some of these have already been discussed in this chapter under the heading of tertial harmony. Another type includes chromatic appoggiature such as in altered chords, also unresolved. A third type includes appoggiature sounding simultaneously with their notes of resolution. These types also occur in various combinations, and certainly a number of chordal phenomena we have already discussed earlier, such as major-minor chords and certain fourth chords, occur in contexts that permit them to be treated as appoggiatura chords.

EXAMPLE 31–63: Stravinsky, *The Firebird*, Finale

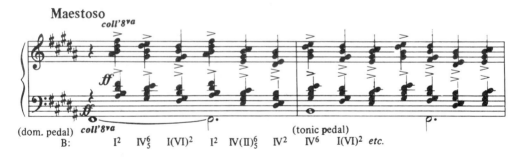

The vertical structure of the example above is no more complex than simple nondominant sevenths and added-sixth chords, framed by parallel sixths. It is their closely packed arrangement, in the form of triads with attached neighbor notes, and their nonsystematic resolution, that brands these as diatonic appoggiatura chords.

Short appoggiature in close texture with their notes of resolution appear as special ornaments called *acciaccature* (Italian *acciaccare*, "to crush") in Baroque harpsichord music; Domenico Scarlatti's sonatas furnish some startling examples. Chopin's *Etude* in E minor, Op. 25, No. 5, is a later example of acciaccatura style. In all these cases the appoggiatura, usually the semitone below, is sounded on the strong part of the beat like any other appoggiatura (in other words, it is not a true grace note), the note of resolution coming either simultaneously or immediately afterward. The developments after common practice extended this principle to allow appoggiature of equal duration with their simultaneous notes of resolution, a technique that seems to foreshadow tone-clustering.

EXAMPLE 31–64: Dvořák, *The Noon Witch*, Op. 108

The following example suggests a roughly strummed guitar.

EXAMPLE 31–65: Albéniz, *Ibéria*, Book I: No. 3, *Corpus Christi in Seville*

The augmented sixth chord over a dominant pedal, occasionally found in common practice, may be cited here as a type of appoggiatura chord, representing a secondary dominant sounding simultaneously with the root of its chord of resolution. As an unresolved appoggiatura chord, it may also be regarded enharmonically as a dominant seventh with pedal; as such it was a favorite chord of Ravel. The reader may compare the following example with Example 27–21:

EXAMPLE 31–66: Ravel, *Miroirs*: No. 4, *Alborada del gracioso*

In the example below, the sequence, which is not completely strict, gives the impression of a chromatically descending series of dominants, each an appoggiatura chord to the next. The starred chords are rhythmically stronger, however, and carry the harmonic weight as successive dominants with appoggiatura thirteenth (in the upper voice) and major and minor third.

EXAMPLE 31–67: Ravel, *Gaspard de la nuit*: No. 3, *Scarbo*

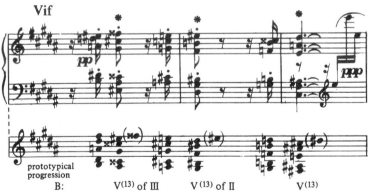

The first harmony of the following example is a dominant seventh with appoggiatura thirteenth and appoggiatura leading-tone (E♯) to the leading tone; the second is a chromatic passing chord (D♯ from D to E; C♯ from C to D; A♯ from A to B); the third is a tonic triad with added sixth and appoggiatura ninth (A); the fourth is a superposition of raised supertonic (like the traditional raised supertonic seventh but without the seventh) over a dominant bass.

EXAMPLE 31–68: Ravel, *Valses nobles et sentimentales*, I

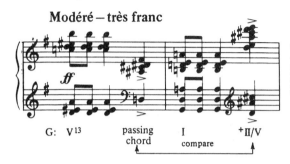

Modéré – très franc

G: V¹³   passing   I   ⁺II/V
                 chord   compare

A favorite resource of jazz harmony is the following sequence of appoggiatura dominants:

EXAMPLE 31–69

D: V¹³   V⁷ of IV⁽±³⁾ C: V¹³   V⁷ of IV ⁽±³⁾
G: V⁷⁽±³⁾   V¹³ of IV F: V⁷⁽±³⁾

The upper voices move in parallel; the bass moves in downward fifths. An early use of the sequence is the following:

EXAMPLE 31–70: Ravel, *Gaspard de la nuit*: No. 2, *Le Gibet*

The dominant seventh and dominant major ninth, both with raised or lowered fifth, were widely employed as independent sonorities in the atmospheric harmony of Scriabin, which in turn had an influence on the early chromatic harmony of Stravinsky. The examples below may be compared for their chromatic and whole-tone relationships.

EXAMPLE 31–71: Scriabin, *Poem of Ecstasy*, Op. 54

EXAMPLE 31–72: Stravinsky, *The Firebird*, Supplication Scene

The closely textured seconds, sevenths, and ninths of the following example result partly from appoggiatura-chord layers, partly from pedal points, and partly from contrapuntal convergences. It is instructive to compare the very different style of this example with that of the preceding, composed only nine years earlier.

EXAMPLE 31–73: Stravinsky, *Symphonies of Wind Instruments*

The following could be cited as one paradigm of the appoggiatura principle in the twentieth century. The first two measures are an unadorned appoggiatura plagal cadence in E minor; the next two are an echo of it, beginning with a complex tangle of notes which slowly slide their way (except for the bass) to consonance.

EXAMPLE 31–74: Prokofiev, *Piano Concerto No. 3*, II

32

Extended Chromaticism

The music of the twentieth century, considered as a whole, shows the widest possible range of different styles, techniques, and compositional philosophies, and we have shown in this book a variety of examples that can in one way or another be called tonal. Tonality in music is in part a formal system, by which we mean a kind of organized relationship among tones, with all the dependability, variability, and exceptions that composers have been able to devise. That is what this book is about.

Nevertheless the most distinctive aspect, and the most interesting historical fact, of the music of our own century, is the appearance in music of atonality, or absence of key, the result of more than a century of harmonic evolution and ever-widening exploration of the expressive resources of chromaticism. Though atonal music has not been readily accepted by perhaps even the majority of listening audiences, at least so far, atonality and the compositional techniques that govern it have been the major interest of some composers for nearly eighty years, and of most composers for at least the past thirty years.

The disappearance of tonality was from the start attended, in the works of the first atonal composers, by a search for new formal relationships, for new modes of compositional thought that could support a new music without tonality, and this search was successful. The techniques of atonality are beyond the scope of this book, but it is worthwhile to follow some of the paths that eventually led to the emergence of atonality, if only because they form a logical conclusion to our present study.

We have seen that even in music of the common-practice era there are instances when the impression of tonality, at least on some level, can be temporarily suspended. This means that one or another element of the music causes the obliteration of tonality, or perhaps that the absence of some element results in a failure of the tonality to be sustained. Atonality would then be represented by the systematic application or suppression of these respective elements.

Tonality-Supporting and Tonality-Weakening Elements

The following elements tend to establish tonality or to preserve it:

1. Tone centers, related intrinsically by scale, but established by the compositional process, and including the possibility of major and minor modes.
2. Harmonic progression of triads. In common practice, these are fundamentally the most important organizers of tonality. Dissonant harmonic factors reinforce progressions by their contrapuntal resolutions.
3. Clear cadences. A phrase need not immediately reveal its tonal center, and interest is to be gained by postponing the arrival.
4. Dominant and tonic pedal points and ostinati.
5. Avoidance of notes other than the major and minor scale degrees.
6. Reinforcement of a tone center by its restoration after a temporary departure.

The following elements tend to weaken or disguise tonality:

1. Complex chords, specifically: chords containing multiple non-harmonic tones; chords with obscured root functions (as for instance a ninth chord with the ninth below the root); chords of superposed fourths or fifths.
2. Multiple functions of chords from common practice having neither a major nor a minor triad as the principal component, such as II in the minor mode, VII, V_9^0, etc.
3. Irregular resolutions.
4. Rapid harmonic rhythm.

5. Dense contrapuntal writing.
6. Remote tonal functions; dislocation of the tonal center through extension of the secondary dominant principle.
7. Frequent and continual modulation.
8. Extensive use of modal mixture.
9. Fluctuation of tonal center about a single chord or pivot tone.
10. Use of scales other than major or minor: modal scales, whole-tone, pentatonic, chromatic, and artificial scales.
11. Polychords and polytonality.
12. Harmonies chosen for other than grammatical or contextual significance; tone-clusters.
13. Intentional avoidance of tonality-strengthening elements; atonality.

Most of these elements have already been dealt with at some length in this book; we know that not all of them are mutually exclusive categories. What is plain from the examples of the two preceding chapters is that the various new discoveries of the post–common-practice era were applied by different composers so as to alter, suspend, or even distort the classical perception of a tone center, but not to do away with it entirely. Debussy's music, for instance, is full of examples of pieces beginning in one key and ending in another, or traversing many different keys within a short time without ever employing a V–I cadence, but we have seen that in all such pieces there is most of the time a clear sense of some kind of tone center, even if that center is constantly shifting and even if there is no apparent single background tonality.

The idea of a unified classical tonality replaced by nonclassical (in this case nondominant) centricity in a composition is perfectly demonstrated by Debussy's *Prélude à l'Après-midi d'un faune*. (See Example 32–1.)

The opening melody begins unaccompanied on C♯ and returns to it, outlining the E-major triad at the end. In several reappearances of this melody, the C♯ is differently harmonized, once as a major seventh above a D-major triad (m. 11), once as an added sixth above an E major triad (m. 21), twice as a thirteenth above a V^9 of A major (m. 26, m. 94), and only near the end as the root of a chord, which, ambiguously enough, is equivalent to a V$^4_3$ of F♯ major (m. 100). One reappearance of the melody does not even begin on C♯ but on E, whose presumptive tonality, the relative major of C♯ minor, is like an "alter ego" in this work; the C♯ appears as the root of the accompanying VI^7 of E major (m. 81). This passage is followed a few measures later by a

EXAMPLE 32–1: Debussy, *Prélude à l'Après-midi d'un faune*

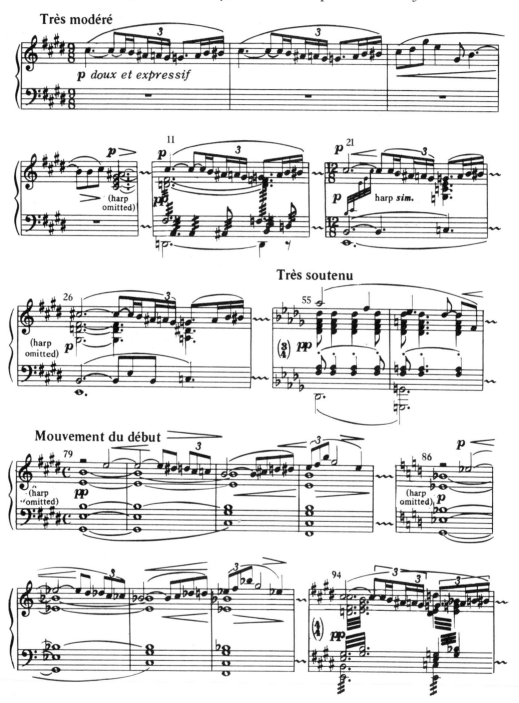

repeat in E♭ major, with no C♯ anywhere (m. 86). The only strong appearance of C♯ as a root-position sonority is in the middle section of the work (m. 55ff.), in connection with a new theme, with the main melody absent from the context; the only connection to the main theme suggested by this passage is the tritone span in the bass. Even the final measures of the piece treat the C♯ as a tone that dissolves rather than resolves. One concludes that the pitch-class C♯ is indeed central to the tonality of the work, but that its centricity is veiled by the varied harmonic functions it is called upon to perform. The centricity derives from its being present so often and from its oblique but definite connection with every fiber of the harmony and form, and not from any classical stature as the root of a systematically recurring triad.

A C♯-centricity of an entirely different kind is illustrated by the following equally familiar example. The C♯ is maintained by constant recurrence in the outer voices, as a chordal component in a texture dominated by inverted ninth chords, polychords, and tone-clusters. Were the C♯ not present, one would probably hear the passage as atonal, without any connection to a tone center. Whatever the chromatic density may suggest about the tonality, Stravinsky's own sketches refer to this passage as "in C♯ major."

EXAMPLE 32–2: Stravinsky, *The Rite of Spring*: Part II, *Sacrificial Dance*

Copyright 1918 Edition Russe de Musique. Copyright assigned 1947 to Boosey & Hawkes, Inc.
Reprinted by permission.

In the following example it is possible to discern a modulating pattern among the imitative entries of the main theme, indicated in the top and bottom voices by the wedge accents. The harmony, however, only tenuously supports the tonalities suggested by the melodic entries, and soon any generalized appearance of tonality breaks down under the weight of the rapid harmonic rhythm and distantly related harmonic functions, not to be restored until the surprise appearance of D major. A partial analysis has been provided, but it is not meant to suggest anything definitive.

EXAMPLE 32–3: Strauss, *Till Eulenspiegel*

A comparable situation, but one in which the very slow tempo makes all the difference, is shown in the opening of the third movement of Bruckner's *Ninth Symphony*.

EXAMPLE 32–4: Bruckner, *Symphony No. 9*, III

This is a characteristic example of late-nineteenth-century chro-matic modulation, one that presents typical difficulties of hearing in terms of classical tonal progressions. Because of the slow tempo, the ear fixes on the individual chords; because of their apparent tonal remoteness from each other, the chord progressions sound like abrupt modulations, at least until the relatively more tonally stable climax on D major is reached. The distant harmonic relationships of the individ-ual chords are further clouded by nonharmonic tones. The chord on the third beat of the third measure, for instance, is more likely to be thought of as an A-major triad (D♭ = C♯) with a D♯ (E♭) appoggiatura in the tenor voice, until its altered dominant relationship to A♭, the downbeat harmony of the next measure, is made clear. A reduced har-monic scheme makes it easier to follow the more distant progressions.

EXAMPLE 32–5

The problem of chromatic density in tonal harmony and counter-point is most vividly illustrated in several transitional works of Schoen-berg, who had already demonstrated consummate mastery of all aspects of tonal composition. The following typical passage from his *String*

EXAMPLE 32–6: Schoenberg, *String Quartet No. 1*, Op. 7

Quartet No. 1, Op. 7, is a work in several continuous movements lasting nearly an hour. The tonality of the work as a whole is loosely organized about D minor, but is far-ranging, with relatively stable tonal areas contrasting with chromatic harmony of the most extreme complexity.

During the greater part of the last movement of Schoenberg's *String Quartet No. 2*, Op. 10, tonality is abandoned altogether, though harmony unmistakably in F♯, the nominal key of the work, does reappear at the very end. Most of Schoenberg's music written after this work can be classified as atonal simply on the basis of its systematic elimination of diatonic harmony and of relative consonance and dissonance. A characteristic example is given here.

EXAMPLE 32–7: Schoenberg, *Three Piano Pieces*, Op. 11, No. 3

In atonality as practiced by Schoenberg and his followers, it is irrelevant to speak of consonance and dissonance. By tonal standards nearly everything is dissonant, strongly tonal intervals such as the fifth generally being concealed within dense textures and intentionally avoided in thin ones. (Octaves occur in melodic doublings, as the above example shows.) There is no diatonic hierarchy; the pitch-classes of the chromatic scale are represented in the note-population on a generally equal basis, subject only to the structural postulates of the individual work. (See Example 32–8.)

In atonality there can be no such thing as harmony in the traditional sense. It is obvious that even in atonality different tones sounding simultaneously create harmony, by definition, but a fundamental background for this harmony that is comparable to the assumption of a key, a scale, and roots in tonal music cannot be assumed in atonal music

EXAMPLE 32–8: Webern, *Five Pieces for String Quartet*, Op. 5, No. 4

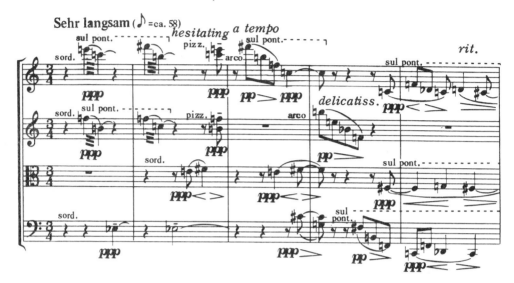

unless the composition itself defines such a background. The attempt was made by Schoenberg, and to a greater extent by his pupil Berg, to provide comparable definitions by means of specific recurring vertical combinations of motives, or by the use of motivic chord progressions. In the following example, the initial motive group recurs at three later points in the piece, including the last measures, the open D–A fifth being a prominent underpinning, and the D alone appearing as a bass support at other points.

EXAMPLE 32–9: Schoenberg, *Five Pieces for Orchestra*, Op. 16:
No. 2, *Vergangenes*

It is possible, though not particularly useful, to point to this motivic unit in its various transformations as constituting the basis of a vague D major–D minor background to the piece, with all the other pitch-classes hovering around a D major-minor sonority even if not exactly gravitating toward it. It would be more accurate to say that the piece is "in D-*Vergangenes*," indicating that the occasional emphasis on D as a quasi tone-center is but one of the defining conditions of the piece.

Berg's compositional practice differs from Schoenberg's most notably in that it regularly employs, within an atonal context, harmonies that derive in sound and structure from tonal harmony, even going so far as to include these on an important structural basis.

In the example below, it is possible to relate much of the harmonic substance of the orchestral accompaniment to the successive and overlapping transpositions of a single intervallic cell, a major third plus a semitone in the opposite direction, or to the retrograde of the same cell.

EXAMPLE 32–10: Berg, *Five Orchestral Songs on Picture-Postcard Texts of Peter Altenberg*, Op. 4, No. 2

Sie - he, Frau - e,   auch — du brauchst Ge-wit - ter - re - gen!

In the fifth measure the ascending overlapping statements outline two simultaneous diminished seventh chords, and this structuring seems to justify the appearance in m. 7 of a complete dominant ninth sonority, whose upper four factors are also a diminished seventh chord. This dominant ninth does not refer to any key, and it carries no express tonal implication other than its own isolated sound; nevertheless, it is the structural centerpiece of the song. The descending layer of thirds that follow it cleave to the pattern of the basic cell in reverse order, again outlining diminished seventh chords, and the final pitch of the accompaniment, like the initial, is identical with the "root" of the centerpiece chord. Thus within this atonal song one perceives a certain F-centricity, perhaps on an abstract, not easily heard basis. Certainly it is not a tonal centricity in any diatonic sense, but one could hardly deny that the F is structural, and that the diminished seventh structures are harmonic in the sense defined by the composition itself.

The influence on music of the twentieth century of the atonal works of Schoenberg and his followers has been enormous, not so much for the fact of atonality as for the comprehensive principles of form that evolved concomitantly with it in their music. The most potent of these has been the technique of the twelve-tone series, in which all the pitch relationships of a given composition are referable to a predetermined special ordering of the twelve pitch-classes of the chromatic scale. One of the first twelve-tone serial works by Schoenberg is shown in part in the following example. The series is used in all parts of the piece, most clearly in the upper melody of the first four measures. The order numbering beginning with zero is a convention of contemporary twelve-tone analysis.

EXAMPLE 32–11: Schoenberg, *Five Piano Pieces*, Op. 23: No. 5, *Waltz*

Used by permission of Edition Wilhelm Hansen A / S, Copenhagen.

Berg's last work, his *Violin Concerto*, provides a fitting close to this chapter on extended chromaticism and to this textbook on tonal harmony. The *Violin Concerto* is chiefly based on a twelve-tone series deliberately selected for its tonal implications. In this work tonality and atonality, as we have defined them, are merged in such a way that neither predominates; if the two domains are opposite by definition, Berg nonetheless has successfully combined them in a personal and compelling manner. The example below, from near the beginning of the work, displays the tonal harmony that the series implies. (Some expression marks have been omitted.)

EXAMPLE 32–12: Berg, *Violin Concerto*, I

By convention, the basic series of any twelve-tone work is the prime, abbreviated P_0, meaning prime without transposition.

The final movement of the *Violin Concerto* is a set of variations on the chorale *Es ist genug* (compare Example 16–17). Berg's twelve-tone harmonization makes use of the eleventh and third transpositions of the prime series and the ninth transposition of the inverted series, with a few slight modifications; the last four notes of the eleventh transposition give the first four notes of the chorale in B♭ major, the relative major of the basic "G minor" form of the series. Berg's phrase is answered by a repeat of the melody in Bach's own harmonization (Chorale No. 216, transposed to B♭.)

EXAMPLE 32–13: Berg, *Violin Concerto*, II

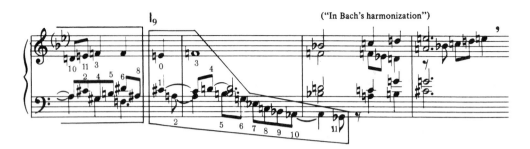

Afterword

By the time you have worked your way through most of this book, you will already have an idea of what further study in music theory will be good for you. If you are a college student majoring in music, you will most likely take courses in counterpoint, analysis, orchestration, or composition as well, and a good knowledge of this book is a good a preparation for those subjects. But the main purpose of this book, as set forth in the Introduction, is worth noting once more: to understand how music has been written in the past.

By far the most important part of that understanding is learning the music itself. If you love music, then you should learn as much music as you can, by daily listening and study, with or without the aid of a book. Whether you are a music major or a practicing professional or simply someone who enjoys music as an avocation, you will already be studying the masterworks as an important part of your own life. As the original Conclusion to this book read: 'It is not to be denied that the acquisition of a consummate knowledge of the practice of composers is a lifetime's work. *Ars longa, vita brevis*, but consolation may be derived from the thought that intellectual and artistic rewards are to be had at all stages along the way."

Appendix I

Acoustical Basis of the Scale: The Harmonic Series and Equal Temperament

It was known to the ancient Greek mathematicians that the simpler intervallic relationships between tones exactly correspond to simple ratios, in small whole numbers, of lengths of a vibrating string. If a plucked string sounding a certain tone is shortened, for instance, to exactly half its initial length, the resulting tone sounds an octave higher than originally, assuming that the tension on the string is kept constant. The same string shortened by only a third of its length (that is, so that two-thirds remain) sounds a perfect fifth higher; other simple proportions yield other intervals. The simple intervals and the ratios of their string-lengths can be easily correlated by using a monochord, which is essentially a string with one fixed bridge and one movable, mounted over a suitable ruler; many college physics departments possess one. If a monochord cannot be procured, intervals can be measured on a suitably long musical string, such as one of the strings of a double bass or cello, using a tape measure or yardstick (a tape measure graduated in centimeters is most convenient).

If we set up a string of arbitrary length (call it 1) between two fixed bridges and divide it by means of a third bridge placed between, we can obtain the tones represented by the lengths $\frac{1}{n}$ and $1 - \frac{1}{n}$, that is, the lengths on either side of the movable bridge, n being an integer.

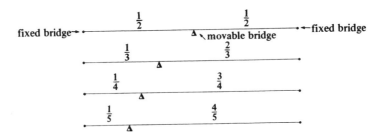

Let us say that the undivided string (length 1) sounds C two octaves below middle C, corresponding to the open string that is the lowest note of the cello. Then we will find that the lengths of the segments shown in the diagram above sound as follows:

EXAMPLE A–1

The process of division cannot be carried much further without our running into impracticably short string-lengths. Assuming that we could accurately measure them, however, the increasingly smaller $\frac{1}{n}$ lengths would yield the following tones (sixteen of them are given here, but theoretically the number is infinite):

EXAMPLE A–2

harmonic number: 1 2 3   4 5 6 7 8 9 10 11 12 13 14 15 16 *etc.*

sounding length: 1 $\frac{1}{2}$ $\frac{1}{3}$ $\frac{1}{4}$ $\frac{1}{5}$ *etc.*

These tones are called the *harmonic series* for low C; the numbers are the ordinals of the *harmonics* in the series. The number of each tone is also the denominator of the fraction representing the length of the string segment producing the tone. (The asterisks indicate tones that by musical standards are grossly out of tune, for reasons that will soon become clear.) An older terminology, still widely used, calls the series the *overtone series*, but numbers the notes differently; the second harmonic is the first overtone, the third harmonic is the second overtone, etc., while the first harmonic is called the *fundamental*.

Harmonics are generated by all natural vibrating systems. A vibrating string under normal conditions sounds not only the fundamental tone but simultaneously all the other harmonics together—at least theoretically. Harmonics above the fundamental are present in the tone, but only in much lesser strength than the fundamental, and their relative strength decreases with higher harmonic number, in most cases vanishing completely above the sixteenth harmonic. The relative strengths of the harmonics above the fundamentalcontributes to our perception of timbre and instrumental individuality; the distribution of these relative strengths results in a characteristic wave-shape that can be accurately measure in a modern acoustics laboratory. The shape of the wave form of a sustained middle C on an oboe, for instance, as seen on an oscilloscope is quite different from that of a middle C played on a piano. A "pure" tone, that is, a fundamental tone without any overtones, is represented by a sine wave (the graph of the function $y = \sin x$), and can be generated electronically; it has a plain, undistinguished, humlike sound. (A tuning fork generates a nearly pure tone.)

Harmonics, Interval Ratios, and Equal Temperament

The harmonic series as shown in the preceding example consists of tones related intervallically to a particular tone, the C two octaves below middle C. They are also related intervallically to each other, of course, but this intervallic relationship remains constant regardless of what the fundamental may be. For instance, the first six harmonics of F♯ below middle C would be:

EXAMPLE A–3

It is easily verified by experimenting on differently tuned strings that the ratio of string-lengths for *any* particular interval must be constant, assuming that the tension and density of the string remain constant.

The Greek theorists beginning with Pythagoras (fl. c. 531 B.C.) were able to correlate intervals with numerical quantities only by measuring strings. In more modern times, when it became known that sound is propagated by waves in the air, it became possible to measure tones by their frequency of vibration; it was then ascertained that the ratios of the measured frequencies were identical with the Pythagorean ratios of string-lengths. For instance, two tones an octave apart differ in frequency by a factor of 2.

On a somewhat more sophisticated level, we can determine that the frequencies of tones in the musical scale correspond logarithmically to the integers. This is easy enough to see with the octave relationships. If we start with a given tone of frequency f, the octave above it will have a frequency $2f$, the octave above that will have a frequency $2^2 \cdot f$ or $4f$, the next octave $2^3 \cdot f$ or $8f$, and so forth. These coefficients correspond to the numbers of the harmonic series, as Example A–2 shows. To take another example, the interval of an octave plus a perfect fifth (that is, a perfect twelfth) is represented by the ratio of $\frac{3}{1} \cdot f$ or $3f$, that is, the upper tone has three times the frequency of the lower. The tone two octaves above that upper tone would then have 2^2 times that frequency, and thus $2^2 \cdot 3$ times the frequency of the original tone, or $12f$. (Refer again to Example A–2.) The principle emerging from these empirical observations is that when intervals are added, their frequency ratios are multiplied. This is exactly comparable to a logarithmic procedure, using 2 as the logarithmic base.

The multiplication property suggests that it should be possible to obtain tones that are not found in the harmonic series on C, and thereby generate the entire chromatic scale over a given range. For instance, we might generate twelve different pitches by starting with the lowest C of the piano, and tune upward with perfect Pythagorean fifths, thus:

EXAMPLE A–4

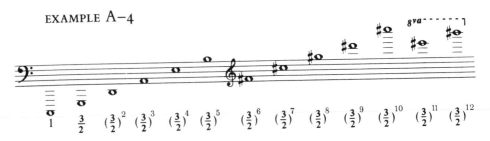

Since each of these fifths has the frequency ratio of $\frac{3}{2}$, by successively adding the fifths we multiply the lowest frequency by successive factors of $\frac{3}{2}$. The numbers in Example A–4 are the multipliers, the lowest C being the unit frequency. (Its actual frequency according to international standard pitch is 32.70 cycles per second.) The series of eleven superposed fifths gives all twelve pitch-classes ending with the high E♯; if we tuned the corresponding notes of a piano to the indicated frequencies it would then be a simple matter to tune all the other notes from them by octaves up or down.

Unfortunately, such a procedure yields very unsatisfactory results. To see why, let us compute the frequency of the next fifth up in the series, the high B♯, whose frequency relative to the low C would be $(\frac{3}{2})^{12}$. Enharmonically this should be equivalent to the highest C on the piano, seven octaves above the lowest, corresponding to the C arrived at this way:

EXAMPLE A–5

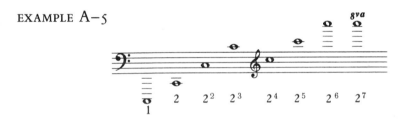

Working out the unwieldy fraction $(\frac{3}{2})^{12}$, or $\frac{531441}{4096}$, we obtain 129.746, which is significantly greater than 2^7, or 128. This means that the B♯ obtained by tuning upward from the low C by fifths will be audibly sharper than the C obtained by tuning upward by octaves. The difference between the two pitches obtained in this way, expressed as the intervallic ratio 1.014, is called the *Pythagorean comma*. This is slightly less than $\frac{1}{4}$ of a semitone—an easily audible difference.

A comparable comma could not have been avoided by tuning instead by perfect fourths, as the following demonstration shows.

EXAMPLE A–6

The ratio of the perfect fourth, $\frac{4}{3}$, multiplied twelve times, comes out to be less than five octaves by a factor of 1.014, just as in the previous instance, and the terminal D♭♭ will be annoyingly lower than the corresponding C.

Only a little more exploration is necessary to ascertain that *none* of the ratios representing simple intervals will yield a division of the octave, or of a series of octaves, that is free from commas.

EXAMPLE A–7

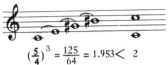

$$\left(\frac{5}{4}\right)^3 = \frac{125}{64} = 1.953 < 2$$

comma: 1.024, almost a quarter-tone

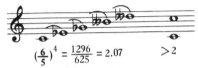

$$\left(\frac{6}{5}\right)^4 = \frac{1296}{625} = 2.07 \qquad > 2$$

comma: 1.037, more than a quarter-tone

The practice result of any of these tunings is that notes progressively higher in the stack of repeated intervals become progressively more out of tune. Even F♯, the seventh tone of the perfect-fifth series, will be audibly sharp as the third of a D-major triad, and D♯, considered enharmonically, will be totally unacceptable as the third of a C-minor triad.

The multiplicational inequities inherent in the intervallic ratios can be demonstrated within the harmonic series itself.

EXAMPLE A–8

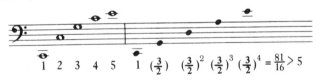

$$1 \quad 2 \quad 3 \quad 4 \quad 5 \quad 1 \quad \left(\frac{3}{2}\right) \quad \left(\frac{3}{2}\right)^2 \quad \left(\frac{3}{2}\right)^3 \quad \left(\frac{3}{2}\right)^4 = \frac{81}{16} > 5$$

The ratio of this difference, $\frac{81}{80}$, called the *syntonic comma*, reveals a startling fact. In the case of the other commas, it was plain that a notational difference existed between B♯ and C, and between D♭♭ and C, and we might suppose that these notational differences resulted from the natural differences in the way the frequencies were generated. In the case of the two E's in the example above, no such notational difference exists; they are both the same E, just as B♯, D♭♭, and C all designate the same note-class on the piano. What, then, is wrong with the measurements? For plainly the ratios we have computed represent different quantities.

Eventually we may come to reexamine the harmonic series as notated in Example A–2. One property that may have escaped our attention is that the intervals between adjacent harmonics get progressively smaller, or seem to. Certainly this fact is plain enough from their frequency ratios; $\frac{10}{9}$ or 1.111. . . , for example, is obviously smaller than $\frac{9}{8}$ or 1.125. But this is not apparent notationally; in the example, the distance C to D is a major second as we know it, and D to E is also a major second. Thus there is an inequity between the harmonic series that we can generate and hear, and the musical notation we have chosen for it. To put it another way, our familiar notational system cannot accurately represent the notes of the harmonic series, or at least not all of them. We know that the musical notation we use, though complicated and cumbersome to learn, is adequate to represent the music in our ordinary experience; it is perhaps not a little alarming to realize that it is intrinsically at variance with the acoustical realities. It is disconcerting enough to know that we cannot tune a piano, or indeed any instrument with fixed pitches, by combining pure intervals; how can we rescue our notational system from the same kinds of defects?

An answer is found in the historical compromise known as *equal temperament*, invented in the early sixteenth century or perhaps earlier, but not put into wide use until J. S. Bach's time (Bach in fact did much to popularize it). In equal temperament, the octave is divided into twelve exactly equal semitonal intervals, meaning that every semitone in the octave, regardless of where it is situated, is represented by a constant ratio. This ratio is $\sqrt[12]{2}$ to 1, or 1.05946. . . . The tempered major second thus has the ratio of $(\sqrt[12]{2})^2$ or $2^{\frac{2}{12}}$, the minor third $2^{\frac{3}{12}}$, and so on up the chromatic scale, so that the octave ratio becomes $2^{\frac{12}{12}}$, or 2. The multiplier $\sqrt[12]{2}$ is an irrational number and thus cannot be expressed as the ratio of two integers; therefore the equally tempered semitone cannot be the exact interval between *any* two tones in the harmonic series. (It can be pretty closely approximated, however, by $\frac{18}{17}$ = 1.0588, as was suggested in 1581 by Vincenzo Galilei, a composer who was the father of the great astronomer.) What this means is that of all the intervals in the tempered chromatic scale only the octaves will be precisely in tune with the intervals of the harmonic series. From the standpoint of "ideal" intonation, as measured by the harmonic series, this is a general disadvantage; from the standpoint of practical musical performance and notation, however, the advantage is immense. Commas vanish; the intonational differences between intervals are being shared equally throughout the scales, and are too small to be readily noticed in performance. As for our system of musical notation, we realize that its diatonic basis permits a subsystem of chromatic notes with sharp signs and flat signs, and that equal temperament perfectly accommodates these notes when enharmonic equivalence is assumed. (Without the assumption of equal temperament and enharmonic equivalence there would for one thing, be no circle of fifths, but rather a spiral of fifths, implying the theoretical possibility of key signatures with infinitely many sharps or flats.)

A little calculation shows that the ratio of the tempered perfect fifth (7 semitones) is equal to $2^{\frac{7}{12}} = 1.498 \ldots$, which is very slightly flatter than 1.500, the Pythagorean fifth. The equally tempered major third is $1.2599 \ldots$, slightly sharper than the major third of the harmonic series, 1.25. The student will find it a profitable exercise, much facilitated by a pocket electronic calculator, to compute all the tempered multipliers and to compare them in various multiples with the interval ratios of the harmonic series, as well as with those obtained by superposing different and like integral ratios. It is also worthwhile to study the old tuning systems, such as mean-tone tuning and just intonation, comparing their intervallic ratios with the equally tempered ones, to see quantitatively how these systems were only partially satisfactory even in their own time; the relevant descriptions will be found in the various music dictionaries and in most treatises on musical acoustics.

Difficulties

Some considerable questions remain. The harmonic series, which is sometimes called the *chord of nature*, is more than just a physical fact; it also represents intervallic relationships that to a large extent agree with what we need for music. It is therefore natural to ask: how does the ear actually perceive "pure" intervals as opposed to tempered ones? How, for instance, does a singer, or a player of an instrument with adjustable pitches such as a violin or a trombone, actually manufacture the tuning of the notes to be produced? Does the performer instinctively imagine and produce a tempered pitch, or a harmonic-series pitch, or something else? Is the hearing of the pianist, who most of the time will not have to worry about such matters, fundamentally different from that of a violinist? Why is it that in actual practice pianos are not tuned to equally tempered pitches throughout their entire range? Most important of all, why do the scales and intervals of our music exist at all, or, to put it another way, why did Western music come to choose these particular relationships based on twelve pitches per octave? (We must remember that throughout this book we have completely ignored, for no good reason other than Western practicality, the large repertory of non-tempered and unequal tunings in non-Western music.)

There are no simple answers to these questions. The results of many years of research in psychoacoustics have not yielded much that is not still subject to widespread debate. The subjective phenomena of hearing involves more complex relationships than the relatively straightforward arithmetic we have dealt with here. Controlled acoustical measurements under actual conditions of performance have shown a great variability in the intonational preferences of highly skilled musicians, preferences that are influenced by a number of different factors but that are certainly not the product of chance. Furthermore, these preferences may be very different for even the same performers when measured in the laboratory with electronically synthesized tones. What is evident above all is that the musician attempts to solve intonational problems by musical sense, meaning by comparison and judgment, not by theory or computation.

The complexities of acoustics and hearing are therefore inescapably different from the complexities of music itself. However systematic and simplifying the equally tempered system may be (or for that matter the Pythagorean or any other tuning system), it is only a practical, and therefore partial, solution to the question of musical tuning. Thus equal temperament, like everything else in this book, is incomplete as a theoretical foundation for the study of music. The inequities and incompletenesses we have been discussing may have more to do with the philosophy of music than with anything else. The equally tempered system, so different from nature, is symbolic of the whole art of music; more than any other, music is the sublime artificial art, the creation of the human mind.

Appendix II

Special Exercises
Based on Bach's
Chorale Harmonizations

The exercises that follow consist of phrases taken from Bach's 371 chorale harmonizations with most of the notes removed. The object of each exercise is not specifically to restore the original notes—though that might be a possible result—but rather to devise a coherent and pleasing solution, applying deductive reasoning and principles of harmony and voice leading, and exercising one's musical intuition. After the student has completed each exercise, he may compare his results with Bach's original and evaluate the differences between the two.

The following rules apply to these exercises:

1. All the phrases are in common time, a few with upbeats. All complete measures are printed here in equal width, so that there should be no difficulty in determining which beat a given note comes on.

2. All phrase endings are marked with a fermata, indicating that no motion should occur in any of the parts until the next phrase begins.

3. The chorale melodies themselves are mostly composed of quarter-note values; a few eighth notes, and some half notes at cadences, may be incorporated, but no values smaller than the eighth note.

4. All durations given here are like those in the originals. A quarter note, therefore, should not be interpreted as one of a pair of eighth notes which has suffered erasure of the other eighth note. No dotted or syncopated values are used except where actually indicated or clearly implied.

5. Sometimes a bass figure is included, with or without notes to fit it. The absence of such figures does not necessarily mean that root position is called for. On the other hand, where figures are given, the usual conventions in reading them apply; e.g., a 6 is understood to mean $\frac{6}{3}$, but not $\frac{6}{4}$ or $\frac{6}{3}$.

6. Slurs are employed to indicate melismas, that is, more than one note per syllable of text. They are omitted for melismas of two successive eighth notes, being understood. Rests are not to be used except where indicated, and then only in all parts.

Exercises of this type, further examples of which are not difficult to construct, are valuable for developing skills in chorale harmonization. They attempt to provide simultaneous emphasis on problems of harmony and counterpoint, in such a way that the ear perforce will search for melodic lines concurrently with specific harmonic points.

1. Chorale No. 152, *Meinen Jesum lass ich nicht, weil*

Use continuous ♪♪ in the bass, except as noted.

2. Chorale No. 256, *Freu dich sehr, o meine Seele*

3. Chorale No. 263, *Jesu, meine Freude*

4. Chorale No. 85, *O Gott, du frommer Gott*

5. Chorale No. 108, *Valet will ich dir geben*

6. Chorale No. 326, *Allein Gott in der Höh' sei Ehr*

7. Chorale No. 83, *Jesu Leiden, Pein und Tod*

8. Chorale No. 131, *Liebster Jesu, wir sind hier*

Index of Musical Examples

This index locates every musical example in this book cited from actual works; it also provides the birth and death dates of the composers. For Schubert's works, "D." numbers, referring to Otto Erich Deutsch's Thematic Catalogue, may be useful when the reader wishes to consult published scores or identify recordings; similarly, some of the "BWV" numbers of Bach's works are provided for pieces that might otherwise be difficult to identify in the collected editions. Haydn's Piano Sonatas are listed by the Hoboken's catalogue numbers. The "K." numbers, from Köchel's catalogue of Mozart's works, are so frequently employed that they are given in the main text as well as here. The student will find it helpful to become familiar with these bibliographical devices, since they are in wide use in libraries and scholarly works, and (except for Bach) are chronologically arranged. Opus numbers, whether provided by the composer or by the publisher, are often unreliable guides in this respect; Schubert's *Erlkönig*, Op. 1, for example, is D. 328, and his *Gretchen am Spinnrade*, Op. 2, is D. 118.

Index

abrupt modulation, 230, 235–38, 460
  see also remote tonal relationships
a capella counterpoint, 286
accented passing tones, 117
accent, 199
  agogic stress as, 189
acciaccatura, 257, 521
accidentals, in figured bass, 85–86
accompaniment, melody and, 287–95, 308
acoustical basis of scale, 545–53
  difficulties of, 552–53
  equal temperament and, 551–53
  harmonics and, 547–52
  interval ratios and, 548–51
added sixth, triad with, 365–69, 483
Aeolian mode, 53, 468
agogic stress, 189
Alberti bass, 167
alto clef, 312–13
anacrusis, 98, 207
analysis:
  of accompaniments, 288–92
  harmonic, 299–314; *see also* harmonic analysis
  of melody, 103–5, 109–10, 111, 141
  of short pieces, 214–16
analytical reduction, 103, 288, 297
antecedent and consequent, 102, 211–12
anticipation, 121–22, 307–8
antiparallel harmony, 497
appoggiatura chord, 126, 520–26
  in cadences, 173, 176–77, 181–82
  chromatic, 446–50, 521, 523
  dominant sequences of, 524–25
  layers of, 525
  pedal points and, 521–22
  six-four as, 164
  unresolved, 522
appoggiatura, 117, 122–26, 308, 383–91
  with delayed resolution, 385
  with notes of resolution, 521–22
  unresolved, 385–87

arabic-numeral notation, 71–72
arpeggiating six-four chord, 166–68
arpeggiation of chord factors, 67–68, 96, 106, 109, 115, 120
artificial scales, 485, 493–95
atonality, 463, 495
  as practiced by Schoenberg and his followers, 535–41
  tonality vs., 527–29
attendant chord, *see* secondary dominants
augmented fifth, 436–39
  V^7 of IV with, 436–38
  as secondary dominant, 436–38
  on subdominant, 438
augmented fourth, resolutions of, 245
augmented interval, 8, 25, 427
augmented six-five-three chord, *see* German sixth chord
augmented six-four-three chord, *see* French sixth chord
augmented sixth (interval), 25, 427
augmented sixth chord, 419–33
  definition of, 420–21
  over dominant pedal, 522
  exceptional forms of, 430–31
  inversions of, 427–28
  irregular resolutions of, 428, 430
  modulating with, 428–29
  regular resolutions of, 421–26
  secondary dominant function of, 417; *see also* Italian sixth chords
augmented triad, 14, 490–92
authentic cadence, 56–59, 172–73
auxiliary six-four chord, 163–64
auxiliary tones, 118–21

balance of phrases, 102
"barber-shop" progression, 262
basso continuo, 84
binary form, 213

Books That Live In Music

THE NORTON MANUAL OF MUSIC NOTATION *By George Heussenstamm*
THE MUSIC KIT SECOND EDITION *By Tom Manoff*
Regular and CAI versions
SCALES, INTERVALS, KEYS, TRIADS, RHYTHM, AND METER *By John Clough and Joyce Conley*
BASIC HARMONIC PROGRESSIONS *By John Clough and Joyce Conley*
A NEW APPROACH TO EAR TRAINING *By Leo Kraft*
A NEW APPROACH TO KEYBOARD HARMONY *By Allen Brings et al.*
A NEW APPROACH TO SIGHT SINGING THIRD EDITION
By Sol Berkowitz, Gabriel Frontrier, and Leo Kraft
SIGHT SINGING: PITCH, INTERVAL, RHYTHM *By Samuel Adler*
EAR TRAINING AND SIGHT SINGING *By Maurice Lieberman*
MOSTLY SHORT PIECES *Edited by Mark DeVoto*
THE NORTON SCORES FIFTH EDITION *Edited by Roger Kamien*
GRADUS SECOND EDITION *By Leo Kraft*
HARMONY FIFTH EDITION *By Walter Piston*
Revised and Expanded by Mark DeVoto
WORKBOOK FOR HARMONY FIFTH EDITION *By Arthur Jannery*
INTRODUCTION TO SCHENKERIAN ANALYSIS *By Allen Forte and Steven E. Gilbert*
ANALYTIC APPROACHES TO TWENTIETH-CENTURY MUSIC *By Joel Lester*
STRUCTURAL FUNCTIONS OF HARMONY REVISED *By Arnold Schoenberg*
TWENTIETH-CENTURY HARMONY *By Vincent Persichetti*
COUNTERPOINT *By Walter Piston*
THE STUDY OF COUNTERPOINT *By J. J. Fux (Ed. & Tr. by Alfred Mann)*
SONATA FORMS REVISED *By Charles Rosen*
ORCHESTRATION *By Walter Piston*
THE STUDY OF ORCHESTRATION SECOND EDITION *By Samuel Adler*
WORKBOOK FOR THE STUDY OF ORCHESTRATION SECOND EDITION *By Samuel Adler*
A GUIDE TO MUSICAL STYLES *By Douglas Moore*
A GUIDE TO MUSICAL ANALYSIS *By Nicholas Cook*
ANALYSIS *By Ian Bent*
MUSICAL FORM AND MUSICAL PERFORMANCE *By Edward T. Cone*
PERSPECTIVES ON MUSICAL AESTHETICS *Edited by John Rahn*
THE ACOUSTICAL FOUNDATIONS OF MUSIC REVISED *By John Backus*
THE NORTON/GROVE CONCISE ENCYCLOPEDIA OF MUSIC *Edited by Stanley Sadie*
THE PIANO *By Philip R. Belt et al.*
VIOLIN FAMILY *By David D. Boyden et al.*
THE ORGAN *By Barbara Owen and Peter Williams*
EARLY KEYBOARD INSTRUMENTS *By Edwin M. Ripin et al.*
CHORAL CONDUCTING *By Abraham Kaplan*